Divided Waters

Divided Waters

Bridging the U.S.-Mexico Border

Helen Ingram, Nancy K. Laney, and David M. Gillilan

The University of Arizona Press   Tucson

The University of Arizona Press

Copyright © 1995
The Arizona Board of Regents
All Rights Reserved

♾ This book is printed on acid-free, archival-quality paper.
Manufactured in the United States of America

00 99 98 97 96 95   6 5 4 3 2 1

Library of Congress Cataloging-in-Publication Data
Ingram, Helen M., 1937–
Divided waters : bridging the U.S.-Mexico border / Helen Ingram,
Nancy K. Laney, and David M. Gillilan.
  p. cm.
Includes bibliographical references and index.
ISBN 0-8165-1513-1 (cloth).—ISBN 0-8165-1564-6 (paper)
1. Water rights—United States. 2. Water rights—Mexico.
3. Water-supply—Arizona—Nogales. 4. Water-supply—Mexico—
Nogales (Sonora) 5. United States—Boundaries—Mexico.
6. Mexico—Boundaries—United States. I. Laney, Nancy K. II. Gillilan,
David M., 1960–   . III. Title.
HD1694.A3 1995
333.91′00972′1—dc20   95-13626
CIP

To Rosalva Gallardo, who was herself a bridge across the border.

Contents

List of Acronyms   ix
List of Figures   xi
Acknowledgments   xiii

Chapter 1   Global Trends and Border Consequences   3
Multiplying Borders   3
The Greening of the Globe   9
Global Economic Integration   15
The Grass Roots: Demand for Local Participation and Control   19
Policy Design for the Future   22
The Global Problem in Microcosm   25

Chapter 2   Shared Encounters: Ambos Nogales   28
The Origins   29
Patterns of Growth   33
Interdependent Economies   38
The Border Culture   46

Chapter 3   The Troubled Waters of Ambos Nogales   50
Natural Water Resources   50
Water Resources Systems   58
Water Quality   98

Chapter 4   Divided Neighbors   104
Four Families   105
Socioeconomic Dividing Lines   110
Perceptions and Attitudes about Water   116
Social and Economic Linkages Across the Border   129

Transboundary Linkages: The View from Nogales, Arizona 134
Differing Perceptions of Water Issues in Nogales, Arizona 137

Chapter 5 Stranded Communities and Failed Crossings 146
Who Is Responsible for Sewage in Nogales Wash? 147
Lessons from Nogales 160
The Mexican Perspective 165
Differing Perceptions of Public Health and Environmental Issues 166
Changing Times in Mexican Water Regulation 167
The Path toward Decentralization and Shared Goals 178
The IBWC: Hope for the Future or Outdated Institution? 180
The La Paz Agreement: Adequate Basis for Binational Action? 194
Ambos Nogales and the EPA 197
An Evaluation of the EPA and SEDESOL as Binational Actors 200

Chapter 6 Reinventing the Border: A Framework for Transboundary Water Management 203
Global Forces Revisited 203
Borders: Maelstroms or Bridges? 205
Border Links 216
Bridging Borders through Improved Institutional Design 220
Criteria for Successful Border Institutions 222

Appendix A Implementation of the Border Environment Cooperation Commission and the North American Development Bank 231

Appendix B Proposal for a U.S.-Mexico International Boundary Environmental Commission: A Binational U.S.-Mexico Border Environmental Management Institution 234

Notes 243
Bibliography 252
Index 258

Acronyms

ADEQ	Arizona Department of Environmental Quality
ADWR	Arizona Department of Water Resources
AGMA	Arizona Groundwater Management Act (1980)
AMA	Active Management Area
AMCHAM	American Chamber of Commerce in Mexico
BECC	Border Environmental Cooperation Commission
BEP	Border Ecology Project
BIP	Border Industrialization Program
CILA	Comisión Internacional de Limites y Aguas (International Boundary and Water Commission)
CNA	Comisión Nacional del Agua (National Water Commission)
COAPAES	Comisión de Agua Potable y Alcantarillado del Estado de Sonora (State of Sonora Potable Water and Sewerage Commission)
COLEF	El Colegio de la Frontera Norte (College of the Northern Border)
EPA	U.S. Environmental Protection Agency
GIS	Geographical Information System
IBEP	Integrated Environmental Plan for the Mexico-U.S. Border Area
IBWC	International Boundary and Water Commission
INEGI	Instituto Nacional de Estadística, Geografía e Informática (National Institute for Statistics, Geography, and Information)
NAFTA	North American Free Trade Agreement
NGO	Nongovernmental organization
NIWWTF	Nogales International Waste Water Treatment Facility
NPDES	National Pollution Discharge Elimination System
NWD	Nogales, Ariz., Water Department
PCE	Perchloroethylene (tetrachloroethylene)
PRI	Partido Revolucionario Institucional (Institutional Revolutionary party)
SARH	Secretaría de Agricultura y Recursos Hidráulicos (Ministry of Agriculture and Water Resources)

SEDESOL	Secretaría de Desarrollo Social (Ministry for Social Development)
SEDUE	Secretaría de Desarrollo Urbano y Ecología (Ministry for Urban Development and Ecology)
SIF	Sistema de Información Fronteriza (Border Information System)
TCE	Trichloroethylene
VOC	Volatile organic compound
WPA	Work Projects Administration

Figures

1.1 The border region on either side of the U.S.-Mexico boundary   7
1.2 A state of emergency declared by the City of San Diego on September 7, 1993   13
1.3 Aerial map of Ambos Nogales   26
2.1 Population growth in Ambos Nogales, 1930–1990, and estimates for Nogales, Son., through 2012   35
2.2 Fruits and vegetables passing through the Port of Nogales, 1987–1992   40
2.3 Employed population in Nogales, Son., 1990   42
2.4 Estimated number of maquila employees in Nogales, Son., 1990   43
2.5 Labor costs in Mexican factories as a percentage of total U.S. labor costs for manufacturing   44
3.1 The upper Santa Cruz River and upper Río Magdalena (Los Alisos) watersheds   51
3.2 Climate of Nogales, Ariz.   52
3.3 Nogales, Son., water supply wellfields, July 1993   71
3.4 The price of household water in Ambos Nogales   82
3.5 Social inequity in access to water in Ambos Nogales   83
3.6 Effluent release from the NIWWTF to the Santa Cruz River   95
4.1 Zones supplied with potable water by pipas; and the percentage of residents without access to water supply or sewer systems   117
4.2 Number of hours per day during which inhabitants of Nogales, Son., receive water through the COAPAES system   118
4.3 Percentage of residents of Nogales, Son., who believe that contaminated water may adversely affect their health   119
4.4 Residents' perceptions of water quality in Nogales, Ariz.   126
4.5 Residents' perceptions of the degree of seriousness of water contamination in Nogales, Ariz.   127
4.6 Increased purchases of bottled water in response to perceptions of worsening water quality in Nogales, Ariz.   128
4.7 Household income diversity by language preference, Nogales, Ariz.   135

4.8 Residents of Nogales, Ariz., who transport water to friends or relatives in Sonora   136
4.9 Goods and services purchased in Nogales, Son., by Nogales, Ariz., residents   137
4.10 Nogales, Ariz., residents' perceptions of NWD water quality   138
4.11 Nogales, Ariz., residents' perceptions of water contamination   138
4.12 Nogales, Ariz., residents' political actions in response to water problems   140
4.13 Nogales, Ariz., residents' perceptions of the level of government most responsible for water policy   141
4.14 "National" versus "binational" orientations of Rio Rico and Nogales, Ariz., residents   143
5.1 Environmental themes in Ambos Nogales newspapers   167
5.2 Sources of information for articles on the environment in Ambos Nogales newspapers   168

Acknowledgments

This book is the capstone of a binational research project that began in 1989. The project was sponsored by the Ford Foundation and conducted at the Udall Center of the University of Arizona. By 1994 the project had produced more than 175 documents, including published and unpublished papers and conference presentations. Consequently, this book reflects not just the work of the authors but also the cumulative knowledge and insights provided by the many individuals involved in the project. As a binational enterprise, the book draws heavily on the knowledge and expertise provided by the Mexican counterparts of the Udall Center: El Colegio de La Frontera Norte (COLEF) and the Instituto Tecnológico de Sonora. Roberto Sánchez and Francisco Lara at COLEF were important sources of information and perspectives on water management in Mexico.

The interdisciplinary research team coordinated by the Udall Center is the source of the broad expertise that informs this book. Simon Inge, Tod Rasmussen, and Jim de Cook developed much of the hydrological information on which Chapter 3 is based. Stuart Marsh consulted on the GIS maps. Irasema Coronado provided much of the social and historical data in Chapters 2 and 4. Melinda Laituri, Barbara Morehouse, Shelby Tisdale, Brad Cloud, David White, Vera Pavlakovich, Gary Hansen, Greg Saxe, and Ron Sokota, among others, produced crucial background documents. Other individuals, especially Dick Kamp and John Audley, provided important ideas at key junctures.

Large team efforts seldom succeed without a maestro to orchestrate the blending together of the many parts. Our maestro was Robert Varady, who also doubled as a careful reader and critic. Among

Varady's most important accomplishments was the recruitment of Lenard Milich, whose enormous talent for editing and manuscript preparation are evidenced on every page. Although the authors hold Milich blameless for any faults in this book, they gratefully share full credit for turning a simple report into a real book.

Divided Waters

Chapter 1

Global Trends and Border Consequences

Multiplying Borders

Our shrinking planet hosts a growing number of nations. Along with the rapid political reconfigurations of the 1990s, new boundaries are proliferating like lines on a fractured mirror. At the same time, the distances between nations are being narrowed through migration, travel, communications, and trade. The collapse of communism in the Soviet Union and eastern Europe and the virtual disintegration of several African states have been accompanied by drastic changes in the political landscape. New, often ethnically based nations are in the process of inventing themselves and securing their borders. Between late 1991 and mid-1993, the dissolution of two great heterogeneous federations, the Soviet Union and Yugoslavia, into many ethnic republics, as well as the amicable separation of Czechoslovakia, expanded the number of international boundaries by 46 (Udall and Varady, 1993).[1] By their very nature, borders create stress and contradictions, and the increasing number of borders is cause for concern. Where the peripheries of nations come together, experience suggests that both problems and possibilities exist.

Boundaries are legal constructs invented by humans to serve a variety of important purposes. Political control cannot be asserted without setting a boundary inside of which a regime governs. Rights cannot exist unless a boundary separates those who have rights from those who do not. Formerly united peoples divide as a way of resolving disputes resulting from irreconcilable interests, allowing each new nation to go its own way. Less internal conflict may exist when borders are drawn to include people with common interests or to exclude those with different backgrounds and points of view.

Boundaries can be flashpoints over issues that neighbors have in common, such as environmental pollution. Natural resources are especially likely to present problems because of their increasing scarcity and value. Further, national boundaries often intersect the boundaries of natural systems, and actions taken by one nation that affect the atmosphere, oceans, airsheds, watersheds, aquifers, wildlife migration corridors, and other shared resources are bound to affect the interests of other nations.

What should be optimally treated as a unified whole is managed instead through different and often conflicting regimes. Boundaries fragment legal and political power, with the result that there is no single jurisdiction with the power to make and enforce decisions. Throughout Eurasia, for example, the number of trustees of threatened resources such as the Black, Aral, and Caspian Seas and the Danube River has multiplied severalfold. What were once difficult internal problems for the Soviet Union and its eastern European sister states have become even more complex international issues.[2] There are other costs associated with drawing boundary lines as well. Drawing boundaries has the effect of marginalizing the things closest to the line, designating them as remote from the core. The breakdown of law and order and the decline of civilizing influences are often associated with frontier regions. It is no accident that from the time the Akkadian Empire constructed a wall of fortresses known as the Repeller of the Amorites almost 4,050 years ago (H. Weiss et al., 1993), powerful interests have fortified themselves against change by building walls and arming outposts along borders.

But if boundaries can separate, they can also connect. They can bridge differences and bring divergent interests and attitudes closer together, functioning as points of contact and cooperation where greater diversity and opportunity for innovation exist. Frontiers are often testing grounds that illustrate the vulnerability of a system and the advantages of change. The Berlin Wall, after all, represented a desperate act by a threatened regime, and the permeability of the border leading to the dismantling of the wall signaled the regime's end. Boundaries, more than other places, provide the geographic context for challenging established ideas. Possibilities expand at the frontier. At their best, borders are places where conventional approaches are questioned; stereotypes dissolve in the face of reality, and new understanding emerges. A boundary region that shares and combines the characteristics of the nations it joins can soften differences between the nations. The mutual advantages of commerce and exchange are often most salient in arenas where buyers and sellers meet face to face. Great cosmopolitan cities like Venice and Hong Kong constructed at the margins of nations have capitalized on their openness to free exchange among diverse cultures. Negative stereotypes tend to disappear among neighbors who are economically interdependent.

Whether the creation of new borders will lead to an increase in global conflict or to greater recognition of the advantages resulting from increased recognition of diversity will depend largely on the ways border relationships, cultures, and institutions evolve. Global forces too strong to resist, including environmental consciousness, trade, and communications, tend to decrease the distance between neighboring nations. Consequently, what happens at borders is critical to the global future. Studying environmental issues in particular border zones brings into sharp focus the critical factors that are likely both to create conflict and to lead to its resolution.

Water, once a plentiful resource, is now often polluted and in short supply. The problem of supplying adequate clean water to urban areas has become critical in many parts of the world, according to the World Resources Institute and the World Bank. Already 1.5 billion people on the planet are without safe drinking water.[3] Control over natural resources, including water, is the motive for a number of regional conflicts. The world population now exceeds 5 billion—approximately five times what it was 200 years ago. Demographers project a doubling to 10 billion in half a century or so. Environmental systems that were able to sustain lesser resource use and waste loads are now overextended, and the degradation promises to become much worse. The multiplying population has increased the worldwide demand for land, air, water, food, and fiber, and the demand now presses close upon the supply. People are spilling over boundary lines in search of better lives.

But even as the world's population is exploding and the environment is deteriorating, consciousness about and concern for environmental sustainability and biological conservation are becoming more widespread. The United Nations Conference on the Human Environment held in 1972 in Stockholm, which established the UN Environment Programme, ushered in a new era of global environmental concern. Since then, hundreds of international agreements have been concluded, regulating, for example, ocean dumping, trade in endangered species, and air and water pollution (E. B. Weiss, 1993).

Among the environmental issues most distinct at borders, none is more significant than water. Almost 40 percent of the world's population lives in river basins shared by more than two nations (Vlacos et al., 1986). Transnational water resources offer a good focus for studying the border environment not only because water is usually among the most important shared environmental issues, but also because water is a transcendent resource. All forms of life depend on it. Water is fundamental to economic activity, and the presence of ample supplies of high-quality water determines whether and where sustainable development can occur. Water is critical to human health, and the control of waterborne diseases has been an overarching priority of civilized human settlements since at least the time of Frontinus, the water commissioner of Rome in A.D. 97.

The best case-study material for exploring water as a boundary issue is found where there is both a long historical record and where the ingredients for conflict and cooperation exist. The U.S.-Mexico border presents such a case. The United States and Mexico offer a number of starkly contrasting features that easily lead to misunderstandings and conflict, among them the following:

- Disparity in infrastructure development, such as roads, sewers, schools, hospitals, and transportation;
- Different legal systems with different patterns for distributing revenue to states and localities;
- Different politics and decision-making structures;
- Sharply different levels of prosperity and per capita income;
- Great variation in numbers and power of nongovernmental and environmental organizations;
- Different cultures, social structures, and customs;
- Different perceptions of environmental quality and degrees of protection;
- Different motives and interest in removing trade barriers.

Such abstract contrasts become real sources of conflict when they

Global Trends and Border Consequences   7

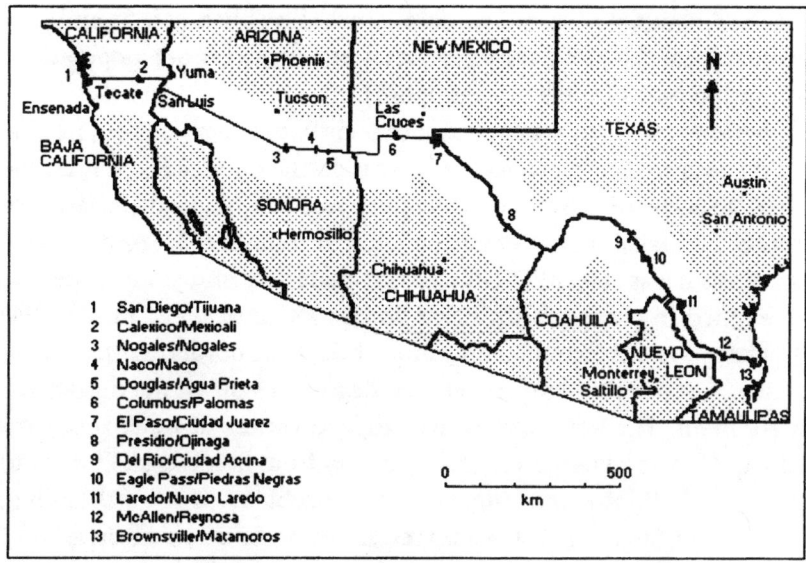

Figure 1.1   The border region, a 100-kilometer-wide strip on either side of the U.S.-Mexico boundary, showing the 13 pairs of major twin cities. *Source*: EPA and SEDUE, 1991.

are placed in a border context where the dissimilarity is marked. The disjuncture between the two nations—one postindustrial, the other developing—is startling to anyone who passes through a border crossing, especially as regards differences in environmental quality. The U.S.-Mexico boundary bisects a variety of natural systems, including wildlife migration routes, habitats, water basins, and aquifers. The 13 pairs of border twin cities (fig. 1.1) share common airsheds, and particulate matter and other pollutants move freely across the boundary. Both mobile and stationary sources of air pollution create problems. Long lines of cars at ports of entry and the lack of effective emissions controls on automobiles adversely affect human health (EPA and SEDUE, 1991). Some factories in Ciudad Juarez burn tires for fuel.[4] Pesticides sprayed on crops in the Mexicali Valley drift on the prevailing winds to affect U.S. and Mexican populations. The border has numerous national parks, recreation areas, and wildlife areas populated with migratory species, 460 of which are endangered, threatened, or candidate species for listing (U.S. Fish and Wildlife Service, 1992). Disease vectors are also transnational, and environmentally related disorders—including birth defects and pulmonary, cardiac, and skin diseases—affect the border populations of both nations (Udall Center, 1993a).

Actions affecting a shared resource or natural system on one side of the line are bound to have an effect on the other side. Neither the legal concept of national sovereignty nor the physical presence of fences can halt systemic environmental degradation. Hazardous substances such as solvents, acids, caustic materials, and paint wastes are generated in great quantities by border industries, but no effective tracking system exists to monitor their transborder flow.[5] Transnational water problems reflect the degraded state of the border environment. The boundary is marred by a variety of water problems along the 3,200 kilometers (2,000 miles) from San Diego/Tijuana to Brownsville/Matamoras (fig. 1.1). These problems, it is worth noting, are not unidirectional: the sources are as often north of the border as south of it. Many problems relate to water quality, including biological and chemical contaminants; but in this largely dry area, problems of water supply also exist. Groundwater basins are seriously overpumped, and large populations must rely on scarce, undependable water supplies.

Among the natural resource and environmental conflicts between the United States and Mexico, water has been the most troublesome. Historic contests over the water supply continue into the present but have come to be superseded by controversies over water quality. The United States was the first to develop the water resources of both the Colorado River and the Rio Grande (Río Bravo), and in its dealings with Mexico has held stubbornly to the "prior appropriations" doctrine of "first in time, first in right." Water is a fighting matter not only among but within Western states, and political leaders who represent the interests of U.S. water users historically have been hesitant to give Mexico one drop more than absolutely necessary.

Even though environment and water resources are contentious issues on the U.S.-Mexico border, the relationship has its bright side. The two nations have peacefully, if not entirely equitably, settled disputes for more than a century through treaties and executive agreements. Even while the two nations were at odds concerning relationships with Cuba and access to and pricing of Mexican petroleum, they could agree in principle (through the 1983 Reagan–de la Madrid Accord) to act jointly to protect the border environment. An old and honored organization, the International Boundary and Water Commission, exists to settle routine differences over water allocation. In addition, border residents are bound by their shared history of Spanish colonial rule and their distinct border culture, and they have been able to develop many informal problem-solving arrangements. The 1990s appear to be an especially hopeful period in U.S.-Mexico relations. Seldom during the long association between the two countries has the spirit of common destiny and collaboration been more evident; and rarely have the two disparate neighbors been so willing to pledge resources to tackle shared problems.

This book is based on the premise that a close examination of an important set of issues on the U.S.-Mexican border holds valuable lessons for dealing with global trends and issues, including the rise in environmental consciousness, the integration of the global economy, and aspirations for self-determination. The remainder of this chapter examines the impetus for each of these worldwide movements and how they bear on the U.S.-Mexico border region. We consider first the ways that mounting environmental degradation and the worldwide dissemination of information regarding environmental disasters, such as the Chernobyl nuclear accident and the *Exxon Valdez* oil spill, have increased the sense of common risk. Industrialization and the rise of the global marketplace are taken up next, along with contradictory theories of the effects of economic integration on environmental quality. Subsequently, the chapter turns to the rising discontent among citizens in many countries over the inability of national governments to implement laws and respond to local demands for participation and control. In each case we will trace the consequences of these interacting forces on the U.S.-Mexico border. Finally, we will establish some principles for designing policies that are suited to particular border circumstances.

The Greening of the Globe

Environmental problems have become so large that they can be intelligently grasped and dealt with only on a scale that transcends national boundaries. Greenhouse gases threaten to alter climate and cause a rise in sea level worldwide. Pressures on shared resources such as river basins and coastal fisheries are growing. Massive deforestation in one region can alter the rainfall in another and the carbon balance globally (EPA and SEDUE, 1991). Disconnected human activities carried on in locations that are geographically and politically separate have a collective and cumulative impact on whole systems.

Further, the line between national and international environmental problems is fast disappearing (e.g., Dickinson, 1992). Resource deterioration in many nations is so severe that it registers in neighboring countries in the form of acid rain and high levels of other air pollutants, increased flooding and siltation, and the disappearance of migratory species. It is no longer possible for any nation to be confident that its domestic environmental laws can ensure an ecologically sound and sustainable future for its citizens. More than ever before, developed nations have a direct interest in the environmental degradation taking place in developing nations, especially those with which they share borders.

Technological advances such as the Green Revolution in agriculture, which involves heavy fertilizer and pesticide use, were once heralded as the palliative to population growth, but the new technologies have also introduced new sources of transnational pollution. Energy- and chemical-intensive manufacture, transportation, and agriculture increase energy use and waste loads.

Technological innovations in communications that have raised individuals' awareness and aspirations have concomitantly facilitated the globalization of environmental consciousness. The environmental costs of development in lesser-developed nations draw international attention from environmentalists and the broader public. Mexico is a case in point. Its forests, which are being harvested at rates far exceeding sustainability, are decreasing by more than 405,000 hectares (1 million acres) annually (Sand, 1990). The Mexican government's investment policy has encouraged rapid industrialization and urbanization at the expense of the countryside. By 1990, almost 20 million inhabitants, or nearly one quarter of Mexico's population, were concentrated within the metropolitan area of Mexico City. Pollution from smokestack industries and millions of motor vehicles have fouled the air, endangering public health.

Water resources in Mexico have also been negatively affected; 77 percent of Mexico's river basins are sufficiently polluted to jeopardize public health. Beaches and lakes have become unsafe and unsightly as a result of the dumping of untreated wastes. Oil spills in the Gulf of Mexico threaten marine life and vital fisheries (*World Resources 1990–91*). Water treatment plants in the border region have the capacity to treat only 16 percent of the municipal and industrial wastewater generated there. Many Mexican border cities, such as Ciudad Juarez—which generates 83,300 cubic meters (22 million gallons) of raw sewage a day—have no wastewater treatment system at all (Mumme, 1991). U.S. border cities feel threatened by the ever-escalating volume of sewage affecting their immediate environment (see fig. 1.2).

The deterioration of the environment in Mexico and other developing nations concerns environmentalists everywhere. Once believed to represent a sentiment affordable only by the healthy and wealthy few in developed countries, the environmental movement now extends in some degree to all classes in all countries. The 1992 United Nations Conference on Environment and Development held in Rio de Janeiro brought together heads of government and their representatives with 8,000 journalists and the representatives of 1,400 nongovernmental organizations (NGOs). The citizens' organizations clearly pushed a more ambitious agenda for action than did professional diplomats and military officers.[6] Many U.S.-based environmental groups now have foreign offices and counterparts, and their programs include preserving tropical rainforests and endangered species through such mechanisms as debt-for-nature swaps and setting strict environmental conditions for international loans. International environmental organizations now have considerable political clout.

Public consciousness of environmental threats has emerged slowly in Mexico. At Stockholm in 1972, the Mexicans supported the general Latin American position that environmental degradation was caused by First World consumption and that strict pollution controls were luxuries that poor countries could not afford. More recently,

RESOLUTION NUMBER R-282544, ADOPTED ON September 7, 1993

A RESOLUTION OF THE CITY OF SAN DIEGO DECLARING THE EXISTENCE OF A STATE OF EMERGENCY WITHIN SAID CITY RELATING TO THE ESCALATED DISCHARGE OF RAW SEWAGE ACROSS THE INTERNATIONAL BORDER INTO THE CITY.

WHEREAS, upwards of fifteen million (15,000,000) gallons of contaminants and raw sewage are flowing daily across the international border into the City of San Diego; and

WHEREAS, the raw sewage causes contamination of the Tijuana River Valley and the ocean beaches, thereby threatening the health, safety and welfare of the citizens of San Diego; and

WHEREAS, this flow continues to escalate due to increased water availability and use in the City of Tijuana; and

WHEREAS, this flow is the acknowledged responsibility of the federal governments of the United States and Mexico; and

WHEREAS, the International Boundary and Water Commission and the U.S. Environmental Protection Agency are coordinating both interim and long term measures to provide for the treatment and disposal of this raw sewage; and

WHEREAS, the City of San Diego desires to assist both state and federal agencies in expediting treatment of this international sewage to protect its citizens from existing harm and potential disease; and

WHEREAS, pursuant to Section 8558(c) of the California Government Code, the flow of this renegade sewage is "beyond the control of the services, personnel, equipment and facilities of the political subdivision" of the City of San Diego; and

WHEREAS, pursuant to the authority of the charter of the City of San Diego and Section 51.0106 of the San Diego Municipal Code, the City Manager of the City of San Diego has requested the Mayor and the City Council to proclaim that a state of local emergency exists; and

WHEREAS, pursuant to Section 8625(b) of the California Government Code, the Governor may be requested to proclaim a state of emergency in the area affected and make available any state or federal assistance to the City of San Diego; and

WHEREAS, pursuant to Sections 28 and 94 of the San Diego City Charter, in the event of an emergency affecting public health and safety, the City Council may authorize the City Manager to enter into contracts requiring the expenditure of necessary sums on hand in the City Treasury and available for necessary emergency assistance; NOW, THEREFORE

BE IT RESOLVED, by the Council of The City of San Diego, that the request by the City Manager to the Mayor and Council to declare a state of local emergency pursuant to Section 51.0106 of the San Diego Municipal Code is hereby approved.

BE IT FURTHER RESOLVED, that the Governor of California is hereby requested to proclaim a state of emergency in San Diego, pursuant to Section 8625(b) of the California Government Code and Section 51.0106a.2 of the San Diego Municipal Code.

BE IT FURTHER RESOLVED, that the City Manager, pursuant to Sections 28 and 94 of the San Diego City Charter, is hereby authorized and empowered, on behalf of said city, to provide all necessary assistance to federal and state agencies for the diversion, treatment and disposal of international raw sewage as may be required.

APPROVED: JOHN W. WITT, City Attorney

Figure 1.2 A state of emergency was declared by the City of San Diego on September 7, 1993, as a consequence of escalating sewage flows across the U.S.-Mexico border.

however, many Mexican intellectuals have begun to reevaluate that position; they have come to realize that their government's subordination of ecological issues to industrialization has not led to real progress for the people whose environment has been adversely affected (Caldwell, 1993). Environmental organizations such as El Grupo de Cien have criticized the Mexican government for failing to enforce sanctions against private and public industries whose activities endanger the public health. Although Mexican environmentalism in the 1980s and 1990s has had a different tone than that exhibited by its counterparts in the developed world (Graham, 1991), Mexicans in public opinion polls express a strong interest in the environment as they define it. A 1991 poll found that 60 percent of Mexicans consider the environment a high priority.[7]

Action by the Mexican government to protect the environment in Mexico has lagged and is perhaps primarily preemptive—that is, motivated by a desire to co-opt demands for even stronger action and to forestall grassroots activism (Mumme, 1991). In contrast with its slow progress on the home front, however, the government of Mexico has been a strong supporter of international environmental accords. A list of high-profile environmental concerns published in U.S. newspapers by the Mexican government included such topics as acid rain, desertification, loss of species, contamination of the oceans, and atmospheric change (Mumme, 1991). The United States and Mexico have signed bilateral accords that address urban air pollution in Mexico City and regulate the transport of hazardous wastes, among other issues (Graham, 1991).

How the rise of global green consciousness will affect particular places like the U.S.-Mexico border is far from clear, but it is in just such settings that the success of the international environmental movement will be most severely tested. In Mexico itself, the focus of environmental concern has been on Mexico City, whose pollution problems have been highly publicized; the city is also the home of most Mexican environmentalists. While many U.S. national environmental groups express great interest in the global environment, few leaders of such groups are acquainted with problems on the U.S.-Mexico border. It was not until the early 1990s, when the North American Free Trade Agreement (NAFTA) became an issue, that the national press and environmental groups expressed concern about the degraded border environment, although the problem has existed for decades. A growing alliance between Mexican and U.S. environmental groups has had a strong impact on the side agreements forged to support NAFTA (Mumme, 1991; E. B. Weiss, 1993), but it is unclear what priority the alliance gives to the border environment.[8] Countering the fierce historical competition to exploit natural resources, especially water, the existing accords between the United States and Mexico to protect the border environment provide an alternative precedent for increased cooperation and real progress on border cleanup.

Global Economic Integration

The increasingly unified world economy has made it more and more difficult for any nation or group of nations to remain absolutely independent. The worldwide integration of manufacturing and commerce with international banking and finance has resulted in unprecedented economic interdependence. No nation can remain isolated and maintain economic parity. Every nation is now forced to compete against every other nation within complex linked blocs and networks.[9] This trend is responsible for the rise of the European Economic Community (now the European Union), which at least partly prompted the creation of NAFTA. Economic performance has become key to the political survival of national leaders.

While both the environment and economics are forces favoring global integration, the relationship between economic interdependence and environmental quality is not obvious. Free-market advocates, for example, maintain that very few industries change locations primarily in pursuit of lenient environmental regulations. They cite evidence such as the U.S. General Accounting Office study that found that only 1 to 3 percent of the wood furniture manufacturers in the Los Angeles area migrated to Mexico between 1988 and 1990, and then only in part because of less stringent environmental regulations (Sjöstedt, 1993). Further, there appears to be a close relationship between economic progress and environmental aspirations. As the economies of nations grow, their citizens come to expect better lives. With greater access to entertainment and education through radio, television, movies, and videos comes greater exposure to environmental values, and citizens are being socialized to expect a cleaner environment. With stronger economies, governments and industry are in a position to respond positively to environmental problems. By this reasoning, free trade will not lower environmental standards to the least common denominator; it will instead spread the demand for improved environmental quality (U.S. General Accounting Office, 1991).

On the other hand, a strong argument can be made that the globalization of the economy is resulting in environmental degradation despite the efforts of the international environmental movement. Market forces drive producers to seek locations with low environmental standards and low labor costs, and nations and localities are reluctant to impose either regulations or taxes for fear that industry will relocate. According to this perspective, as globalization progresses, national governments lose control over what used to be national economics. As goods, capital, and labor flow across their borders without restraint, the concept of a national economy loses its meaning. Decision making within the integrated economy is increasingly dictated by transnational corporations that are beyond the reach of governments and are restrained only by the forces of markets in which the major competition is among a few gargantuan oligopolistic firms. The pressures of competition drive these firms to base their production facilities where total production costs are the lowest and to produce products to sell in the markets where income is the highest—but with no incentive or obligation to help maintain those higher incomes (e.g., Leonard, 1988).

Greater profits to transnational corporations do not necessarily lead to the kind of economic progress that supports a cleaner environment. There is a growing global income gap between the rich, who control capital and technology, and the poor, who have only their labor and the low wages it brings. Increased national income will not lead to mass popular demand for environmental improvement if profits are inequitably distributed. The worldwide distribution of environmental risk is closely related to poverty and political powerlessness; the poor are disproportionately subjected to environmental insults and are more likely to be the primary victims of environmental degradation. The relationship between economic growth and environmental quality is also unclear because conventional measures of economic progress, such as gross domestic income or product, do not take into account the depletion of natural resource capital. Further, conventional measures of economic progress treat expenditures on pollution cleanup like other investments, with the odd result that the more a nation is forced to spend on cleaning up pollution, the wealthier it appears to be (Korten, 1991). If better economic tools were used to examine the perceived economic miracles in global traders such as Japan, Taiwan, and Malaysia—tools that took national and international natural resource depletion and degradation into account—there would be smaller positive, and perhaps even negative, balances. A case study of integrated economic and environmental accounting performed for the Mexican economy in 1988 transformed a positive net capital formation of 11 percent to a loss of 2 percent when the depletion of natural capital was included in the analysis (Repetto, 1993). Such findings strengthen the arguments of those who maintain that the global economy is driving countries away from sustainable development, and that economic progress today is coming at the expense of the environment and the natural legacy of future generations. In short, it is far from certain that the movement toward freer trade will cause global environmental indicators to move in a more optimistic direction.

Borders are particularly likely to be affected by the movement toward worldwide economic integration because they separate national economies. In some cases, borders separate areas with high wages and a strong economy from areas where workers are willing to work more cheaply. Nowhere in the world are the economies of adjacent countries at such markedly different levels as in the United States and Mexico. The costs to industry of environmental regulations, while ordinarily a small percentage of production, are determined by national governments. Unquestionably, environmental regulations are more stringent in the United States than in Mexico. The U.S.-Mexico border, then, is a crucible in which the forces of economic and environmental integration are coming together. And it is exactly in places like this that the future could be decided: Will the environmental progress made in the United States since the 1970s spread to other countries, or will economic competition to reduce production costs drive down the levels of environmental protection to some least common denominator?

The global economic forces dictating the relocation of labor-intensive production processes from industrialized regions in developed nations to areas of cheap labor have led to enormous population pressures on limited border resources. The plight of the Mexican factory worker is not unique to the border, but it is particularly critical, and visible, there.

Mexico's rapid urbanization has cost its citizens dearly. In 1930, two-thirds of all Mexicans lived in rural areas, but by 1980 two-thirds lived in the cities (van Tongerin et al., 1991). Until the mid-1970s the Mexican government devoted very few resources to urban planning, and urban growth was often in the form of unplanned, unregulated, and poverty-ridden illegal settlements established by squatters (Bennett, 1995). The government started to invest in urban infrastructure in the 1970s, but the process had barely begun before the economic crisis of the 1980s forced severe cutbacks. The shortage of adequate housing in urban areas is especially acute. In 1992, the federal housing agency, Infonavit, estimated that 7 million Mexicans qualified to receive subsidized housing, but only 50,000 units were being built per year (Herzog, 1990a). At that rate, it will take 140 years just to meet the existing demand. Because the government has so few resources with which to meet housing and other infrastructure needs, procurement of basic services is often left to individuals, many of whom also lack the necessary resources. Employees in many Mexican cities lack the money to pay for housing even if it is available. The gulf between the standard of living in the United States and Mexico is sharply defined at the border. This is true even though U.S. border residents are relatively poor; approximately 20 percent of the U.S. border residents live below the official poverty level, as compared with only 12 percent in the nation as a whole. Of 28 border counties, 21 have been designated economically distressed. Mexican border residents are poorer. Residents south of the border average approximately one-seventh of the average income per capita of U.S. border residents. The low wage rate along the border has been the catalyst for the industrialization and concomitant population boom chronicled in Chapter 2.

Even with bonuses, most Mexican workers employed by border industries earn too little to meet their basic needs. Their real wages, discounted for inflation and peso devaluation, have been constantly decreasing since the late 1970s. The only affordable housing close to workplaces is in *colonias*, the squatter settlements that have cropped up in many border cities. Such areas usually have inadequate water, unpaved streets, poor drainage, and little access to schools, medical facilities, transportation, or the other amenities that make a high-quality life.

The construction of the necessary environmental and other infrastructure and the cleanup of already polluted soils and water will be expensive. The positive side of the economic boom along the border is that it is creating resources that could underwrite investments in the environment. The mechanisms through which such financing decisions are to be made, and who is to pay, are the major issues.

**The Grass Roots:
Demand for Local Participation and Control**

The complex problems brought about by the current reconfiguration of national boundaries may have a bright side: it will be easier to assign responsibility for pollution. The verifiable effects of transboundary pollution may provide new leverage for cleanup because international law makes the originating state responsible for cleaning up such pollution. Even so, implementation is often far from certain, partly because both international institutions and national governments are ineffective in these matters. The failure of governments to successfully implement pollution control laws is one of the strongest motivations behind a new worldwide phenomenon, the demand of local people for participation and control over policies that affect their lives and living space.

International agreements, like other laws, are meaningful only if they are implemented. In a world where national sovereignty remains the ruling concept, implementation of laws depends on the commitment, capacity, and perceived legitimacy of governments.

Just as governments are becoming more numerous, they also seem to be losing their power in relative and absolute terms. International governing institutions and national governments have lost power relative to the growing power of multinational business corporations, which have grown robust in the global marketplace. National governments have lost power absolutely in terms of public support. Even Western democracies are coming to be seen as illegitimate because their central institutions are mishandled and they do not deliver what they promise.[10] Scandal has marred the reputation and hampered the performance of many government institutions. Special interests create gridlock, dominate political parties, and make a mockery of parliamentary procedures. Governments seem to be helpless to act in the face of international economic recessions and rising costs for social services, especially for the poor. Increasingly, citizens are looking to private initiatives and local communities to respond to problems rather than relying on national governments. Many laws made at the national level are far removed from the needs of the people. Sometimes laws are based on incorrect technical and behavioral theories. Other laws assume that organizational skills and capacities exist that are not in fact present.

In many countries, the national government's management of the environment is being challenged. Their failure to prevent supposedly extremely unlikely events, such as the failure of nuclear reactors in the United States and the former Soviet Union and the explosion of chemical plants in India and sewers in Mexico, has diminished public confidence in the effectiveness of environmental regulation. An enormous gap exists between symbolic decisions and lofty goals, on the one hand, and actual achievements, on the other. Too often, policy, especially environmental policy, is not implemented. Incentives for policymakers generally bear no relation to reality at the field level. Instead, policymakers are rewarded for setting ambitious goals while they shirk the responsibility of providing the appropriate understanding, tools, and capacity for realistic implementation. Goals and objectives therefore become burdens and impediments to firing-line actors. The logrolling practices of the American pluralist political system result in large government expenditures on wastewater treatment plants and water supply projects that deliver far from optimum returns.

The inability of government at any level to solve problems, and thereby gain the confidence of citizens, is nowhere better illustrated than in the issue of transboundary water resources along the U.S.-Mexico border. Within their respective borders sit two sovereign nations with complete legal rights to regulate water resources and water pollution. Only through mutual consent can these two sovereigns cooperate and coordinate their management of joint resources.

The divisiveness of the international border is exacerbated by the different political systems that exist in Mexico and the United States. The Mexican political system is characterized by a strong national government headed by a powerful president. All water resources are owned by the federal government, and most water supply projects are funded by and regulated at that level. In Mexico, federal investment decisions are not unrelated to the needs of the president and the dominant political party, the Partido Revolucionario Institucional (PRI), to garner votes and reward friends. Strong efforts are currently under way to decentralize and privatize water management, and to fund more infrastructure through user fees.

In the United States, in contrast, state and local governments have long had a strong role in providing and regulating water supply and use. Even where national regulations such as the Clean Water Act apply, states are involved in enforcement. And when water projects do receive funding at the national level, it is often at the behest of members of Congress pursuing their share of pork-barrel projects. While water management in both the United States and Mexico is highly politicized, the character of the politics differs. Neither brand of politics has placed border water problems consistently high on the national agenda. Consequently, the laws promising a clean water supply enacted by each nation and their international agreements to prevent border pollution are not being implemented.

As government has come into disrepute, citizens are increasingly confronting the state at all levels and demanding participation and a voice in decision making. NGOs are placing environmental issues on the international agenda. For example, a group of NGOs in Europe recently established an unofficial international water tribunal to arbitrate conflicts between local populations whose livelihoods depend on water supplies and the industries and public officials who have diverted water for large-scale industrial purposes. Most of the cases brought before the tribunal are there because public authorities have proven incapable of effective action (Hjern, 1992).

Something of a schism has developed between national environmental organizations and grassroots groups, mainly on issues of agenda setting. The "not in my backyard," or NIMBY, movement is really an expression of individuals' aspirations to control their own living space and ensure a safe environment for themselves and their families. Environmental consumerism—both recycling and the systematic choice of environmentally benign products—are actions emerging from the grass roots.

The desire of people to influence the condition of their local environment has particular resonance for residents of international borders. According to one report to the Council of Europe, people in frontier regions face three handicaps: they are usually distant from the capital or regional center, their most favorable trading area is often foreign rather than domestic, and some of the local authorities with whom they have to deal are in another country (Hey and Nolkaemper, 1992). Although border residents have strong reasons to search for understanding and cross-boundary agreements, they often lack sufficient authority to fully implement any cooperative agreements they might negotiate.

Policy Design for the Future

The conflicting interests of the environment and global economics and the demand for local participation and control are pushing our rapidly changing world in an uncertain direction. While much evidence suggests that the environment is deteriorating, global environmental consciousness is increasing. Globalization of trade may raise income levels to a point where environmental quality and pollution control are both desirable and affordable. At the same time, however, poor and disadvantaged populations will be subjected to greater health risks when polluting businesses can move freely across international boundaries. Governments may be able to agree on common environmental standards that apply to large areas of the globe, but they may become less able to deliver on their promises, and effective action may increasingly depend on local initiatives. In an era of linked economics, easy communications, and nascent environmental consciousness, a nettlesome dilemma has appeared. On the one hand, environmental systems are always local but invariably feed into ecosystems on regional, if not global, spatial scales. Remedial or protective actions, therefore, should be coordinated, perhaps centralized, to achieve maximum effectiveness. On the other hand, it is almost axiomatic that insensitivity to local needs increases as the level of decision making becomes more remote and centralized.

International treaties that commit nations to higher environmental standards are one approach to mitigating transboundary environmental problems. The Earth Summit held in Rio de Janeiro in 1992 promoted a number of ideas as strategies "in good standing" for dealing with transnational pollution. Among these ideas were comprehensive global and multinational treaties that include targets and standardization of environmental regulations. Far-reaching reforms of international conventions that recognize the shared nature of the global environment are long overdue. To achieve such reforms, however, national governments will have to relinquish some of their sovereignty to collective bodies that can base their decisions on a perspective of the whole earth, or at least on continents or regions. Some critics suggest that comprehensive negotiating sessions too easily degenerate into public theater, and that the resulting treaties may be nothing more than words on paper. Other views are even more critical of such international approaches, claiming that they are actually harmful and costly, not just inefficient. These analysts believe that the focus on high-level negotiations of new, more comprehensive environmental regulations is misguided. Instead they support the creation of grassroots local institutions built from the bottom up that take into account the motivations, interests, and resources of the actors, the nature of the problems, and local traditions for problem solving (Orianne, 1973).

Many of the barriers to international solutions—for example, national sovereignty and fragmented national institutions that jealously guard narrow missions—are also impediments to binational community-based action. Further, local actors often lack the necessary expertise, authority, and capacity—including money.

Consequently, the environmental quality they are able to deliver often does not reach the minimal levels that should be guaranteed to all people wherever they reside, not just along borders.

Designing institutions is not like writing on a blank slate, and it would be foolish and arrogant for policy designers to begin anew. The challenge for designers trying to improve on what already exists is to thoroughly understand the context in which they are operating. While good ideas can come from previous experience in a number of different arenas, the specific history and setting of a place may make a policy that has worked elsewhere inappropriate and non-transferable. Further, wholesale dismantling of existing institutions is both unlikely and probably undesirable. Not only do existing institutions represent centers of power that will react negatively to threats, they are also repositories for past knowledge and experiences.

Another objective for policy designers is to nest existing and new institutions at all levels—local, regional, national, and international—and to appropriately place authority at each level according to knowledge, political will, and resources. Each locality has its own problems, its own social, political, and economic structures, and traditional ways of resolving disputes. It is unlikely that a detailed blueprint for resolving local problems can be fashioned by officials at national or international levels. At the same time, efficient and sustainable environmental protection is not likely to result from local initiatives funded from national treasuries or international funding mechanisms who issue blank checks.

Policy designs for managing transboundary resources should not be evaluated according to their elegance, simplicity, or fidelity to some universal model or ideal. Good policy design contributes to three key public needs: progress in problem solving that will make tomorrow's challenges easier than today's; representation of sufficient interests, so that the policy has a positive balance of support and is politically feasible; and empowerment of the people affected, so that they can become engaged and better able to resolve their own problems (Ostrom et al., 1992).[11]

A guiding principle for thinking practically about the kind of nested policies and institutions we envision is that context is of the utmost importance. Designing policies and institutions for borders will require unique methods and procedures. We support the argument that areas surrounding national borders can be considered as units of analysis in their own right. Important perspectives are obscured when border areas are perceived only as peripheral areas of nation-states. When these areas are viewed as the center of concern, new possibilities for dealing with their problems will arise (Ingram and Schneider, 1990; Schneider and Ingram, 1993).

The Global Problem in Microcosm

Much can be learned about transboundary water resources by examining a specific representative case in microcosm. From several viewpoints—including hydrology, politics, economics, demography, culture, and social structure—the U.S.-Mexico border and the twin cities of Ambos Nogales are an exceptionally instructive example (fig. 1.3). While Ambos Nogales shares most of the problems of larger border communities such as San Diego/Tijuana and El Paso/Juarez, its problems remain on a manageable scale. The key to global environmental improvement is likely to be found in successfully meeting challenges in serious but tractable situations like those found in Ambos Nogales (Nogales, Mexico, and Nogales, Arizona).

While the twin communities of Ambos Nogales are smaller than many of the other binational cities, their experiences, environmental problems, and difficulties with water management are entirely representative. As Chapter 2 explains, the population growth associated with border industrialization has severely stressed the communities and their surroundings. Ambos Nogales eloquently illustrates the elevated exposure to environmental pollution and the concomitant health risks that are all too often characteristic of poor communities. Smoke from burning dumps mixed with flying dust from unpaved roads in Nogales, Son., spreads a brown haze over both Nogaleses on most days. Particulate matter concentrations have exceeded annual health standards every year since monitoring began in 1985 (Alger, 1984–85). And in the spring of 1991, Nogales Wash, which flows through both communities, caught fire in Nogales, Son., about two miles south of the international border. Gasoline or diesel fuel

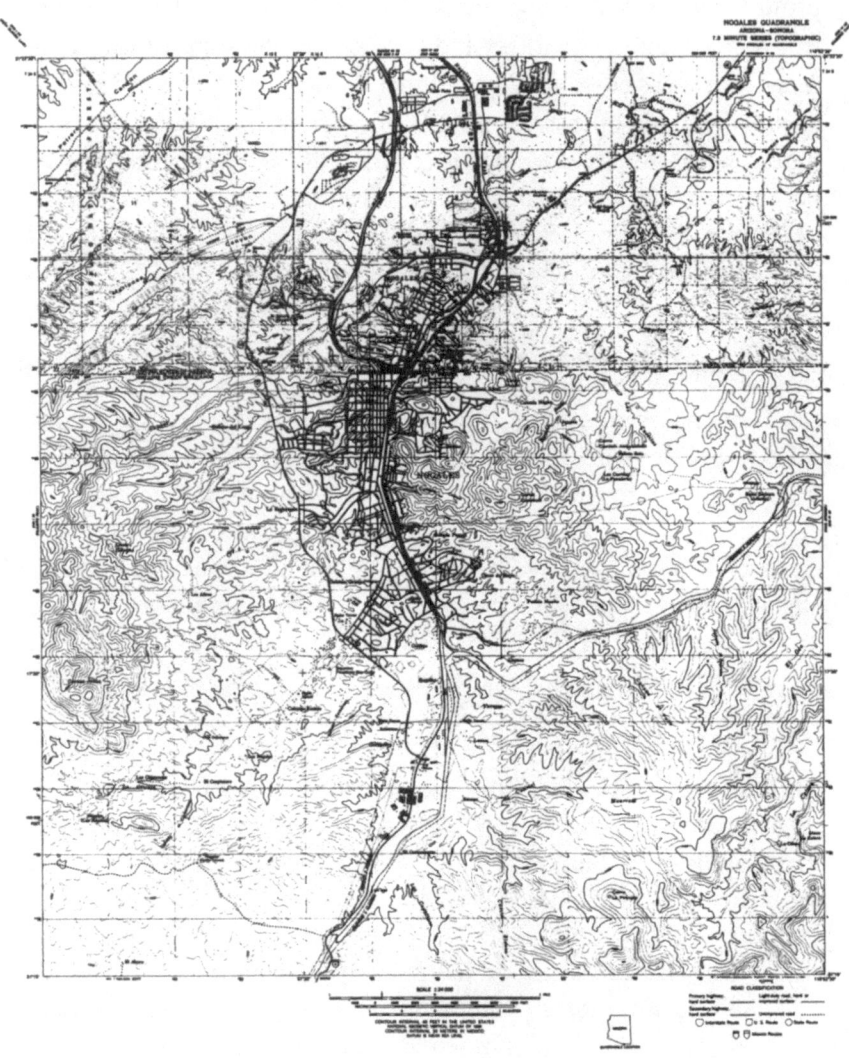

Figure 1.3 Aerial map of Ambos Nogales. *Source*: U.S. Geological Survey, 1981.

leaking from a nearby filling station that discharged spills and wastes directly into the wash was thought to be responsible.[12]

Ambos Nogales provides the full spectrum of binational water problems: surface and groundwater contamination, inadequate and insecure water supply, inequitable distribution of water resources, flooding, and endangered riparian habitats. Chapters 3 and 4 explore in depth the nature and consequences of these water problems. The challenge we hope to meet in this book is to design policies to resolve the existing water problems in Ambos Nogales that, while adequately representing important interests, empower local residents to participate as well. While the solutions for Ambos Nogales are unlikely to be directly transferable to other areas, the same problems and forces encountered in Nogales must be confronted elsewhere. Context, as we stated above, is critical. In Chapter 2 we describe the historical and cultural milieu that distinguishes border communities in general, and Ambos Nogales in particular, from other places.

The physical characteristics of watersheds, aquifers, aridity, drought, and flooding must be included in any design for the future, as must past human attempts to harness natural forces for water supply and wastewater systems. These are the subjects of Chapter 3. Physical characteristics are no more real or important than social relationships, practices, and attitudes, however, and all these factors combine to affect what humans do with water. Chapter 4 examines the different people who use water in Ambos Nogales and how their expectations and coping mechanisms for overcoming water problems differ. Water and politics are everywhere intertwined, but the pattern of the braid varies. No pattern is more complex and convoluted than the fragmented legal and institutional structures encountered at the border. The confusion and contradiction of laws, administrative practices, and political incentives are the subjects of Chapter 5. In Chapter 6 we provide the design elements we believe must be included before successful improvements can occur at both the institutional and the resource management levels.

Chapter 2

Shared Encounters: Ambos Nogales

Throughout the nearly 400 years since Europeans arrived in the geographical area that now is the border between the United States and Mexico, Native Americans, Spaniards, Mexicans, and Anglo Americans have intermingled. Through the centuries and through shifts in cultural dominance, their interactions have resulted in mutual exchanges of languages, foods, and economic goods and services. Against the backdrop of a common history during which the various groups struggled to establish themselves, fighting both each other and the harsh, predominantly arid land, a distinct border region emerged. Widely referred to as La Frontera, it is a region of rich diversity that is unlike any other place in either the United States or Mexico. While the people who inhabit the region have a great deal in common, they also exhibit sharp divisions. There are other lines of demarcation besides the political border, and a stratified system of advantage and disadvantage exists here (Velez-Ibañez, 1994). This stratification is nowhere more noticeable than in the differential access to ample high-quality water at affordable prices.

The idiosyncratic and complex relationships in La Frontera and the region's remoteness from national capitals generate misunderstanding and neglect. Public policies made in national or international forums often inadequately address local problems and frequently do not work well. In fact, many of the policies that emanate from distant centers of government are impediments to effective problem resolution, and they frequently yield unexpected, unintended, and adverse consequences. The drug war is a good example. Launched in Washington, D.C., the campaign to staunch the flow of drugs across the border severely hampered the transborder flow of goods and people unrelated to the narcotics trade. Similarly, regulations on vehicle crossings, conceived in Mexico City to prevent the undercutting of auto sales in Mexico by used cars bought or stolen in the United States, have unintentionally hurt the tourist industry.[1] More to the point here, national policies have failed to protect the environment, and in some cases have actually worsened it.[2]

The context in which a policy is intended to operate should shape its design. This chapter briefly sketches the common history and shared economic and social network in the border region. While the towns and cities on the border have much in common, each also has a story of its own. Ambos Nogales is a classic example of the rich and dynamic history of cultural interaction that has made the border a distinct region.

The Origins

At the time of the Spanish conquest, the indigenous people who occupied the area around what is now Ambos Nogales were primarily Pima and Tohono O'odham who practiced irrigated agriculture or migrated over large areas following the seasonal rainfall. The Spanish conquerors christened the region the Pimería Alta, and during the centuries of their dominance a mission system was developed along the Santa Cruz and Magdalena Rivers, including the missions of San Xavier, Tumacacori, and San Ignacio. The early written history of the people of the area revolves around the personality of the Jesuit missionary Eusebio Francisco Kino, an energetic Italian who was as much explorer as missionary (Spicer, 1992). Until his death in 1711, he waged a campaign to resettle the indigenous people into pueblos that peacefully supported the missions. Even after the Republic of Mexico succeeded the Spanish in taking formal control over the region, the string of missions dotting what is now the border were the major human settlements outside of scattered indigenous rancherías.

Apache predation was among the experiences shared by settlers in this region. The hostile Apaches diminished Mexico's desire to maintain its far northern settlements, over which it had nominal control for less than three decades; and the Apache raids eroded Mexican resistance to the expansionist grazing and mining interests of the United States. The Treaty of Guadalupe Hidalgo (1848), which ended the subsequent Mexican-American War, stated that the United States would prevent the Apaches and other tribes from raiding across the border into Mexico. The international boundary was meaningless, however, to the Apaches, who continued their raiding expeditions far south into the Mexican states of Sonora and Chihuahua. The raiding continued until the 1870s and established a precedent: Policies set in national capitals are often poorly related to the actual experiences and needs of border residents.

The Gadsden Purchase of 1853, or La Mesilla, as it is referred to in Spanish, annexed the territory that came to include Nogales, Ariz., to the United States. The purpose of the $10 million purchase was to facilitate the construction of the transcontinental railroad. The new border made little hydrologic or human sense; it both carved up the Santa Cruz and San Pedro River basins and divided indigenous peoples. At least three quarters of the Upper Pimas became residents of the United States. As much as 60 years later, there were still Pimas in the desert rancherías under the leadership of a headman named Pia Machita who seemed unaware of the change and still professed allegiance to Mexico (Spicer, 1992).

Rail lines replaced missions as the lifelines of the region in the latter half of the nineteenth century. Investors were eager to develop a railroad connecting the eastern United States to the west coast of Mexico, and the logical route lay along the old Tucson, Ariz., to Guaymas, Son., trade road running through the Nogales Valley. The railroad, a joint project of the New Mexico & Arizona Railroad and Sonora Railway, Ltd., was completed in 1882, and the two towns of Nogales sprang up immediately at the Nogales Valley border site where the rails were joined.[3]

The roots of economic interdependence, and particularly northern Mexico's late nineteenth-century economic dependence on the United States, were planted by the policies of Mexican President Porfirio Díaz, who encouraged U.S. investment there. The new railroad opened up opportunities for mining the rich metal deposits of the Arizona-Sonora region and shipping Mexican cattle to U.S. markets. The major transportation lines were built mostly with U.S. capital and were responsible for increasing exports of Mexican raw material and labor to the United States and imports of goods manufactured in the United States into Mexico (Martinez, 1988). The U.S. economy in the late nineteenth century needed agricultural and mineral resources to supply its factories, and new markets for its products. The presence of the railroads, together with additional American capital, led to the expansion of numerous mines in the region, including the massive Cananea and Nacozari mines southeast of Ambos Nogales, as well as the purchase by Americans of several large cattle ranches. Mexican national and state officials strongly encouraged foreign purchases of land and minerals during the period as a means of encouraging the development of its northern border, and most of the labor in the establishments was provided by Mexicans (Heyman, 1991).[4]

Nogales, Ariz., soon became a supply center for miners and ranchers and a place of refuge during Apache raids.[5] By 1883, just one year after the railroad had been completed, the town was estimated to be home to around 400 people; another 400 people lived in the town of Nogales, Son. The town was incorporated as the city of Nogales, Ariz., in 1898, and it became the seat of Santa Cruz County when the county was formed one year later.

Ambos Nogales was well positioned to take advantage of international trade opportunities, and it became known as the "Key City to the West Coast of Mexico." As such, it attracted a truly international set of residents. The valley's first settler is said to have been Jacob Issacson, an itinerant peddler from Russia who established a trading post and resthouse along the Tucson-Guaymas stage route in 1880, before the railroad was completed. He soon moved on, but the men who came to stay during the next few years were natives of at least 14 different states and 11 foreign countries. Some brought their wives or sent for them, but many married girls from Sonora, laying the foundation for the present bicultural and largely bilingual community.

Just as the city had been founded in response to the desire of distant powers to open new trade routes, its existence continued to be influenced by economic forces originating outside the region. Among the more significant early events was the Panic of 1893, which caused Eastern investment capital to dry up and silver prices to decline. Nogales survived, but its economy suffered greatly when several of the nearby mines closed.

A burgeoning trade in produce was also inspired by national markets. The produce trade started modestly in 1910, when iced boxcars carrying vegetables grown in Sonora passed through Nogales en route to nearby cities like Tucson. By 1939, demand from outside the region had caused trade to expand to the point that 5,000 carloads of winter vegetables destined for Canadian and Eastern markets passed through the city. Nogales also continued to be a focal point for the shipment of cattle from western Mexican states.

The Mexican Revolution of 1911 resulted in a U.S. Army detachment being sent to Nogales, Ariz., to watch developments in Mexico. Pancho Villa captured Nogales, Son., from Francisco Madero's forces during the revolution and then threatened Nogales, Ariz., closing the international crossing to all traffic. The success of the insurgency movement in the north during the revolution was part of a long-standing pattern: Remoteness from the central government in Mexico City fostered regionalism and independence. Norteños have demonstrated their strong dissatisfaction with national policies at more than one point in Mexican history (Martinez, 1988).

The U.S. Army built a military post on the outskirts of the city and stayed for more than 20 years. The new post, which at its peak was the base for 12,000 troops, was an economic and social boon for the town; its closing in 1932 was correspondingly detrimental.

Nogalensians in the 1930s and 1940s were subjected to a variety of other economically detrimental events that were largely beyond their control. Even before the military post closed, the 1929 Six Weeks' Revolution in Mexico had disrupted the Mexican economy and seriously reduced the flow of trade goods through Nogales. The U.S. Tariff Act of 1930 raised duties to the point of causing a practical embargo, stimulating retaliatory action by Mexico. Subsequent tariff acts and the devaluation of the peso cut trade to a minimum, and business throughout Nogales declined drastically.

The Great Depression resulted in further job losses in Nogales, Ariz., and a series of floods caused severe property damage and claimed several lives (see Chapter 3). World War II once again caused trade with Mexico to be greatly reduced. If not for the construction of a large flood control project by the International Boundary and Water Commission (IBWC) and other federal spending through the

Work Projects Administration, the city's economy would have collapsed completely.

World War II also provided the seed for some of the city's future salvation, however, as American tourists unable to visit Europe began to "discover" Mexico in increasing numbers. The travel and entertainment industry had been important in Nogales, Ariz., from the beginning, with hotels, restaurants, and saloons catering to a variety of army troops, traders, travelers, and businesspeople in addition to miners and ranchers. After 1945 the industry started to cater to an increasingly civilian clientele, and the tourism industry joined international trade as an important part of the city's economy.

Patterns of Growth

Nogales, Arizona

At the time of its incorporation in 1898, the West was wide open, Arizona was still 14 years away from becoming a state, and the 1,500 residents of the city of Nogales constituted the Arizona Territory's fifth largest city. In 1990, the U.S. Census showed that Santa Cruz County had grown to almost 30,000 residents but accounted for less than 1 percent of the state's 3.7 million residents. Though much larger today than in its early years, Nogales is still a small community.[6]

Nogales's multinational origins are still apparent in the names of streets and businesses and the existence of a few small ethnic enclaves, but most Nogalensians are Hispanic—78 percent of the county's residents and 92 percent of the city's residents, according to the 1990 U.S. Census. Hispanic residents undoubtedly formed a significant proportion of the city's population at its founding, given that the Treaty of Guadalupe Hidalgo in 1848 and the Gadsden Purchase in 1853 made instant American citizens of the many Mexican residents living within the borders of present-day Arizona. In addition, little if any effort was made to physically separate the two cities of Nogales in the early years, and residents of either nationality were free to build homes or establish businesses on whichever side of the line they chose. A 1930s-era guidebook to Arizona mentions the existence of several Mexican neighborhoods in Nogales, Ariz.

Nogales originally was under the jurisdiction of Pima County, which includes a huge area of south-central Arizona and is dominated by the city of Tucson, 97 kilometers (60 miles) to the north. The citizens of Nogales thought that their situation and interests were not very similar to those of Tucson residents, and, further, they believed their taxes were mostly being spent elsewhere in the county, and in 1899 they persuaded the state legislature to create a new county with Nogales as its seat. Then as now, Santa Cruz County was Arizona's smallest county, covering only 3,260 square kilometers (1,260 square miles), more than 60 percent of which belongs to either the U.S. Forest Service or the state of Arizona. Figure 2.1 shows population growth in Nogales, Ariz., from 1930 to 1990.

Nogales, Sonora

People moved to Nogales, Son., for many of the same reasons that they came to Nogales, Ariz. Commodities moved in both directions across the border—minerals and cattle to the United States, and finished goods to Mexico—and customs brokerage and import-export business opportunities were available in both cities. The economy of northern Sonora was booming as the result of American investment in the development of natural resources, and much of the labor at the mines, ranches, and railroads in both Arizona and Sonora was supplied by Mexicans. Some of the Mexicans commuted to their jobs from Mexican border cities such as Nogales rather than living at job sites, and there were many opportunities for business establishments of all kinds to supply workers during their occasional forays to town.

The population of Nogales, Son., grew for other reasons as well. Northward migration from the interior of Mexico had long been encouraged by both the Spanish and Mexican governments as a means of retaining control of the northern frontier. Though not substantial enough (or timely enough) to secure that goal, migration to the north did occur, especially once jobs in American-owned enterprises became available. Following the establishment of a new political boundary after the Gadsden Purchase, the border became a natural stopping point, and Nogales, like other border cities, became the "end of the line" for many Mexican migrants. For all these reasons,

Shared Encounters: Ambos Nogales   35

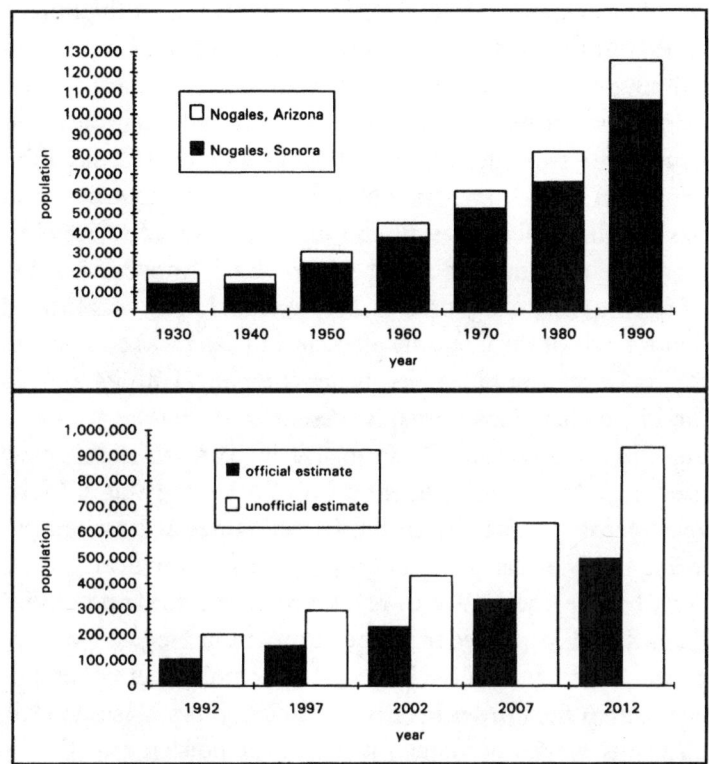

Figure 2.1 *Top*: Population growth in Ambos Nogales, 1930–1990. *Sources*: Respective decennial censuses. Many people with considerable knowledge of Nogales, Son., consider the official population figure for that city to be underestimated by at least 100 percent. *Bottom*: Official and unofficial projected population estimates for Nogales, Son. *Source*: COAPAES.

the population of Nogales, Son., grew quickly, and by the turn of the century it was substantially larger than Nogales, Ariz.

The decision to reside in the Mexican city rather than the American one appears to have concerned preference more than obligation, because little (if any) effort was made to restrict movement across the boundary. There was no restriction at all on immigration until 1917, and from 1917 to 1929 only minor paperwork and a small fee were required to cross into the United States. The U.S. Border Patrol was not even created until 1924, and its mandate was to prevent the immigration of Chinese, not Mexican, laborers across the Mexican border. Further evidence of the initial inconsequence of the border is the fact that until 1898 the Nogales railroad depot was housed in a single building that straddled the international boundary, as did some business establishments, and commerce flowed freely back and forth between the two cities. One of the city's first residents, John Brickwood, built his saloon straddling the border so that he could sell drinks on the American side and cigars on the Mexican side, thereby avoiding customs duties on both articles. Johnny Jund, a dispenser of fine liquors, discovered that his establishment was located on the Sonora side of the line only after the building was completed. A description of the two cities' first water company, with its wells in Sonora and its owners in Arizona, is presented in Chapter 3.

Although many Sonorans chose to live in Nogales, Son., many others used the city as a point of entry into the United States. Mexicans moved across the border to the United States at least temporarily during the Mexican Revolution (1910–20), many fleeing rural villages that had been engulfed in revolutionary turmoil and bloodshed. When the Mexican Federalist government in Nogales was uprooted by the Constitutionalists in 1913, the Federalists set up temporary offices across the border in Arizona, in Nogales's Masonic Hall. Other Mexicans moved permanently across the border, establishing residences in Nogales, Ariz., or seeking opportunities elsewhere in the United States. Emigration from Mexico to the United States was particularly pronounced during the 1920s.

The population of Nogales, Son., reached 15,605 in 1930 but then leveled off during the Great Depression (INEGI, 1990a).[7] The new tariffs and the resulting reduced trade between the two countries caused as much difficulty for residents of Nogales, Son., as they did for residents of Nogales, Ariz. Copper prices plunged, and thousands of laborers were laid off by the large copper mines in Sonora. Wholesale and retail establishments went out of business as their customers lost their jobs. Unemployment was common, and exacerbated by the fact that job opportunities in the United States began to disappear when U.S. officials started to deny entry visas on the grounds that emigrants were too likely to become wards of the state. The number of unemployed grew even larger when U.S. officials, worried about the impact of Mexican labor on U.S. jobs, began to forcibly repatriate

Mexican emigrants. The repatriates often returned to cities and towns in the interior of Mexico, but many later made their way back to the Mexican border towns.

Nogales began to grow rapidly again once the Depression was over. Cattle exports surged in the late 1930s after the restrictive U.S. tariffs were lifted. The booming postwar economy in the Southwest created a strong demand for Mexican labor. Mexicans holding "green cards" were allowed to work in the United States, and U.S. jobs were important sources of income for Mexican border city residents. Many unemployed Mexicans found work in the United States in the *bracero* (laborer) program, under which Americans were legally allowed to hire contract labor from Mexico for a variety of jobs, primarily in agriculture. The program, which ran from 1942 to 1965, attracted especially large numbers of unemployed Mexican laborers to the border during its first 10 years, when contracting offices were located in border cities like Nogales. The state of Sonora grew rapidly, at an average rate of 3.4 percent per year during the 1940s, but the city of Nogales grew even faster, at a rate of 5.4 percent per year, reaching a total population of 26,016 in 1950.

The next wave of U.S.-financed jobs for Mexican laborers developed in the mid-1960s, just as the bracero program was winding down. The Border Industrialization Program (BIP), initiated in 1965, provided jobs within Mexico, just as the American-owned mines and ranches had done between 1882 and 1930. This time, however, it was the labor itself, rather than raw materials, that American and other foreign investors were interested in developing. As part of the BIP, the Mexican government allowed foreign companies to own and operate manufacturing plants in Mexico at which imported parts and materials would be assembled by Mexican laborers. The finished goods were sent back across the border, with only the value added in Mexico (consisting almost entirely of the labor of the Mexican workers) being taxed. The assembly plants are commonly known as *maquiladoras* or *maquilas*, after the Spanish *maquilar*, which refers to the share of the flour that a miller withholds in payment for services rendered.

The first maquila in Nogales began operation in 1967. The number of plants grew steadily during the next several years, but then slowed considerably as American companies responded to a 1974 economic downturn in the United States by shutting down or reducing their operations in Mexico. Though maquila operations slowly built back up during the remainder of the decade, it was not until the early 1980s that their growth became dramatic. Major peso devaluations in 1976 and 1982, and numerous other devaluations during the years 1982–87, made Mexican labor increasingly attractive to American companies, which built new plants and expanded operations at existing plants. By 1990 there were about 75 maquilas in Nogales, employing 16,840 workers out of a total workforce of 38,936.[8]

In the 1980s the population of Nogales surged once again, growing at an annual average of 4.8 percent after two decades of annual growth averaging 3 percent or less. Nogales, Son., was home to 68,076 people in 1980, and 107,936 in 1990. Figure 2.1 depicts population projections for Nogales, Son., through 2012.

Interdependent Economies

Nogales, Arizona

The economy of Nogales, Ariz., is still largely based on industries related to the city's border location. Visitors from Mexico spent an estimated $268.5 million in Santa Cruz County in 1991, accounting for approximately two-thirds of the county's retail sales (Hopkins, 1992). Nogales, Ariz., merchants generally consider all of Santa Cruz County and Sonora to be their market area, and many customers come from even farther away. More than 80 percent of the Mexican residents who shop in Nogales, Ariz., live within 17 kilometers (10 miles) of the border, but almost 30 percent of Mexican expenditures in Nogales, Ariz., are made by people who have traveled more than 338 kilometers (200 miles).

The extent to which Nogales, Ariz., merchants benefit from border industrialization is illustrated by the findings of a survey of maquila employees in Nogales, Son. The employees spent an average of 30 percent of their earnings on the U.S. side of the border, mainly in Nogales, Ariz. Official estimates indicate that although the overall population of Nogales, Son., is at least five times that of Nogales,

Ariz., the daytime population is more evenly distributed as shoppers, workers, businesspeople, and visitors cross the border in their daily activities or in search of goods and services not available, not as cheap, or not of equivalent perceived quality on the other side. During a normal day, the population of Nogales, Ariz., increases to approximately 40,000, about double the official count. Ambos Nogales is now subject to global markets and distant sources of capital and investment, and Nogales, Ariz., is economically dependent on its Mexican counterpart.

The sale of goods and services to Mexican residents benefits residents of Nogales, Ariz., in many ways. A large proportion of city and county revenues is obtained from sales taxes, so the Mexican visitors fund many local public expenditures.[9] Retail trade is in many ways the backbone of the county's economy, employing 23.9 percent of the labor force in 1990. These jobs exist year-round and help create other jobs because of the "multiplier" effect: Those employed by the retail trade have money to spend on other local goods and services. A model constructed by economists at the University of Arizona indicated that in 1991, a total of 4,425 jobs in the county (of a total employment of 11,286) may have been attributable to the expenditures of Mexican visitors (Hopkins, 1992).

The wholesale trade industry is the county's second largest source of employment, accounting for 11.6 percent of the workforce in 1990. This industry too is strongly affected by the county's proximity to Mexico, as seen from the fact that the proportion of the county's jobs found in wholesale trade, 3.9 percent, is three times higher than that found in the state of Arizona as a whole. Many types of goods have crossed the border at Nogales since the two cities were founded, and customs brokerages and U.S. Customs offices have always been conspicuous in the Nogales economy. In 1939, for example, three quarters of the business volume in Nogales was from merchandise sales to Mexico and the handling and warehousing of products from Mexico's west coast.

Produce is now mostly trucked rather than shipped by rail, and the Mexican produce trucked through Nogales now accounts for approximately half of all the winter vegetables consumed in the United States (fig. 2.2). The dozens of warehouses in Nogales, Ariz., that

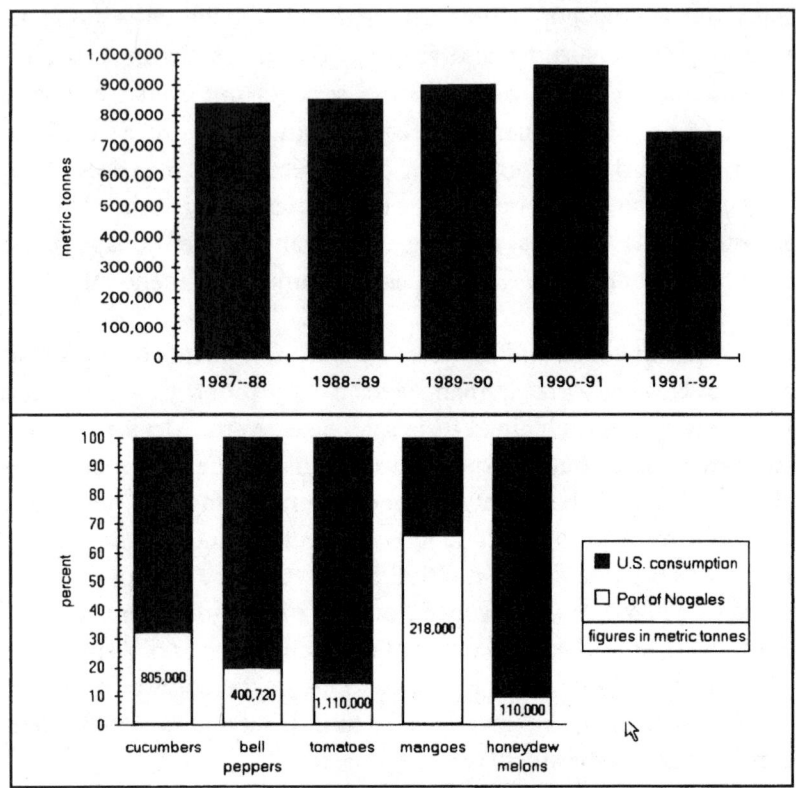

Figure 2.2 *Top*: Fruits and vegetables passing through the Port of Nogales, 1987–1992. *Bottom*: Specific fruits and vegetables passing through the Port of Nogales as a percentage of total U.S. consumption (figures in metric tonnes). *Source*: U.S. Customs, Arizona Port of Entry data.

store and process the produce are important employers during the winter produce season (November–April), when 600 trucks per day cross the border.[10] The movement of manufactured goods across the border became important with the development of the maquiladora program in the 1960s. Parts and materials are shipped to Mexico, and finished goods are returned to the United States.

Although many of the recent settlers were attracted there by economic opportunity, Nogales, Ariz., is not a well-to-do area. Twenty-two percent of the families in Santa Cruz County in 1990 were identified as living below the poverty level—twice the rate for the state of Arizona as a whole.

Nogales, Sonora

The current economic status of Nogales, Son., can be understood only in the context of the broader national economy. Industrialization in Mexico proceeded rapidly during the post–World War II years, and economic growth led to steadily higher standards of living for Mexico's citizens. The economy started to slow in the 1970s, however, and in 1976 the peso was devalued for the first time in 23 years (Heyman, 1991). Fortunately for Mexican residents, who had grown accustomed to steadily improving conditions, the economy was soon revived by the discovery and development of vast oil resources. In the late 1970s the future looked extremely promising to Mexican citizens, government officials, and foreign investors alike. The Mexican government borrowed large sums from international banks on the strength of its oil exports, and the national debt grew from $4.5 billion in 1971 to $19.6 billion in 1976, and reached $80 billion by 1982.[11]

In the early 1980s, worldwide oil prices suddenly dropped, along with Mexico's high expectations of economic growth. Mexican industry owners found it difficult to make payments on their enormous loans, foreign reserves dwindled, and the government was forced to suspend debt payments. Investor confidence was shattered, and capital to finance future investments disappeared. In 1982, the new administration of President Miguel de la Madrid was forced to undertake an austerity program in which public spending was slashed. Unemployment levels rose and inflation soared, causing real wages and standards of living to decline. La Crisis had begun, and it was to last for two years.[12]

La Crisis hit Mexican border residents especially hard. Standards of living near the border depend heavily on exchange rates, since prices for almost all goods at the border are implicitly or explicitly based on the value of the U.S. dollar. When La Crisis hit, the peso came under severe pressure and was allowed to fall freely. Major peso devaluations occurred in 1982 and again in 1987; altogether there

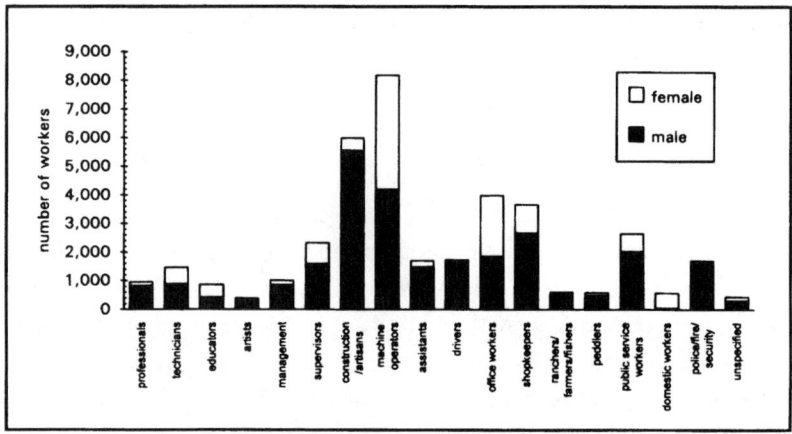

Figure 2.3 Employed population in Nogales, Son., in 1990. *Source*: INEGI census, 1990. The INEGI census probably underestimates the true numbers. Some percentage of the technicians, artisans, managers, supervisors, and professionals are employed by maquilas, but exactly how many is not known.

were more than a hundred devaluations between 1976 and 1987, and purchasing power declined to levels not seen since the Great Depression (Heyman, 1991).

The high unemployment and low wages resulting from the weak peso devastated Mexican residents, but the same conditions were extremely attractive to foreign investors. As described earlier, growth of the maquiladora industry boomed following the start of La Crisis in 1982, and the maquilas now dominate the economy of Nogales.

There is no question that the maquilas are the major source of jobs in Nogales; a recent census conducted by the maquila industry indicated that maquilas employ 43 percent of the city's workforce (figs. 2.3 and 2.4).[13] There are questions, however, as to just how much the maquilas actually benefit the local economy. Because they are foreign-owned, a substantial portion of the maquilas' profits accrue outside the country and thus are not used for consumption or investment that would stimulate the local economy. Similarly, the profits are not available for local taxation and do not contribute to the revenue base that supports public expenditures. And since workers in the maquilas primarily assemble parts that have been shipped

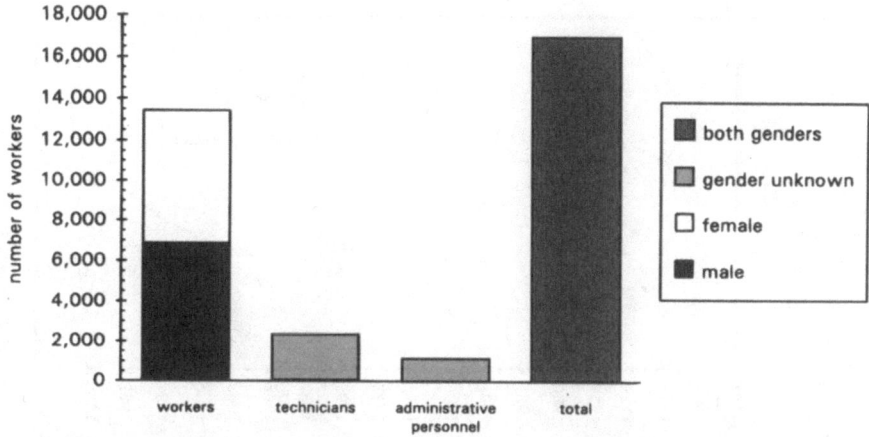

Figure 2.4 Estimated number of maquila employees in Nogales, Son., in 1990. *Source*: Francisco Lara, COLEF-Nogales, pers. comm., 1993.

into the country, the maquilas generate very little local business among wholesalers and other suppliers. A survey of Sonoran maquiladoras indicated that less than 10 percent of the materials processed by the maquilas was of Mexican origin (Pavlakovic and Silvers, 1988). Because they have so few links to other businesses, provide very little to the tax base, and contribute little to the pool of capital available for other investments, the maquilas have a diminished multiplier effect in the local economy.

Even employees of the maquilas find it difficult to finance anything beyond mere survival. Work hours vary from one business to the next, but a "typical" maquiladora employee works eight hours per day, six days per week. Mexican law mandates that workers receive an additional day's wages for Sunday, though they do not work that day, and that they receive vacation pay, holiday pay, and Christmas bonuses. Depending on the particular employer, they may also receive fringe benefits such as attendance and punctuality bonuses, transportation subsidies, cafeteria subsidies, life and medical insurance, supermarket vouchers, and other cash benefits that in 1988 added almost an additional 50 percent to their annual wages. While the list of paid days and fringe benefits sounds impressive, it is important to keep in mind that all of it is based on the legal minimum

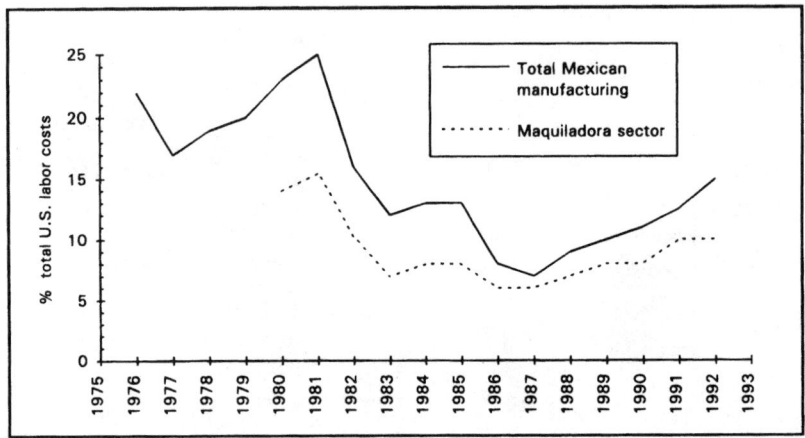

Figure 2.5 Labor costs in Mexican factories as a percentage of total U.S. labor costs for manufacturing. *Source*: U.S. Department of Labor, Bureau of Labor Statistics, Joint Economic Committee of Congress.

wage, which amounts to only a few dollars per day—just over $4 per day for unskilled workers in 1993 (fig. 2.5). Despite all the fringe benefits, then, the minimum wage does not provide a very high standard of living. In 1988, the average maquiladora salary, including fringe benefits, was less than $1,700 per worker per year (AMCHAM, 1988).

The maquila workforce in Nogales, as elsewhere along the border, is largely young. More than a third of the city's population is age 14 or younger, and only 3.1 percent are 65 or older. Almost all workers in the maquilas are under 30, and many are much younger. The workers leaving the factories at the end of the day look more like high school students leaving their classrooms than factory workers. Most of the positions in maquilas are low-skill, low-wage, production-line jobs that are often filled by women.[14] Little advancement is possible from these positions, and it is common to find women who have worked at the same kind of job for minimum wages for several years. The few higher-paying jobs that require technical expertise are usually filled by men. The highest-paying managerial positions are often occupied by Americans who moved down with their companies; many of them live across the border in the United States rather than in Mexico.

The turnover rate is extremely high because the work is tedious and workers feel that they have little to lose. Workers "drop out" temporarily for a variety of reasons ranging from boredom, to a desire to visit hometowns, to the need to take care of sick children. When they want to return to work, they simply look for jobs in another factory. A comment from one maquila manager indicates the magnitude of the turnover rate: "We got ours down to a manageable level, a little below 100 percent. At our worst, we've had a 400 percent [annual] turnover rate."[15]

Maquiladoras pay a variety of payroll taxes on the wages and fringe benefits they pay to their workers. The major payroll taxes are social security (10.5 percent), housing (5 percent), and education (1 percent) taxes. In 1988, payroll taxes accounted for 18.7 percent of the total labor costs paid by the maquiladoras. Though the figures sound substantial, they actually have very little impact on the standard of living of local residents, for two reasons. First, because salaries—and total payrolls—are so low, so too are the payroll taxes. For instance, the housing tax amounted to just $65.49 per worker per year in 1988. Second, the taxes are collected by the federal rather than the state or local government. Although a proportion of the funds is supposed to be returned to the states, based on population size, this does not always occur. For instance, a member of the Sonora Maquiladora Association claimed that money in the federal housing fund financed by the housing tax was being used to rebuild housing in Mexico City after the devastating 1985 earthquake instead of being returned to the border.[16]

Despite their importance, however, the maquilas are clearly not the only source of employment in Nogales, Son. (see fig. 2.3). Customs and export brokerage services have always been a part of the Nogales economy, as has tourism. A 1930s-era guidebook depicts Nogales, Son., as depending heavily on international trade. It describes a city full of curio shops, sidewalk vendors selling leather goods and other handicrafts, and scores of cantinas and restaurants. Much the same scene exists today in downtown Nogales; those who don't venture very far from the boundary line are not likely to see anything else. Despite the many jobs and occupations available, however, the jobless rate in Nogales, Son., is reported to be very high (47.8 percent).[17]

The Border Culture

Contact among different ethnic groups and nationalities, bolstered by the continual flow of people, goods, tourists, and information across political boundaries, has created what some social scientists identify as a border culture (Stoddard and Hedderson, 1987). Others claim that some twin cities such as Brownsville/Matamoros and Laredo/Nuevo Laredo constitute a community in the sense that, although they maintain separate political systems, they share a "we" feeling, they believe that what is good for one city is good for the other, and they act accordingly (Sloan et al., 1977). Ambos Nogales remains what it was at its founding, a diverse but coherent culture.

International division of labor is not simply a transfer of labor power, it is also a transfer of culture across international boundaries, and thus an indicator of deepening economic, social, and geographic interdependence (Herzog, 1990b). The steady stream of laborers migrating out of Mexico has fed border cities for several generations, and a unique regional social system whose family structures, culture, social interaction, and factors of production are fused has evolved across the boundary.

Transnational linkages are bolstered by a common language of sorts. It is not uncommon in the border region for speakers to switch from English to Spanish and back again in a single conversation depending on the topic and their language abilities. More than 80 percent of Nogales, Ariz., residents speak Spanish, and, as we elaborate in Chapter 5, the ability to communicate in Spanish is related to a number of attitudes about water. Bilingualism is obviously linked to family background; approximately 60 percent of Nogales, Ariz., families are binational and have members on the other side of the line (Francisco Lara, COLEF-Nogales, pers. comm., 1993).

For some immigrants from the interior of Mexico, Ambos Nogales is only a jumping-off place for movement farther north into the United States. And for some U.S. residents and retirees, few of whom ever learn Spanish, the border is simply an inexpensive place to live with a good climate. But many other residents contribute to and participate in the regional ethnicity. Binational, bilingual families use their family ties to cope with poverty and discrimination in housing, jobs, groceries, schooling, and medical attention (Velez-Ibañez, 1988).

Informal networks established through frequent interaction provide mechanisms that border residents use to cope with the stresses of rapid population growth, low income, and the elevated health risks resulting from pollution. During times of stress, cross-border networks become viable links to social, economic, and psychological survival. Accordingly, people seek goods and services on whichever side of the border offers the best value and most culturally comfortable service. The easy crossing of the regulars is symbolized by the hole in the international fence, within clear view of the international border crossing, that was used by residents of Ambos Nogales who found the long walk to the official gate inconvenient—until an "impermeable" solid-steel fence was erected in 1994.

The kin network that links binational families is but one of several informal structures that facilitate cross-border interchange. Firefighters, police, and disaster rescue operations regularly cross the line in emergencies. Public health officials have developed lines of communication to exchange equipment, diagnoses, and sometimes patients. Academic and government researchers trade information and peer-review comments, eschewing formal channels and procedures. And as Chapter 3 explains, Nogales, Ariz., water flows across the border through a variety of unofficial means, including a hose over the fence from a fire hydrant during drought emergencies. Transnational informal networks are clearly used by a significant proportion of Ambos Nogales residents, and the usefulness of such networks for resolving problems is not always officially acknowledged.

Some Mexican border residents, called "national fronterizos" by O. J. Martinez (1990), have minimal or superficial contact with the United States either because they are indifferent to their next-door neighbors or because they are unwilling or unable to function in any substantive way in another society.[18] A similar group of Anglo newcomers to the border on the U.S. side clearly exists, as the data we present in Chapter 4 illustrate. Such groups look to their national capitals for policies that will lessen the severity of problems associated with the border. From the perspective of residents who share the border culture and are adept at employing informal networks, however, the policies that emanate from the national capitals are frequently impediments to effective problem resolution. The industrial and urban policies of both nations have aggravated rapid population growth in border cities; national governments have stimulated the location of maquilas in border cities that possess inadequate water resources and are in fragile environments; and, worse, these industrial policies have not invested anything in national infrastructure or environmental protection. As a consequence, housing shortages, lack of education and health facilities, and inadequate transportation networks accompany and aggravate environmental degradation. The problems have become so severe that Mayor Hector Mayer Soto of Nogales, Son., favors a moratorium on new maquilas in his city.[19]

Ethnic, racial, and cultural diversities have become important issues both among and within nations. Diversity can generate disputes, from which harmful stereotyping and worse can evolve; or, diversity can come to be accepted as natural, positive, and beneficial to society. At its worst, as the carnage of the early 1990s in Bosnia-Herzegovina, Nagorno-Karabakh, and Rwanda illustrate, the conflict resulting from diversity is manifested in "ethnic cleansing." At its best, diversity leads to greater empathy and richer deliberations among peoples who offer different experiences and models for solving problems. The U.S.-Mexico border offers an opportunity for both nations to come to terms with divisions that exist not just at the border but also internally.

This border also offers to the world a generally positive model for very different cultures and economies to coexist side by side. In few places do two nations of such different levels of economic development share a common boundary; yet for more than 200 years the two nations have settled their disputes mainly peacefully. That is not to say that relations among Native Americans, Anglos, Mexican Americans, and Mexicans have been without conflict—conflict that often resulted in the unequal distribution of opportunities and resources. As we discuss in Chapter 4, such stratification is obvious in the differential access to ample, affordable, high-quality water in Ambos Nogales.

The ability of people to maintain ties, bridge their differences, forge informal networks, and develop a common culture underlies the relative success of La Frontera. This chapter has described the historic, economic, and cultural ties that bind these people together through their shared encounters. The chapter has also portrayed the mounting stress on the time-honored patterns of peaceful problem resolution. The entire U.S.-Mexico border in general, and Ambos Nogales in particular, is under pressure from the enormous population growth and the influx of newcomers who may not share the time-honored traditions. The increasing demands on limited resources are reflected in emerging struggles over water resources.

Chapter 3

The Troubled Waters of Ambos Nogales

The history of Ambos Nogales has been strongly influenced by the region's political, economic, and social conditions. But the surrounding physical environment and the natural resources it contains have been just as important to the growth of Nogales and its residents. Water is of particular importance in this semiarid land, for it has shaped both the earth and the lives of those who live on it. The natural water resources of Ambos Nogales and the ways they have been used and developed to support the area's residents are the subjects of this chapter.

Natural Water Resources

Surface Water Drainages

The two cities of Nogales lie within a small valley 24 kilometers (15 miles) long but only 0.8 kilometers (0.5 miles) wide. Nogales Wash, a small watercourse that runs through the valley, meanders across the valley floor on its journey from the higher southern end to its confluence with the Santa Cruz River to the north. Along the way Nogales Wash is joined by numerous tributaries from the surrounding hills, particularly on the west side of the valley (fig. 3.1).

The southern end of the Nogales Valley is quite rugged, and hills rise steeply from both sides of the valley floor. Farther north the eastern hills diminish in height until the Nogales Valley eventually merges into the neighboring and much larger Santa Cruz River valley. The Santa Cruz River valley and its tributaries form a watershed that is the dominant hydrographic feature of the central portion of southern Arizona and northern Sonora.

The Santa Cruz and Nogales Valleys are bisected by the international boundary, so that portions of each lie within both the United

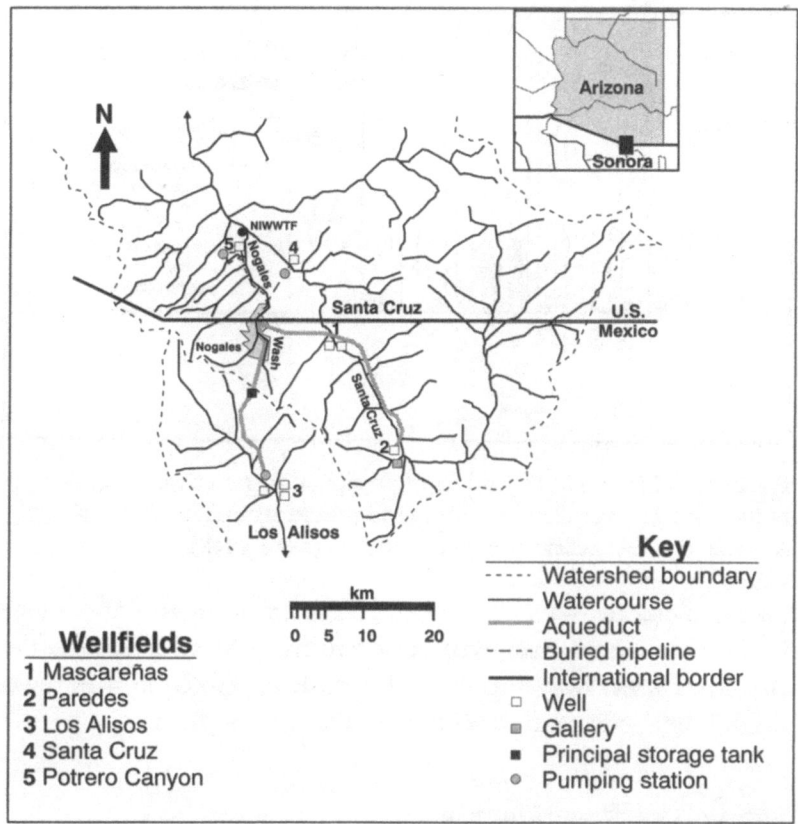

Figure 3.1 The upper Santa Cruz River and upper Río Magdalena (Los Alisos) watersheds. The major sources of the Ambos Nogales water supply are shown, with the exception of the 14 urban wells in Nogales, Son., which provide about one-fifth of the nominal supply for the Sonoran sector of the city. The NIWWTF is at the confluence of the Santa Cruz River and Nogales Wash. *Sources*: COLEF and Nogales, Ariz., Water District.

States and Mexico. Like the Nogales Valley, the Santa Cruz Valley is higher in the south, so the Santa Cruz River flows generally from south to north. The origin of the Santa Cruz River is in Arizona's San Rafael Valley, about 80 kilometers (50 miles) east of Nogales, and the river initially flows south into Mexico before turning to the west and then north and flowing back into the United States. From that point the river continues to flow northward to its confluence with the Gila River just south of Phoenix, passing through metropolitan

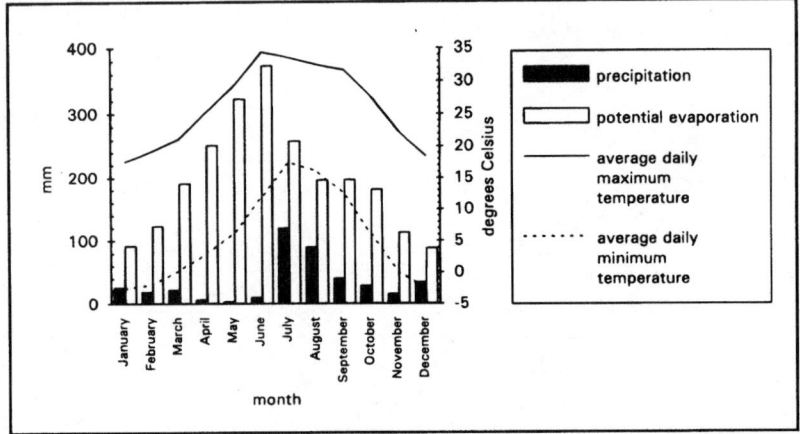

Figure 3.2 Mean monthly values of precipitation, potential evapotranspiration, and average daily maximum/minimum temperatures for Nogales, Arizona. *Sources*: Sellers and Hill, 1974; Sellers et al., 1985.

Tucson along the way. Interestingly, during peak flood times, water in the Santa Cruz River eventually returns to Mexico, because the Gila River flows west into the Colorado River, which in turn flows south into Mexico and the Gulf of California (see fig. 1.1).

Climate, Floods, and Drought

The climate of the Nogales area, like that of much of the U.S.-Mexican border, is semiarid. Figure 3.2 shows the annual distribution of precipitation, potential evapotranspiration, and diurnal temperature ranges in Nogales (Sellers et al., 1985; Sellers and Hill, 1974). The average annual rainfall is only 430 millimeters (16 inches) while potential evaporation—the amount of water that, if available, could be evaporated—averages more than 2,280 millimeters (90 inches). Most of the precipitation that does occur evaporates soon after hitting the ground, if not before, so surface watercourses are usually dry. Though maps of the region show many rivers and streams, in reality most of these are ephemeral, containing water only during or immediately following major storms. Even the Santa Cruz River is dry in many reaches and contains only minimal flows in others.

Local conditions are strongly influenced by seasonal and annual variations in climate. Hot, dry conditions predominate during much of the spring and summer, while moderate and sustained rains are common in winter. More than half of the annual precipitation typically falls during only two months of the year, July and August, when monsoon storms from the south enter the area. The monsoons are capable of dropping large quantities of water in very short periods, but the relatively scarce vegetation and thin desert soils of the Nogales and Santa Cruz Valleys are not able to detain and absorb such large quantities of water. As a consequence, runoff from monsoon storms can quickly fill or overfill local watercourses. These rapidly arising flash floods have the potential to scour out existing channels or even to forge completely new ones, so floodwaters generally run thick with sediment and debris.

Before humans settled and built their homes in the Nogales and Santa Cruz Valleys, flash floods affected only the natural environment, and only flora and fauna adapted to deal with these occasional high-flow events, or even dependent on them, lived on the floodplains. Human activity, much of it in the last century, has caused important changes. Transportation routes and utility lines, which generally follow the natural contours of the land, have been built along local watercourses, and cities have been built on the floodplains—often the first areas to be developed because of their relative flatness. The Nogales Valley floodplain was an especially likely area for development because it covers virtually the entire valley floor. As a consequence of these patterns of development, even relatively minor storms now disrupt the usual flow of people and goods, and high flows from heavier storms have caused extensive property damage and occasional loss of human life.

Drought, though usually less dramatic than floods, can be equally severe. In some years the summer monsoons or the more moderate winter cyclones (which are more important than the monsoons to the region's water supply because they occur over a longer period and are thus more easily absorbed and retained in the basin) are greatly reduced or fail to occur altogether. Water sources in the Santa Cruz Valley respond rapidly to climatic anomalies, so water quickly becomes scarce during droughts. As with flood flows, the native flora and fauna are largely adapted to these cycles of drought, but city residents, industries, crops, and domestic animals depend on regular supplies of water. Droughts periodically lead to economic losses and hardship for the growing number of residents in the Nogales and Santa Cruz Valleys.

Groundwater Resources

Though surface water flows in the Santa Cruz River watershed tend to be limited and highly variable, sizable quantities of groundwater are stored in some portions of the valley. Ninety-seven kilometers (60 miles) north of Nogales, the much larger city of Tucson until recently relied on groundwater to supply 100 percent of its water needs, as did several large copper mines and agricultural operations scattered throughout the Santa Cruz Valley. Although groundwater levels in many areas of the valley have been steadily declining, and even though the massive Central Arizona Project was built to bring surface water from the distant Colorado River into the area, large quantities of groundwater will continue to be used in the Santa Cruz Valley for the foreseeable future.

Nogales Valley communities face the same arid climate and limited surface water resources as their northern valley neighbors, but they do not have access to the same federally financed surface-water importation facilities. Nogalensians, too, would like to be able to tap into the Santa Cruz Valley's deep groundwater, but it is not yet known how much, if any, deep groundwater exists in the southern end of the valley. Groundwater is stored in sediments washed into the valley from the surrounding mountains over the course of geologic time. The northern end of the valley is both much wider and has much deeper sediment deposits—up to 3,800 meters deep (12,500 feet) just south of Tucson. By contrast, sediments in the southern valley are consistently less than 490 meters (1,600 feet) deep, and the sediment thickness diminishes dramatically toward the southern edge. Geologic exploration has already indicated that the deep sediments that form substantial aquifers in the northern part of the valley are much less extensive and less permeable in the south. Thus, the potential for finding substantial, economically recoverable groundwater deposits is much smaller in the Nogales area. A great deal of time, money, and expertise are necessary to adequately evaluate the hydrologic properties of material located deep underground, and the lack of these have so far resulted in uncertainty about potential sources of deep groundwater near Nogales.

Several other sources of groundwater are well known, however. Shallow aquifers have been formed by many of the area's meandering streams and rivers, which over time have deposited and reworked the sediments lying underneath and adjacent to their channels. These reworked deposits tend to be extremely permeable, and in some cases they are extensive enough to be capable of storing and transmitting large volumes of water. The aquifer associated with the Santa Cruz River is up to 1.6 kilometers (1 mile) wide and 30 meters (100 feet) thick, while aquifers associated with tributaries such as Nogales Wash tend to be narrower and thinner. Groundwater in these aquifers usually lies less than 15 meters (50 feet), and often less than 7.5 meters (25 feet), below the ground surface.

The shallowness and permeability of these aquifers, which are easily reached by wells and are capable of yielding large quantities of water, have made them valuable sources of water for residents of the Nogales and Santa Cruz Valleys. These same characteristics, however, make them highly responsive to climatic anomalies, because their status is closely linked to the availability of surface water flows. The aquifers are filled, or "recharged," when water on the surface infiltrates into the ground. They are depleted by vegetation, groundwater wells, and discharge into streams. Most recharge occurs during periods of sustained flows, such as those following the steady winter rains. If these rains do not occur, depletions exceed recharge and the aquifers are slowly drained. Changes in groundwater storage do not occur as rapidly as changes in surface water flow because water moves much more slowly through the earth than it does on the surface. Nevertheless, unusually wet or dry conditions on the surface are eventually reflected in the level of water found in shallow aquifers.

Riparian Areas

The amount of vegetation growing in a given area of the Santa Cruz Valley depends on the amount of water available there. The high mountains surrounding the valley, some of which reach elevations above 2,750 meters (9,000 feet), support dense pine forests because precipitation at this elevation can be as much as twice that on the floor of the Nogales Valley. Chaparral and oak woodlands grow on the lower mountain slopes, while the drier valley floor, at an elevation of approximately 735 meters (2,400 feet), is covered with a mixture of grasses, widely spaced shrubs, and cacti more typical of semiarid desert areas.

The flora and fauna on the valley floor are sparser and less diverse than those associated with more humid regions. This is true over the entire valley floor except in limited areas where surface or subsurface water is more frequently available. On the edges of the valley's watercourses and marshes the vegetation is much taller, more diverse, and abundant, standing in conspicuous contrast to the surrounding landscape. Cottonwood, sycamore, willow, ash, and walnut (*nogales*) trees thrive, as do a variety of smaller trees, shrubs, grasses, and flowering plants. Soils are much thicker in these riparian areas because of the abundance of organic materials. Rich soils, lower temperatures, accessible water, and higher humidity provide ideal growing conditions for a variety of plants that normally might be found only at higher elevations or in wetter regions.

Riparian areas are in many ways the lifeblood of the desert. Though covering less than 0.5 percent of the land surface in the Southwest, riparian areas are increasingly being recognized as complex and productive ecosystems vital to desert plant and animal life. The diversity and abundance of plants generate a variety of food sources and habitats, which in turn support an assortment of animal species.

At least three quarters of all Southwestern vertebrate species depend to at least some extent on streams and wetlands (Arizona–Sonora Desert Museum, 1991). Breeding bird populations are much denser there than in the surrounding desert, and the wetter areas are essential to migrating birds as well. Riparian areas host a variety of animals such as beavers, bobcats, coatimundis, cotton rats, foxes, rabbits, raccoons, and many reptiles and amphibians. Many species, some of which are rare or endangered, exist only in these specialized habitats.

The existence of healthy riparian areas depends not only on adequate water supplies but on variations in the rate of water flow. Periodic floods are particularly important because they clear the understory vegetation, flush out older soils, bring in new minerals and nutrients, and create sandbars where cottonwoods and other vegetation can take root. Floodwaters also modify existing channels and create new ones so that a variety of habitats are continually being formed and destroyed, providing a high degree of dynamism.

While riparian areas are affected by water flows, water flows in turn are affected by riparian areas. Riparian vegetation consumes large quantities of water. Floodwaters are slowed by the numerous channel obstacles and are reduced in magnitude as they spread out through lower-lying areas. Stream banks and channels in riparian areas absorb water during high flows and then slowly release it after the flows have subsided, so that flood peaks are moderated. And bankside vegetation can hold soil together and reduce erosion so that channels are not modified as quickly or as drastically as they would otherwise be.

In recent years the amount of riparian habitat in the Nogales and Santa Cruz Valleys, and in the Southwest in general, has been severely reduced as the growing human population has developed those areas for other uses, altered the natural timing and magnitude of flows, and consumed an ever larger share of the region's scarce water. Before widespread human development, perennial flows in the Santa Cruz River supported extensive riparian vegetation along almost its entire length; today, river flows and riparian vegetation are primarily found only downstream of the local sewage treatment plant. The situation is similar in the Nogales Valley, where the two Nogaleses have been built on top of much of the former riparian area, and artificial channelization designed to control floodwaters has eliminated the water supply for much of the remaining vegetation. Many of the marshes and wetlands that formerly supported lush vegetation, such as the groves of walnut trees that gave the cities their name, have long since disappeared as groundwater tables have fallen below root zones as a result of nearby groundwater pumping. While there is no record of the amount of riparian habitat lost specifically in the Nogales and Santa Cruz Valleys, current estimates claim that only 5 to 10 percent of the original riparian areas in the whole Southwest still exist (Arizona–Sonora Desert Museum, 1991).

Water Resources Systems

Desert plant and animal life depend on natural water resources to survive, and so, of course, do the area's human inhabitants. The timing, magnitude, and location of natural water flows do not always correspond with the needs of people, however, so residents have expended enormous effort to construct systems that alter both the geographic and temporal flow distributions. These interventions in the hydrologic cycle usually produce their intended results, but they may also generate a number of unintended and environmentally damaging reactions as well.

The following sections of this chapter describe the water resources systems that have been built to meet the needs of the residents of Ambos Nogales and discuss the impact of these systems on the environment. Our focus is on the urban water supply, wastewater removal, and flood control and drainage systems that constitute some of the most important services offered in urban areas.

Water Needs and Consumption

The amount of water used by residents of the Nogales Valley varies widely. On average, residents of Nogales, Ariz., tend to use much more water per capita than their neighbors in Nogales, Son. Further, there is much less variation in the rate of consumption among households on the Arizona side of the border than there is among households on the Sonora side. To understand the impact that varying levels of water consumption have on people's lives and to gain a perspective on different water usage rates, it is useful to examine how much water is needed for basic survival, and to compare this with the amount of water customarily used by people in other parts of the world.

Recent research indicates that human survival and major health benefits can be achieved through the use of 20–40 liters (5–10 gallons) of water per capita per day, provided that the water is accompanied by adequate waste disposal and sound hygienic practices (Bahl and Linn, 1992). While considerably more water can be consumed if it is available, only after water availability exceeds 80 liters (20 gallons) per capita per day will water be used for such basic purposes as improving personal hygiene (World Bank, 1992).

In addition to meeting the most basic needs, water can be used to flush toilets, wash clothes, water lawns and gardens, operate evaporative coolers, wash cars and streets, fight fires, operate municipal parks and swimming pools, and supply a variety of commercial and industrial needs. Some of these uses are more important than others, and water consumption rates are frequently lower where incomes are low or water is scarce, and higher when incomes are high and water is plentiful.

Households in developing countries typically use 15–30 liters (4–8 gallons) per capita per day if residents have to go outside the home to obtain their water. Lower-income households consume water at rates near the bottom of that range, while residents who have water connections to their homes typically use 50–125 liters (13–33 gallons) per capita per day. By comparison, consumption of publicly supplied water in the United States is much higher, averaging 693 liters (183 gallons) per capita per day in 1980 (Frederick and Gibbons, 1986). The average water consumption in the Western United States is 45 percent higher than in the Eastern states (Solley et al., 1983), and consumption rates in the United States are two to four times higher than in France, Germany, the United Kingdom, and Sweden (Rogers, 1983).

As the following sections show, these striking disparities in consumption rates and other water services are very evident in Ambos Nogales. In large part, the disparities are due to the differing capabilities of water resources systems and institutions to deliver water to city residents.

The Development of Water Systems in Ambos Nogales

Water supply. Water supply systems in the early days of the two cities were quite rudimentary. Settlers who moved into the valley after the railroad was completed in 1882 founded the two cities literally on top of the original water supply—the banks of Nogales Wash. Water was captured by shallow wells dug into the underlying aquifer and was either used at the site or carried home by hand or wagon. Very little wastewater was generated, and outhouses or latrines were used to dispose of human wastes.

In 1896, a private company based in Nogales, Ariz., installed pumps at three of its wells in Nogales, Son., and began to deliver water to residents on both sides of the border through a simple distribution system. This arrangement continued until 1911, when the city of Nogales, Ariz., purchased the private company and, with public funds, developed a well outside the Nogales Valley at a site northeast of the town in the much larger aquifer underlying the Santa Cruz River. This project included the construction of a pumping station and pipeline to carry the water 8 miles up Proto Canyon from the well to the city. The new public water system was built by and for residents of Nogales, Ariz., so most residents of Nogales, Son., continued to use private wells or carried their water from a central communal well.

Development of the new well in the Santa Cruz River aquifer soon paid off for residents of Nogales, Ariz., as drought conditions in 1921–23 caused wells in the southern end of the Nogales Valley to dry up. In what later became a familiar pattern, residents of Nogales, Son., were forced to buy water from their Arizona neighbors until the drought ended.

Disparities in the water supply systems on the two sides of the border grew as the city of Nogales, Ariz., used public funds to install a new turbine pump in its Santa Cruz well, to build several miles of new water lines, and to treat its water with chlorine to protect residents from a Mexican typhoid epidemic. A few Sonoran businesses located near the border were able to receive water from the Nogales, Ariz., Water Department, but otherwise the water supply situation in Nogales, Son., remained essentially unchanged.

It was not until 1940 that the Mexican federal government came to the aid of Nogales, Son., and brought water into the city from the Santa Cruz Valley. The government built an infiltration system and pump station at the Santa Cruz River aquifer southeast of Nogales and laid a 29-kilometer (18-mile) pipeline between the system and the city. The government made further improvements in 1948, when it installed a pump in the central communal well, and in 1949, when it built the first (and current) water distribution system.

Wastewater removal and treatment. The early development of wastewater removal and treatment systems in the two cities showed comparable disparities. In 1946, the director of the Sanitary Engineering Division of the Arizona Department of Health reported that Nogales, Ariz., was practically 100 percent sewered but that except for a few downtown businesses near the border (which were connected to a short sewer line terminating in the Arizona system), Nogales, Son., still had not developed a sewer system and had to rely on inadequate cesspools and outhouses. Then, describing a situation that is still familiar to city residents today, he went on to state: "The situation then is this, that the sewage disposal south of the border is on top of an impervious rock foundation permitting, during the rainy season at least, drainage of contaminating material to the storm drain, and down the streets on both sides of the line toward the Santa Cruz River. This of course, creates a definite public health hazard to the population on both sides of the line of this important community."[1]

The landscape gradient that causes sewage to flow across the border into the United States also affected the proposed location of sewage treatment facilities. The Mexican health department had developed preliminary plans for a sewer system in the early 1940s, but the town's topography and location made it obvious that a treatment plant and its sewage outfall line would have to be located across the border, in the United States.[2] At the same time, Arizona officials noted that the existing Nogales, Ariz., sewage disposal plant had become "entirely unsatisfactory. It is old, obsolete, odoriferous, and the methods of treatment are a hazard to public health.... Occasionally the effluent has escaped into a wash or other natural drainage [Nogales Wash] endangering domestic water supplies below."[3]

This combination of facts had already led to discussions about a wastewater treatment facility that would be shared by both cities. In March 1940, the Mexican and U.S. sections of the International Boundary and Water Commission (IBWC) began drafting a report on the international sanitation problem,[4] and in 1946 the U.S. Congress authorized the construction of an international wastewater treatment plant. The total construction cost of the plant, estimated to be $400,000, was to be shared equally between the national governments of the United States and Mexico.[5] The city of Nogales, Ariz., agreed to assume the responsibility for operating and maintaining the plant, projected to cost $12,000 per year, with Mexico contributing an amount proportional to its share of the sewage to be treated, or $3,000 per year. The Nogales, Ariz., city officials expected that the U.S. government would actually pay most of the city's operation and maintenance costs, as it did for a sewage treatment plant in Douglas, Ariz., under an agreement established through the efforts of Arizona's senator, Carl Hayden.[6]

The first international wastewater treatment facility for Ambos Nogales was completed in 1951 at a total cost of $580,000. It was located 2.4 kilometers (1.5 miles) north of the boundary and had a treatment capacity of 6,000 cubic meters (1.6 million gallons) per day. Initial flows were 379 cubic meters (100,000 gallons) per day from Nogales, Son., and 2,600 cubic meters (700,000 gallons) per day from Nogales, Ariz.[7] As city officials had expected, the federal government underwrote a substantial portion of the operating costs, requiring the city to simply "contribute an equitable proportion."[8]

Drainage and flood control. The control of floodwaters in Ambos Nogales was another responsibility shared by the governments of the two countries. The two cities were built almost entirely on the narrow valley floor and were extremely susceptible to damage from periodic flooding. Major floods had been recorded by the IBWC in 1905, 1909, 1914, 1915, 1926, and 1930; the 1930 floods claimed five lives and caused extensive property damage. A document prepared by the IBWC for Senator Carl Hayden in 1932 concluded that the flood problem in Ambos Nogales required an immediate solution and recommended that the two federal governments design a joint flood control project (U.S. Department of the Army, 1987).

The proposed flood control project, consisting of 5 kilometers (3.1 miles) of covered channel and 2.1 kilometers (1.3 miles) of lined channel, was subsequently built by the IBWC during the 1930s and 1940s. Water flowing down Nogales Wash now enters the 6.7-meter-wide (22 feet), 3.7-meter-high (12 feet) Nogales Wash Covered Channel 1.6 kilometers (1 mile) south of the border in Nogales, Son., travels underneath the streets of downtown Ambos Nogales, and exits 1.4 kilometers (0.9 miles) north of the border in Nogales, Ariz. A second covered channel several hundred feet to the west, the Arroyo Boulevard Covered Channel, sometimes referred to as the West Channel, similarly collects water at two inlets on the Sonoran side of the city and then carries it to a point 1.3 kilometers (0.8 miles) north of the border in Nogales, Ariz. Both covered channels empty into open, concrete-lined canals which, after continuing several hundred feet further north, merge into a single canal. From there Nogales Wash is lined with concrete for another 1.8 kilometers (1.1 miles) before it once again flows into its natural channel (U.S. Department of the Army, 1987).

Development of water resource systems in Ambos Nogales. Urban water resource systems must be adapted and enlarged to meet the needs generated by urban growth, and as Chapter 2 discusses, both Nogaleses have grown considerably since their original water systems were put into place. The populations of the two cities grew at approximately equal rates for the first several years following their founding, but starting early in the twentieth century Nogales, Son., began to grow much more rapidly than its northern neighbor. By 1941, Nogales, Ariz., had a population of approximately 6,000 while Nogales, Son., had approximately 15,000 residents. By 1961, six years before Nogales's first maquiladora was built, these figures had increased to 9,500 and 40,000 people, respectively (see fig. 2.1).

The difference in growth rates became even greater after the maquiladora program brought thousands of new residents to Nogales, Son., looking for economic opportunities. Growth during the 1980s was especially dramatic; official Mexican census figures indicate that the population of Nogales, Son., grew 58 percent from 1980 to 1990, to a total population of 107,936. The accuracy of the "official" population figures has been called into question, however, and both the growth rate and the total population may be considerably understated. Virtually all of the unofficial estimates indicate that the population is much larger than that. The population of Santa Cruz County, Ariz., two-thirds of whom live in the city of Nogales, grew

33 percent during the same decade to a 1990 population of 29,676, leaving no doubt that the Arizona city is much smaller than its Sonoran neighbor.

Rapid growth in Ambos Nogales, though due largely to economic policies originating at national and international levels, has placed enormous burdens on local urban services. The problem is exacerbated by the fact that new residents typically require services immediately on reaching the city, while revenues from increased sales and property taxes, or from federal and state distributions, lag considerably behind.

In some cases the extension of services may be funded directly by both new and existing residents through connection fees and cost-of-service charges. This has largely been the case in Nogales, Ariz., where in recent years new residents have had to pay sizable sums and negotiate a maze of regulations in order to acquire services, although the city has, by and large, managed to provide these new residents with the services they need. The same has not been true in Nogales, Son. The faster population growth in the Sonoran city has placed proportionately greater burdens on local services. The federal and state governments traditionally have been responsible for constructing and operating new infrastructure, but resources from Mexico City and Hermosillo reach Nogales only sporadically and have not kept up with the city's rapid growth. Though much of the increase in the demand for services is a result of migrants arriving in Nogales to look for work in the maquiladoras, the maquiladoras themselves have not been asked to help relieve the infrastructure deficit. Since the maquilas are an important source of foreign exchange for the Mexican economy, the government is loathe to do anything that might reduce the attractiveness of Mexico as a site for maquiladora operations.[9]

The result of these institutional problems is that residents of Nogales, Son., are often left to fend for themselves when it comes to securing access to urban services. New residents who have come to Nogales from areas of the country where economic conditions are even worse often arrive with virtually nothing, and the situation is even more difficult for them. Some of the migrants are not able to find the work that they had hoped for because the working-age population already greatly exceeds the number of available jobs. Since many of the jobs that do exist, including those in the maquiladoras, pay only minimum wages, even those lucky enough to find employment cannot afford the services they need.

As we describe in the sections that follow, the expansion and adaptation of urban water services in the two cities have proceeded at very different paces and with different degrees of success.

Water Supply in Nogales, Arizona

The Nogales, Ariz., water supply system has for the most part continued to grow with its population. Most water customers in the city are supplied by the Nogales Water Department (NWD), which in the last several years has built or acquired two major wellfields outside the city, several smaller wells along the Nogales Wash, and a number of large storage reservoirs. A much smaller number of water customers are supplied by one of two small private companies—the Valle Verde Water Company and the Town and Country Mobile Home Park—or by their own private wells.

The city's original well site at the Santa Cruz River has been expanded to include several wells with a total capacity of 6,800 liters (1,800 gallons) per minute. The city also bought out a private water company just northwest of town, at the bottom of Potrero Creek, and developed a wellfield there with a total capacity of 8,300 liters (2,200 gallons) per minute. These two wellfields supply virtually all of the potable water distributed by the NWD (see fig. 3.1). Additional nonpotable water is pumped from several wells along the Nogales Wash inside the city for turf irrigation and other uses.

In 1987, 6.4 million cubic meters (5,219 acre-feet) of water, or an average of 810 liters (216 gallons) per capita per day, was pumped for municipal purposes in Santa Cruz County. "Municipal purposes" includes all water supplied by small or large water companies to households, businesses, and industries. An additional 1.7 million cubic meters (1,385 acre-feet) of water was pumped from private wells for other "industrial" purposes, most of it to water golf courses at Kino Springs, Rio Rico, and the Tubac Country Club. An estimated 1.2 million cubic meters (1,000 acre-feet) of water was pumped from more than 700 small, privately owned wells for domestic, small commercial, and stock-watering purposes (ADWR, 1990). During past droughts, the water tables underlying the wellfields have dropped significantly, but not to the point that water supplies for the city have been seriously threatened.

The quality of the water supplied to residents of Nogales, Ariz., from both public and private companies is very good. The water is chlorinated to kill biological contaminants and in the past has easily met water quality standards. Water pumped from some of the wells near Nogales Wash has been contaminated to some degree (this is discussed in greater detail below), but that water was used only for irrigation or other nonpotable uses. Some residents with their own wells situated near Nogales Wash or near the Santa Cruz River downstream from the river's confluence with the wash may be threatened by contaminated water, but it is not known how many people, if any, use their wells for drinking water.

The NWD has been able to fund new water supply development and infrastructure through public bonds backed by revenues collected from its water customers. In 1992, residential customers within the city limits paid at least $9.80 per month, commercial and industrial customers paid $10.40 per month, and customers outside the city limits paid $14.56 per month.[10] There have been no major problems in building or acquiring the infrastructure necessary to supply the city's new and existing water customers with all the water they need. Most of the challenges faced by the NWD have concerned regulation of water use.

Several provisions of Arizona's 1980 Groundwater Management Act (AGMA) have placed limitations on the use of water in the Nogales area. The AGMA was designed to address serious problems of groundwater "mining" (withdrawals in excess of natural recharge) in several of the state's more heavily used groundwater basins, as well as to help pave the way for federal funding of the massive Central Arizona Project, which brings water from the Colorado River to central Arizona. Four groundwater basins experiencing significant overdraft (those underlying the Tucson, Phoenix, and Prescott municipal areas, and the one under mostly rural Pinal County) have been designated active management areas (AMAs), which means that water users there are subject to a number of water use restrictions. Nogales is included within the Tucson AMA, despite the fact that it is 97 kilometers (60 miles) from Tucson, because both cities are within the expansive Santa Cruz River groundwater basin and the AGMA mandates that active management area boundaries correspond with the outer limits of groundwater basins. Because AMAs are political entities of the state, the boundaries of the Tucson AMA end at the international border even though the hydrologic basin continues into Sonora.

The city of Nogales has "service area rights" to pump all the groundwater it needs within its service area, subject only to per capita limitations on water use that are specified by a series of increasingly strict management plans. Per capita water use in Nogales, Ariz., has been much higher than in Tucson, and it also exceeded the limits set by the first of a series of management plans designed to achieve AGMA goals. As a result, the city was fined $80,000 in 1989 by the Arizona Department of Water Resources (ADWR), which administers the Groundwater Management Act. The fine was later waived after the city proved that it was instituting new conservation measures. The second management plan, covering the years 1990–2000, calls for a maximum per capita daily water use of 732 liters (175 gallons) by 1992, and 615 liters (164 gallons) by 1995.

Part of the city's problem in meeting the reduction quotas set by the management plans may be caused by excessive "lost" water; that is, water that is pumped into the system but never reaches (or is not registered by meters at) intended sites of use. Virtually all water systems have leaks, and not all meters are continuously functional. Normal loss rates are expected to be in the vicinity of 10 percent, however, while lost water accounts for 20 percent of all water pumped in Nogales; this discrepancy concerns the ADWR.

Another possible reason for the high per capita water use in Nogales, and one that has been advanced by city officials on numerous occasions, is that the true daily population of the city is considerably understated. As we discuss in greater detail in Chapter 4, thousands of tourists from the United States, as well as visitors and laborers from Mexico, are in Nogales, Ariz., on any given day. Though these visitors consume water while in the city, they are not counted as part of the "official" population used by the ADWR to calculate per capita water use rates.

A further provision of the Groundwater Management Act, and one that has caused even more problems for Nogales, is the requirement that the city must demonstrate that it has a 100-year "assured water supply" before any new development will be allowed. While Nogales has been able thus far to supply adequate water to its residents, it is uncertain that the city will be able to prove that it has an adequate supply for the future. As was mentioned earlier, the existence of deep groundwater sources in the vicinity of Nogales has not been proven, and shallow groundwater sources, although adequate so far, are susceptible to diminution during droughts. Further, since the Santa Cruz River aquifer sources used by Nogales, Son., are upstream from those used by Nogales, Ariz., there is also concern that as Sonoran residents begin to take more water out of the aquifer to meet their growing needs, less water will be left to flow downstream to Arizona.

These conditions, combined with the additional water requirements of its growing population, have made it very difficult for the city to prove to the state that it has the ability to meet its residents' long-term needs. Though the assured water supply provisions of the Groundwater Management Act are based on legitimate concerns about water availability and sustainability, city officials take the stance that the "assured water" issue is a regulatory rather than a physical one.

Nogales has responded to its water problems in two ways. First, the city has been trying to find new sources of groundwater to develop. To this end, the city has hired hydrology consultants to explore possible sources. The results of their work suggest that there may be some recoverable sources of deep groundwater in the area west of the city, but the exact dimensions of these potential supplies are unknown. Second, the city has aggressively sought to acquire additional water rights. The Potrero wellfield, one of the two primary water sources used by the city, was purchased from the Potrero Water Company in 1976, even before the advent of the Groundwater Management Act. The 1988 purchase of the Kino Springs Water Company at the Santa Cruz River was completed primarily because of the city's need to demonstrate an assured water supply.[11] The purchase of Kino Springs also necessitated an expansion in the city's service area, and because Kino Springs includes a golf course requiring heavy irrigation, the purchase also increased per capita water use rates. More recently, Nogales purchased the Guevavi Ranch, a large parcel of land northeast of town in the Santa Cruz Valley, for its water rights. These purchases have cost the city several million dollars.

The status of water rights in the Santa Cruz River watershed is somewhat uncertain pending completion of the state's ongoing Gila River watershed general adjudication. The uncertainty has made it difficult for the city of Nogales to determine exactly what actions it must take to be in long-term compliance with the law, fueling further frustrations for city residents and officials.

Water Supply in Nogales, Sonora

Residents of Nogales, Son., have had a much more difficult time securing water than their northern neighbors. Ever since the water supply system was constructed in the 1940s, residents have had to rely on, and wait for, action from the Mexican federal or state government for additions to the system. Such action has occurred only sporadically, and then only in response to political and economic events largely beyond the influence of local residents.

The driving force behind the water supply problems in Nogales, Son., is the dramatic increase in the city's population over the last few decades. Not only does the presence of more people lead to greater total water demand, the location of many of the new settlements on the sides of the steep hills surrounding the valley has also made the extension of the water distribution system quite difficult. Getting adequately pressurized water to locations at multiple elevations is a difficult engineering problem, and one that the existing system was not designed to address. Water supply pipes have been extended to some upper-elevation neighborhoods, but these additions have increased the stress on other components of the distribution system.[12]

Finding enough water to pump into the system has also been a problem, despite the development of new water sources. Fourteen public wells with a total capacity of 4,920 liters (1,300 gallons) per minute have been developed in the aquifer underlying Nogales Wash within the city. In 1974, a new wellfield with a total capacity of 7,500 liters (1,980 gallons) per minute (Captación Mascareñas) was built in the Santa Cruz River aquifer several miles north of the existing infiltration system. In 1982, the infiltration system, which had experienced declining production due to siltation, was replaced by a new system (Galería Nueva) and another wellfield (Captación Paredes). The gallery and wellfield have a combined maximum capacity of 10,800 liters (2,850 gallons) per minute (COLEF, 1992).

But all of these new sources are vulnerable to disruption. The shallow aquifer underlying Nogales Wash was incapable of supplying residents' needs during dry periods even before the population growth. The aquifer underlying the Santa Cruz River, while larger, also experiences extremely reduced groundwater levels during periods of drought. This problem is more acute in Sonora than in Arizona because of a simple physical characteristic: upstream wells in Sonora draw water from a much smaller drainage area than wells located downstream in Arizona. Several Sonoran wells in the Nogales and Santa Cruz Valleys dried up or experienced drastically reduced rates of production during drought conditions in the late 1980s.

The latest major addition to the water supply was supposed to have solved many of these problems. Captación Los Alisos, a wellfield located 21 kilometers (13 miles) south of the city in the neighboring Río Magdalena watershed (see fig. 3.1), is the only source of water for Ambos Nogales that comes from a completely separate watershed (water transfers from the Santa Cruz Valley to the Nogales Valley simply represent transfers from a watershed into one of its own tributaries). Los Alisos consists of four wells with a total capacity of 9,600 liters (2,535 gallons) per minute. But so far the project does not seem to have accomplished its stated objective. Many residents of Nogales are still without water, and some wonder whether Los Alisos has had any impact at all on the city's water supply situation. Figure 3.3 shows the flow rates of each of the city's water sources as of July 1993; according to the director of the Comisión Nacional de Agua Potable y Alcantarillado del Estado de Sonora (COAPAES), the Sonoran state water and sewer agency, the pumps operate 24 hours per day.

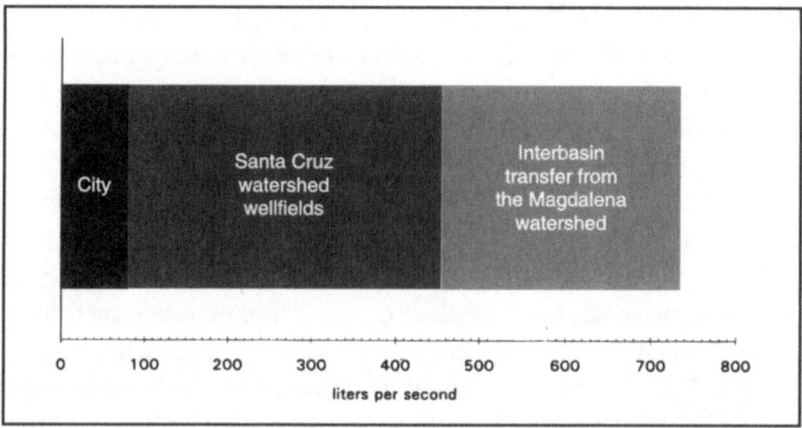

Figure 3.3 Nogales, Son., water supply wellfields, July 1993. *Source*: COAPAES.

Federal funds were used to construct virtually all of these large water supply projects. Responsibility for operations and maintenance, as well as for new connections to the distribution system, lies with COAPAES, whose activities are designed to be financed by revenues collected from its customers. This split in responsibilities between the federal and state governments has been the source of many of the city's water supply problems.

First, COAPAES's revenue collection efforts have been quite ineffective. In 1992, official water rates for residential customers in Nogales, Son., were approximately $0.65 per month for the first 15,000 liters (4,000 gallons), and ranged from $0.19 to $0.44 per 3,750 liters (1,000 gallons) of additional water, depending on the amount used (Comisión Nacional del Agua, 1992). But many customers of the public water system do not have meters on their water lines, and even where meters exist, they are often broken or go unread by COAPAES personnel. COAPAES tried to make up for these deficiencies by billing many of its customers according to flat rates that varied depending on the type of use (residential or commercial) and, for residential customers, the socioeconomic characteristic of their neighborhood. In 1991, these rates varied from $0.48 to $30.65 per month. This cumbersome billing system was abandoned in 1993, and monthly rates were fixed at 50.22 pesos ($14.70) for 43,000 liters (11,360 gallons). Poor record keeping and data management have precluded realistic determinations of who owes money and who does not, and weak enforcement has made it possible for many customers to avoid paying their bills altogether. As a result, COAPAES has frequently been unable to collect enough money to cover the costs of its services, and many necessary operations, maintenance activities, and new connections to the system never take place (COLEF, 1992).

Second, there has been a lack of coordination between the different levels of government responsible for water development and operations. The construction of highly visible water supply projects by the federal government is usually not accompanied by funds for the less visible operations and maintenance activities that are supposed to be funded by COAPAES. New water supplies are sometimes developed without adequate consideration of the infrastructure that will be necessary to distribute and take full advantage of the water produced. Projects are initiated independently by federal or state officials in response to political pressure or the temporary availability of funds rather than as part of a comprehensive and coordinated development plan. At best, this situation results in lowered efficiency and productivity; at worst, the different levels of government may actually operate at cross-purposes.

Third, no mechanism exists for developing the local capacity to identify needs and to plan, develop, operate, and maintain water supply systems. Federal and state agencies are responsible for construction and operations, respectively, so only minimal responsibilities are left to the local government. The federal and state agencies maintain local offices but are driven by agendas arising in Mexico City and Hermosillo rather than in Nogales. Because COAPAES has not been capable of raising sufficient revenues at the local level, residents of Nogales are left to contend with unpredictable outside politics and unreliable outside financing.

The net result of these problems is a public water supply system that frequently fails to function. Though COAPAES officials sometimes claim that virtually all water needs in the city are being met,[13] it is clear that many residents of Nogales, particularly those living in the poorer and higher-elevation neighborhoods, are not connected to the public water system at all. A 1992 survey of neighborhoods found that 17 percent of the population did not have connections to the water supply system (COLEF, 1992).[14] This figure is quite high compared with other large Mexican cities. An average of 97.9 percent of the households in Mexican cities with populations greater than 100,000 have connections to public water systems (Comisión Nacional del Agua, 1992).

But even though 83 percent of Nogales households are physically connected to the public distribution system, many have never actually received any water from it. Some residents have access to public taps but must find ways to carry the water home. Many of the residents connected to the public system who actually receive water cannot rely on its continuous availability. Daily and seasonal variations in system pressure and supplies mean that virtually everyone who relies on the public system for water experiences at least an occasional shortage (COLEF, 1992).

The chronic lack of maintenance causes frequent mechanical breakdowns at pumping stations and multiple breaks and leaks in the distribution system. Production from wells is therefore generally well below capacity and is further reduced by frequent electrical outages. Lack of data on water production and water consumption makes it impossible to determine how much of the water that is pumped into the system is actually used by city residents, but it is likely that a very high proportion of all water pumped into the system is lost without ever having been used. Water is frequently seen running down the streets in Nogales, and leaks from the public water system have been cited as a primary source of flows in Nogales Wash (Udall Center, 1993b).

Water quality has also been a problem. Though COAPAES says that it chlorinates all of the system's sources,[15] health-threatening levels of bacteria have been found at several of the public water system's wells and reservoirs (Udall Center, 1993b). Well sites, transport lines, storage reservoirs, and distribution lines are not always physically secure or isolated from sources of contamination. Contaminated water from broken sewer lines filters into the distribution pipes during the frequent periods of low pressure. Industrial contaminants are also beginning to be found in the water from several wells that supply the public system. These water quality problems, discussed in greater detail below, indicate that even when residents do receive water from the public supply system, it may not be safe to use.

Alternative Water Sources for Nogales, Sonora

Facing a need to obtain at least minimal supplies of water and the inability of the public system to reliably deliver it, the residents of Nogales, Son., have been forced to autonomously develop a number of alternative modes of supply.

Illegal connections. People unable to secure legal connections to the public system (or unwilling to pay for such connections) sometimes create their own illicit connections. New and used pipes are readily available for sale on both sides of the border, and the number of illegal connections is believed to be large. COAPAES has estimated that there may be 3,000 such connections in Nogales, equivalent to approximately 15 percent of the legal connections (COLEF, 1992).[16]

Though water from illicit connections is cheap (only the pipes must be paid for), illicit water users are vulnerable to the same supply problems faced by legitimate customers of the system. Water may be available only intermittently, pressure may be low or variable, and the water quality may be compromised. Owners of illicit connections may be even more susceptible to water quality problems than other customers of the public system if the pipes they use to tap into the system were previously used for carrying anything other than potable water. This type of contamination also has the potential to affect other system customers, since water moves in both directions through the pipes during periods of low pressure.

Private water supply systems. An unknown but potentially large number of industries, businesses, and housing developments have built their own water supply systems. In Mexico, well drilling is regulated by the federal rather than the local government, and information about the number and capacities of these wells is either unavailable locally or contradictory. There is a widespread perception, however, that many of these wells are not registered at any level of government.

Several maquiladoras in the southern industrial park are known to have their own wells in the southernmost reaches of the shallow aquifer underlying Nogales Wash. Less water is typically available near the upper limits of a watershed, but the maquiladoras do not tend to be heavy water users. An advantage of the elevated location of these wells is that very few sources of contamination are located above them.

Several of the newer housing developments also have their own wells and distribution systems. These systems are insulated from some of the problems that plague the public system, but because they use the shallow Nogales Wash aquifer, they are equally vulnerable to drought and potential contamination. They also are susceptible to power supply interruptions and often suffer from inadequate storage capacity. Reports indicate that water in many housing developments supplied by private wells is available only intermittently throughout the day, as is true for many customers of the public system (Francisco Lara, COLEF-Nogales, pers. comm., 1992).

The most common form of private water "system" in Nogales, Son., actually consists of a simple household addition to the public system. The primary function of water supply reservoirs is to level out supply rates in the face of uneven availability or demand. Many customers of the public system have reacted to the public system's unreliability by installing household storage tanks. Typical household storage units are prefabricated, 7,000-liter (1,850-gallon) tanks sold in local stores. Usually the tank is installed on the roof of the house and connected to the public distribution system. The intake valve is left open so that the tank fills when water is available and then slowly drains when it is not. The tank also helps to maintain constant water pressure within the house because of its higher (rooftop) elevation.

Connections to the Nogales, Ariz., public system. Some Sonoran businesses located near the border obtain water from the Nogales, Ariz., public water system. Unlike the Nogales, Son., system, the Nogales, Ariz., public water system is quite reliable; high-quality water is continually available at constant pressure. The NWD currently has four accounts listed at Sonoran addresses, each supplied by a separate water main crossing the border. The origins of these connections are unknown, but they are not recent; they may date back to the earliest years of the city. One of the four accounts is inactive, but two of them are large enough to appear on a list of the 50 largest water customers. The Sonoran customers are billed by the NWD at its standard commercial rates.[17] The water consumption by the listed account owners is much larger than would be expected given the amount of business that they do, so it seems safe to assume that the water is also being used for other purposes.[18] Since these customers pay their water bills promptly, the department has expressed no interest in determining what happens to the water once it crosses the border, and the ultimate delivery points are unknown.

Deliveries by truck. In the early days of the city, people were able to carry their water home from nearby public or private wells. As new residents settled in more distant areas, away from the valley floor, this traditional method of obtaining water became more difficult. Many residents of Nogales, Son., who currently do not have access to either the public water supply system or to private wells, or who wish to utilize as many sources of water as possible, now choose to do what many of their counterparts in developing countries do: they patronize water vendors.

Water vending can take many forms, but in Nogales it consists primarily of the transport and delivery of water by large water trucks, or *pipas*. The trucks fill up at any of several wells on the valley floor and then set out on established delivery routes. Some customers have water delivered on a regular schedule, and others arrange for deliveries as needed. Most deliveries in Nogales are made by privately owned trucks in areas already served, to at least some degree, by the public water system. In these areas the pipa deliveries supplement the supply, and the water is most often stored in the rooftop tanks described above.

Pipas also serve some of the lower-income neighborhoods whose residents frequently do not have even minimal access to the public water distribution system. Usually, the pipa-delivered water in these neighborhoods is stored in 200-liter (55-gallon) drums that residents have scavenged from local industries. Though required by law to deliver water to all areas of the city, pipa drivers are frequently unwilling to make deliveries to lower-income neighborhoods. Access is often more difficult because such neighborhoods are frequently on the steepest hills, far from the valley center, and may not have roads. It also takes more time to fill many small storage drums than to fill a much smaller number of larger ones, so drivers cannot empty their tanks as quickly. Servicios Públicos Municipales, the city's public services department, uses nine publicly owned water trucks to deliver water to areas served regularly by neither the public water distribution system nor private trucks.

Water delivered by the pipas costs more than an equivalent amount delivered through the public distribution system, even assuming that customers of the latter pay their water bills. As of October 1993, the price of 200 liters of water delivered to a 55-gallon drum was 3.5 pesos; in actual fact, the amount paid is usually between 4.5 and 5 pesos ($1.32–$1.47).

The price of a pipa of water is 50 pesos, but the amount paid is usually 60 pesos. The volume delivered may vary from 4,000 to 8,000 liters (1,055–2,115 gallons), but the price is the same; customers pay for the delivery service more than for the water. Payment is made directly to the person who delivers the water, who is usually also the owner of the truck. Depending on the relationship that exists between the *pipero* (pipa owner) and the client, payment is demanded in advance or immediately on delivery, or credit is extended. Clients receive a receipt.

The piperos are under the supervision of the Ministry of Health. They are responsible, first, for the upkeep of La Tomatera (one of the 14 urban wells), from which they draw water, and, second, for chlorinating the water prior to delivery. They pay nothing for the water, but they do pay a city business tax.

The piperos' organization has an agreement with the municipal authorities to deliver water free of charge to schools, firefighters, government branch offices, and, in emergencies, to the sectors of the community experiencing problems with water delivery. During emergencies, the city pays the piperos no more than what is absolutely necessary to maintain the trucks, and COAPAES cooperates with the city and the piperos to ensure that everyone has access to water.

The author of a 1991 study concluded that vending services in developing countries are very flexible, and that they protect consumers from uncertainty better than do piped water supply systems (Katko,

1991). The value of flexibility became evident during the drought in the late 1980s, when several public wells in Nogales, Son., ran dry and deliveries from the public water system were severely reduced. Emergency supplies of water were made available to Nogales, Son., from the Nogales, Ariz., Water Department through a pipe across the border fence running from a metered fire hydrant. Pipas were used to pick up water directly at the end of the border pipe and deliver it to residents throughout the city. The NWD charged the city of Nogales, Son., for this water at its regular commercial rate. In 1989, this arrangement was in operation for some three months and delivered approximately 24.6 million liters (6.5 million gallons) of water across the international boundary.[19]

The pipa system may be flexible, but it is not always reliable. Bad weather or other hazards sometimes create conditions that prevent pipas from making deliveries, and residents on steep hillsides without passable roads may not receive pipa deliveries even in good weather. And because storage capacities are so limited, especially in the poor neighborhoods, deliveries may not be frequent enough to ensure that residents get the minimum daily water necessary to achieve basic health benefits.[20] Obtaining sufficient water is most difficult for those who must rely on the pipas as their sole source of bulk water supplies; generally they are the poorest members of the community.

Water quality problems often accompany shortages. Water from the wells patronized by the pipas is usually not treated with chlorine, and if one of the wells becomes contaminated, then what otherwise would have been an isolated problem is instead spread throughout the city by the pipas. Bacterial contamination is of greatest concern where conditions for growth are favorable, such as in storage drums (almost always located outside) and rooftop tanks exposed to the hot sun. Water that is uncontaminated when it leaves the well can become contaminated after delivery because home storage devices are not adequately isolated from contaminants in the environment. Water quality problems are not as significant for those who use pipa-delivered water as a supplemental water source, but they are enormously important to those who rely exclusively on such water for their household needs.

Contamination by toxic chemicals is another possibility. The trucks themselves, if used in the past to carry anything other than potable water, may be a source of contamination; but the likeliest sources are the 55-gallon drums used to store water. The drums, which are usually obtained near industrial buildings, may have been used to transport and store toxic industrial chemicals. Some of the drums used to store water in low-income neighborhoods still carry labels, in English, that describe the toxic nature of the original contents. The same situation has been found in many other poor communities along the border.[21]

Bottled water. Given the widespread contamination and the unreliability of piped and trucked water supplies, bottled water is popular among Nogales residents. It is widely available in local drugstores and markets on both sides of the border, or homes and businesses can have it delivered for an additional fee. Unlike water from the public distribution system or from the pipas, bottled water is perceived by consumers to be quite safe. A 1991 survey indicated that 39 percent of Nogales, Son., households bought bottled water, and that approximately a third of the water purchased had been bottled in Arizona (COLEF, 1992).

Water bottled in Sonora costs 5 pesos for a 5-gallon bottle (19 liters), or $293 per 1,000 gallons (3,785 liters). A 5-gallon jug bottled in Arizona and delivered costs 15 pesos, or $880 per 1,000 gallons. Drinking water purchased by the gallon in U.S. grocery stores or from vending machines typically costs from 25 to 75 cents, or $250–$750 per 1,000 gallons.[22]

The high price of bottled water limits its use by many residents, even though most people who buy it use it primarily for drinking and cooking, which do not require large quantities. This is especially true of water bottled in the United States, which is perceived by residents to be of higher quality than water bottled in Sonora (COLEF, 1992). Difficulties in transporting the water are also likely to limit consumption, since very few people are able to afford home deliveries. Water is heavy (1 kilogram per liter, or approximately 8 pounds per gallon), and a single 5-gallon bottle, or even a couple of 1-gallon bottles, may be more than some people can carry. This is especially true for people who live far from markets or on steep hills, and those without access to automobiles.

Carried water. Pipas now deliver most of the water to households not connected to the public water supply system, but carrying water by hand or by car is still very much a part of the lives of many Nogales, Son., residents. Some neighborhoods without household connections to the public water supply system do have access to public taps, but area residents must then find ways to carry the water home. In other areas, residents carry water home from taps or hoses in public parks, public rest rooms, or government buildings. Some people obtain water from private taps whose owners either allow them to take the water or don't know that it is being taken.

Obtaining water from across the border also is common. Some residents routinely obtain water from hoses that reach across the border from Nogales, Ariz., with the cooperation of the Arizona property owners and little interference from border guards. Others cross the border for high-water-use activities such as washing clothes and taking showers, or buy water at grocery stores and vending machines and then carry it home. They may take water home after visits to family and friends in Arizona, or receive water from family and friends who visit them. In many cases the quantity of water involved is quite small, but it may be most of the water used for such critical purposes as drinking and food preparation.

Obtaining water by the methods described above requires considerable time and energy. At best, water containers must be filled, loaded into cars, transported, and then unloaded and stored until needed. At worst, water must be captured surreptitiously in small containers and then carried by hand up steep hills and over long distances. Some water sources are available only to people able to make frequent trips back and forth across the border. Though these sources may be important for some residents or for some uses, it is not likely that the total volume of water obtained is very large.

The High Cost of Using Alternatives

There are appreciable economies of scale associated with piped water distribution systems, which are typically the most cost-effective method of delivering water. Alternative water sources can be quite expensive. The high prices are not necessarily due to profit-taking, because delivering water through alternative methods can itself be quite costly. One study of water vending in developing countries indicated that vendors do not make much profit because of the high transportation costs (Katko, 1991).[23] Though we have no data with which to determine profit rates in Nogales, it is apparent that the cost of delivering water by pipas is relatively high. The system requires large amounts of labor and fuel, and significant sums of money are likely to be needed to purchase and maintain the trucks. As a result, the price of water from pipas is extremely high relative to the prices paid by customers of the COAPAES system.

It may be hard to comprehend what price disparities actually mean to the people of Nogales, Son., so an example may help. A household living in a squatter settlement in Nogales would need to fill twenty-two 55-gallon drums each month to obtain 150 liters (40 gallons) of water per household per day (the World Health Organization's recommended minimum quantity for urban areas in the developing world). In October 1993, the cost to the household for this much water delivered by pipa ranged from 77 to 110 pesos, or approximately $22.50 to $32.25. Less money—from 50 to 60 pesos ($14.65 to $17.60)—will buy a better-off household a complete refill of their 1,850-gallon household storage tank, which allows 227 liters (60 gallons) per household per day. In contrast, for a household that has a metered connection to the COAPAES piped distribution system, the standard monthly charge of 50.22 pesos ($14.70) will purchase 43,000 liters (11,360 gallons) of water—if it is available—which amounts to 1,414 liters (373 gallons) per household per day, far beyond personal consumption needs. Should a poor household reliant on pipa deliveries to 55-gallon drums desire this amount of water, it would cost $210 a month, 14 times the price COAPAES consumers pay.

To further illustrate water-pricing differentials, we can extend our example across the border to Nogales, Ariz. As of October 1993, the price of an equivalent amount of water from the public system in Nogales, Ariz., was higher than the price from the public system in Nogales, Son., but incomes are generally higher as well north of the border. A household within the city limits pays a fixed charge of $9.80 per month, which entitles them to 3,000 gallons (11,355 liters), equivalent to about 100 gallons (380 liters) per day. Each additional

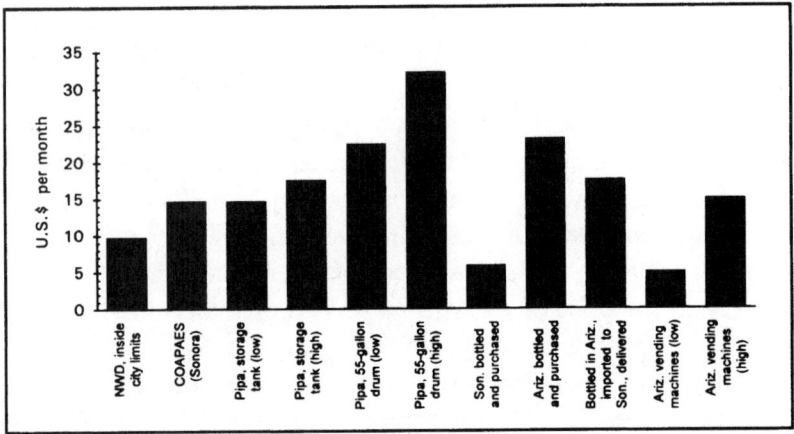

Figure 3.4 Monthly cost of water from various sources. NWD prices reflect the standard unit of 3,000 gallons, billed monthly (1 gallon = 3.785 liters). COAPAES prices reflect the standard unit of 11,360 gallons, billed monthly. Rooftop storage tanks hold 1,850 gallons, and pipa prices reflect a single delivery that fills the tank. Pipas charge more to fill 55-gallon drums. Bottled water prices are based on 20-gallon units (four 5-gallon bottles per month).

1,000 gallons (3,785 liters) costs $1.40. The $22.50 spent monthly on water by a poor household equipped only with 55-gallon drums in Nogales, Son., to satisfy its minimum daily need of 150 liters can buy a household in Nogales, Ariz., 12,000 gallons (45,400 liters), or 394 gallons (1,490 liters) per day. The disparity in cost and service appears even greater when one considers that, unlike the water delivered in Nogales, Son., the water delivered in Nogales, Ariz., is constantly available, delivered under pressure, and of high quality. Figure 3.4 illustrates the different prices that people pay for water in Ambos Nogales.

The true cost of water is not accurately measured by what people pay for it because that figure does not take into account the time and effort expended making arrangements for deliveries, planning to be home when delivery trucks arrive, or carrying water from stores, from public water spigots, or from sources on the other side of the border. However, the enormous disparities among the costs of different sources of water within Sonora and between Sonora and

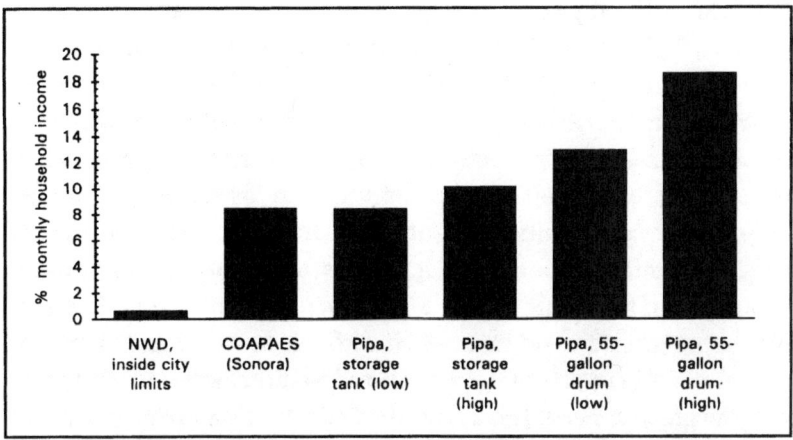

Figure 3.5 Social inequity in access to water in Ambos Nogales, based on the World Health Organization's minimum of 40 gallons per household per day for urban areas in the developing world. Each household is assumed to have two working members, both employed in minimum-wage jobs. Gross pay is $2,080 per year in Nogales, Son., and $17,680 per year in Nogales, Ariz. (exclusive of fringe benefits). The chart shows the percentage of the household's monthly income spent on water and the quantity this sum buys. The variation in water volume is the "basic" amount provided by the delivery institution or service. The poorest people living in squatter settlements are the ones storing water in 55-gallon drums.

Arizona indicate one level of the overall inequity that exists in the residents' access to water.

These disparities in water prices in Ambos Nogales mean that some residents are actually paying significantly more money to use less water than their neighbors. Expressed as a percentage of income, the disparities are even greater: $22.50 a month for a household in Nogales, Son., with even two members employed at minimum-wage jobs is an enormous amount of money to pay for water. Residents with the least access to public water—presumably the poorest residents—are obliged to pay the highest prices. Subsidies inherent in the operation of the municipal system, whether intentionally or not, apparently are going to those who need them least. Figure 3.5 shows the imbalance in social equity that exists because of the different water prices in Ambos Nogales.

The use of alternative water supplies has other costs as well. Water delivered by the pipas or obtained through other means often must be boiled before it can be used. Transporting water involves fuel and container expenses as well as time and physical effort. The use of alternatives may also harm the municipal system. Illegal connections may leak, and they increase stress on other system components, make it more difficult to maintain system pressure, reduce the amount of water available to other system customers, and are a source of contamination. Similarly, household storage tanks can do a good job of balancing supply and demand for individual families, but the open intake valves make it difficult to build and maintain pressure in other parts of the system and to direct water toward areas with the greatest need. It is currently illegal to install new household storage tanks in Nogales for this reason, but the law is widely ignored.

The use of alternative water sources can also have a less direct but more important negative impact on the public water supply system. Substantial personal and financial resources are spent by the residents of Nogales, Son., to obtain water, but whether spent on pipas, household storage tanks, bottled water, or other alternatives, none of the money goes to fund the public water supply system. Rather than being directed toward maintaining and improving the system that has the greatest potential to deliver water cheaply and efficiently throughout the city, the money is instead dispersed among a variety of private water purveyors, none of whom has either the capacity or the responsibility to see that all of the city's residents are adequately supplied. In effect, a vicious cycle has developed: The public system cannot be improved because it does not have adequate resources, but people are unwilling to give resources to the system until it is able to reliably deliver adequate quantities of high-quality water. The end result is that the higher relative expenditure by water consumers in Nogales, Son., is being made in such a way that the disparity in service between the two Nogaleses is likely to widen rather than narrow.

Wastewater Systems in Ambos Nogales

Although the wastewater collection and treatment systems on both sides of the border have been substantially enlarged during the last several decades, the improvements have not kept pace with the rapid population growth, especially in Nogales, Son. Consequently, city residents face many of the same problems in 1993 that they were facing before the first international wastewater treatment plant was completed in 1951.

Wastewater collection. The construction and operation of international treatment facilities has received most of the attention given to wastewater systems in Ambos Nogales. But for individual households and neighborhoods, the status of systems designed to collect and remove wastes is much more important than the status of the treatment facilities at the other end of the pipe. Wastes left in the neighborhood are not only aesthetically undesirable and inconvenient, they are also a source of disease. Wastewater contains microorganisms and viruses that can cause severe diarrhea as well as such life-threatening diseases as cholera, typhoid, and hepatitis. The construction of sewer systems improves public health, reduces health expenditures, and increases productivity and property values. Sewers also enhance water supply investments, since lack of adequate facilities to remove wastes makes additional water more of a problem than a benefit.

Expansion of the wastewater collection system in Nogales, Ariz., has generally kept up with population growth and the water supply system. The 1990 U.S. Census indicates that 67.3 percent of households in Santa Cruz County are connected to the public sewer system, with virtually all others using septic tanks or cesspools. Within the city itself the percentage of households connected to sewers is probably much greater, since most of those using other methods are in rural areas. The continued use of septic systems in areas where population densities are increasing and individual property size is decreasing can cause problems. Effective drain fields require fairly large areas, and local officials are making efforts to expand and extend the sewer system. Despite the need for new connections, very little threat to the public health arises from inadequate sewage disposal on the U.S. side of the border.

The same is not true in Nogales, Son., where there have always been substantial numbers of residents without access to either a piped sewer system or adequate alternatives. As is the case with the water supply system, the residents of Nogales, Son., depend on irregular federal and state government action for the construction of wastewater collection systems. Even where the systems exist, funds for operations and maintenance are scarce. Sewer maintenance is an especially critical activity because of the necessity to maintain smooth, even grades to ensure gravity flow and prevent pipes from becoming blocked.

The Mexican government has made rapid strides in extending the wastewater collection system, and were it not for the overwhelming population growth, almost all residents of the city probably would be connected to the system. However, both the official 1990 Mexican Census and a survey of city residents indicated that only 75–81 percent currently have access to wastewater drainage services, compared with an average 91.8 percent in all Mexican cities with populations greater than 100,000 (COLEF, 1992; Comisión Nacional del Agua, 1992).

About half of the residents of Nogales who do not have access to the municipal sewer system use septic tanks, about one-third use simple latrines, and the remainder use "natural drainages," which essentially means that wastes are disposed of in the environment (COLEF, 1992). All three methods are almost always inadequate in Nogales, Son., because of the thin, relatively impermeable soils, steep hillsides, and high urban densities. Virtually all waste that is not collected by the municipal system sooner or later appears on the ground surface or in city watercourses, where it constitutes an extreme threat to public health.

The extension of wastewater collection systems to more areas of the city in Nogales, Son., presents special challenges. The physical geography that causes such problems with uncollected wastes also frustrates plans for the design and construction of sewer systems, because sewers need to be laid at gentle and precise gradients in order to maintain a nonpressurized gravity flow. Gravity flow eliminates the need for large amounts of energy to operate the system, and nonpressurized conditions are necessary to reduce the potential for leaks and pipe breakages. Urban sewer lines generally follow the existing surface contours, but the large differences in elevation in Nogales, Son., make the design of effective sewer systems very difficult. The extension of sewer services to new areas, a very expensive process, is also frustrated by the lack of reliable information about future sites of growth, population densities, land use, and street layout, but these data are almost impossible to obtain in a city where unplanned and illicit development accounts for much of the recent growth.

Even in areas where sewers have been built, sewer line breaks can pose threats to public health. Much of the sewer system in Nogales, Son., dates from the post–World War II period and has not been very well maintained, so leaks are common. Because only a tiny fraction of wastewater consists of dissolved or suspended solids, it is difficult to distinguish wastewater from fresh water without laboratory analysis; it is likely, therefore, that much of the water in Nogales streets that is assumed to be from broken water lines is actually from broken sewer lines. A 1992 study estimated that between 14 and 21 percent of the population of Nogales, Son., faces health risks due to such sewer line breaks (COLEF, 1992).

Wastewater treatment. Completion of Ambos Nogales's first international treatment plant in 1951 was followed by rapid expansion of sewer systems on both sides of the border, and the new plant was quickly overwhelmed. The Nogales, Son., system expanded faster as a result of the city's faster population growth and the system's extension to previously unsewered areas of the city. The Mexican share of the total influent into the treatment plant rose from 15 percent in 1951 to 40 percent in 1957. At that time, the Mexican government verbally agreed to discontinue making new connections to the system until more treatment capacity was available.[24] Nonetheless, in 1963 the IBWC reported that "since August 1958 the plant design has been continuously exceeded and during a portion of most days it has been necessary to bypass raw sewage to an open stream. . . . During 1960, raw sewage was continuously bypassed all year."[25]

The problem grew even worse. In 1961, 8,000 out of a total of 9,500 residents of Nogales, Ariz., were connected to the wastewater collection system, but only 12,500 of the 40,000 residents of Nogales, Son., had sewer connections.[26] Still, the Mexican government was proceeding with plans to achieve 100 percent coverage. Treatment of such quantities in the existing plant were "unthinkable,"[27] and expansion at the existing site was not possible. U.S. officials therefore began to plan a new plant further downstream.

Meanwhile, Mexican officials were investigating the possibility of building their own plant 11 kilometers (7 miles) south of the city, in the Río Magdalena watershed. Such a plant offered several advantages, among them the facts that the construction money would be spent in Mexico and the effluent could be used for irrigation in Mexico. This plan, however, would require that sewage be pumped up and over the southern end of the valley, a prospect that alarmed U.S. officials:

> It is generally acknowledged that a pump installation is susceptible to failure from various causes. Should the pumping installation of the Mexican Government fail, raw sewage would necessarily discharge into the streets of the two cities and into the Nogales Wash in the major settled areas of Nogales, Arizona. The consequences from such an occurrence would almost surely result in widespread illness of epidemic proportions, not to mention physical damages from overflow of raw sewage and the expense of cleaning after repairs are made.... The Board [convened by the IBWC to make recommendations on future policy] recommends that all possible action be undertaken which will bring a joint international facility of adequate capacity into existence.[28]

U.S. officials also considered the "incidental advantage" that treated effluent could be retained, and used, in the United States.[29]

After considerable discussion and negotiation, in 1967 the Mexican government decided to join with the U.S. government in constructing a new, larger international facility at the confluence of Nogales Wash and the Santa Cruz River, 14.5 kilometers (9 miles) north of the border. The new plant was completed in 1972 with 60 percent of its 31,000 cubic meters (8.2 million gallons) per day capacity assigned to Nogales, Son., and 40 percent to Nogales, Ariz. The design and construction of the plant were funded by the U.S. section of the IBWC (46 percent), Mexico (29 percent), Nogales, Ariz. (17 percent), and the U.S. Environmental Protection Agency (8 percent).[30]

The completion of the new treatment facility in 1972 was followed by a repetition of the entire cycle of events that had precipitated its construction. Sewage flows into the plant once again quickly expanded as the populations of the two cities grew and additional sewers were constructed. The necessity for yet another new plant was recognized as early as 1976 (Ingram and White, 1991), and by 1982 the plant's daily capacity was once again being regularly exceeded. In 1986, the U.S. section of the IBWC proposed expanding the international plant even as the Mexican government once again contemplated building its own treatment facility.[31] U.S. officials again convinced their Mexican counterparts to invest in additional capacity at the international plant instead, and in 1989 construction began on a $10.7 million treatment plant expansion that would increase the capacity to 60,000 cubic meters (15.75 million gallons) per day. Completion of this phase of construction was immediately followed by further modifications that raised the capacity to 65,100 cubic meters (17.2 million gallons) per day.

As of 1994, Ambos Nogales is served by a single wastewater treatment plant, the Nogales International Waste Water Treatment Facility (NIWWTF), located on 33.6 hectares (83 acres) of bottomland at the confluence of Nogales Wash and the Santa Cruz River, 14.5 kilometers (9 miles) north of the border. The facility is operated by personnel from the city of Nogales, Ariz., with support from the IBWC. The operating costs are split between Nogales, Ariz., and Nogales, Son., based on their respective shares of the influent. Many more people are required to run the expanded plant, and its operation is much more expensive now. In part, the higher cost is attributable to the need to comply with increasingly stringent federal water quality standards and to provide information verifying that compliance. The major operations expenditures at the NIWWTF are for labor, energy, and chlorine. In 1991, total operations costs were $1.72 million, of which Nogales, Ariz., paid 45 percent and the Mexican government paid 55 percent.[32]

Despite its expanded capacity and large operations expenditures, the NIWWTF has had problems meeting water quality standards. NIWWTF operations are regulated under the terms of two permits. One permit is based on a federal program, the National Pollution Discharge Elimination System (NPDES), which is designed to protect surface water from point-source pollution threats. The NIWWTF's permit is held jointly by the city of Nogales, Ariz., and the IBWC, and is administered by the Arizona Department of Environmental Quality (ADEQ). ADEQ also administers the second permit, issued under Arizona's Groundwater Quality Protection Act, which is designed to protect the state's all-important groundwater aquifers from contamination.

Before detailing the NIWWTF's water quality and regulatory problems, we think it useful to describe in general terms how the plant is supposed to work. Most of what enters the plant is water; wastewater is typically 99.94 percent water by weight, with the remaining 0.06 percent consisting of dissolved and suspended solids (Water Environment Federation, n.d.). Wastewater comes from sinks, showers, washing machines, toilets, and drains in households, businesses, and industries. Additional water and wastes may enter the system from either planned or unplanned connections to storm sewers, as well as from natural drainage channels. Waste products carried by the sewers include food wastes, soaps and detergents, human and animal wastes, household and industrial cleaners, and a variety of substances generated by industrial processes. Sanitary sewers also often carry enormous loads of sediment, vegetation, trash, and other materials, especially following large storms. Though they account for only a tiny fraction of the sewage, human and animal wastes are of great public health significance because of the pathogens they introduce into the waste stream.

The NIWWTF employs standard primary and secondary treatment processes. Primary treatment consists of screens and settling ponds designed to remove large objects, sediment, and other suspended materials. The wastewater is then moved into separate ponds for secondary treatment, during which microbes degrade dissolved organic wastes and convert them into solids that settle to the bottom of the ponds. This process consumes large amounts of dissolved oxygen and can produce severely objectionable odors if it becomes anaerobic, so aeration of the wastewater is an integral part of the secondary treatment process. Before being released to the Santa Cruz River, the water is treated with ultraviolet radiation to kill bacteria.

The process does not always work as intended, and the number and variety of water quality problems that have occurred at the

NIWWTF over the years are too numerous to document here. Instead, we will let the events of a single year, 1991, illustrate the kind of water quality and regulatory problems that have dogged the plant.

In February 1991, the NIWWTF was cited for chronic excessive levels of suspended sediments in the plant's effluent, caused by wastewater inflow in excess of the plant's rated capacity. The inflow caused wastewater to be released from the plant before treatment was completed. Inflows exceeding capacity have been a persistent problem at the NIWWTF, but this case received added attention because the EPA simultaneously placed a moratorium on the construction of new sewer lines in Nogales, Ariz., until the problem was eliminated.

The moratorium, widely viewed as disastrous for the future development of the city, was especially galling to city residents because much of the excess inflow was attributable to the actions of another federal agency, the IBWC. For the preceding several months, water in Nogales Wash had been contaminated by sewage flowing from broken sewer lines in Nogales, Son. The IBWC's solution to the problem was to pump the contaminated water out of the wash and into the sewage system. Since December 1990, the IBWC had been pumping 3,785 to 11,360 cubic meters (1–3 million gallons) of water per day from the wash directly into the trunk line leading to the NIWWTF.[33] Though excess inflows to the plant were caused in part by the same heavy storms that had caused sewer line breaks in Sonora, there is no doubt that the IBWC's actions greatly exacerbated the NIWWTF's problems.

Lack of capacity was not the only source of permit violations. Later in February the NIWWTF was cited for excessive levels of phenols (derived from household and industrial cleaners), cyanide, and mercury. In general, there are two kinds of industrial wastes: those that are compatible with standard municipal sewage treatment technologies and those that are not. Phenols, solvents, cyanide, mercury, and other heavy metals are among the latter, and they pass through the plant and the treatment processes virtually unaltered. The only way to eliminate them from the sewage effluent is to prevent them from entering the sewer system in the first place. Generally, this is accomplished through better materials management or industrial pretreatment procedures, and the two Nogaleses had signed a pledge in 1988 to institute industrial pretreatment programs on both sides of the border. Nonetheless, many people believed that the contaminants came from industries in Sonora, particularly from the maquiladoras. Since everything that leaves the NIWWTF is the responsibility of the two permit holders (the city of Nogales, Ariz., and the IBWC), the existence of these contaminants in the waste stream caused great concern among Nogales, Ariz., officials.

In July, the NIWWTF was cited for additional violations of both the discharge elimination and groundwater quality permits, this time for "administrative" reasons. Testing for the spectrum of constituents specified in the two permits and preparing reports is time-consuming and expensive, and the city had failed to receive and forward laboratory results in time to meet permit deadlines.

Frustration over the moratorium and repeated permit violations surfaced in August, when the mayor of Nogales, Ariz., defied the EPA by directing city workers to construct a sewer line to connect a new commercial development to the sewer system. Other city officials tried to blame Mexico for many of the NIWWTF's compliance problems by claiming that industrial pretreatment programs were fully in place on their side of the border while nothing at all was being done in Sonora. These claims probably held a good deal of truth; even the IBWC acknowledged that the terms of the 1988 pretreatment pledge were not being implemented in Mexico.[34]

In September, high bacterial levels in the NIWWTF's effluent revealed that the new plant's ultraviolet radiation system was not as effective as it was designed to be. As a result, plant operators decided to start adding chlorine to the effluent on a regular basis rather than using it solely as a backup procedure. The officials responsible for operating the NIWWTF also sought authority to add a new "compliance officer" position to ensure that permit requirements were met and reported on time. These new measures significantly raised the costs of plant operations.

In October, ADEQ approved operations for the expanded NIWWTF even though cyanide, mercury, copper, and phenol concentrations in the effluent were still too high. ADEQ also indicated that it would lift the moratorium on new sewer lines if NIWWTF operators could prove that Mexico was the source of the contaminants. A month later, it became apparent that the "new" NIWWTF was going to have problems meeting standards for nitrogen (in the form of ammonia) because the standards had been tightened considerably after the plans for the expansion had been completed. This raised the specter that the new $10.7 million expansion would be obsolete before it was even built.

The improvements needed to remove the nitrogen were projected to cost over $8 million, but in December the EPA indicated that it would not enforce the stricter standards and also stated that the city of Nogales, Ariz., should not have to be responsible for effluent violations resulting from pollution sources in Mexico. Nogales, Ariz., officials were able to present evidence that the cyanide and mercury arriving at the NIWWTF were in fact from Mexico, and so the moratorium on new sewer lines was lifted in January 1992, even though cyanide and mercury concentrations were still exceeding standards.

Though most of the problems raised in 1991 were eventually resolved, the history of wastewater treatment in the Nogales area indicates that the solutions to these and similar problems are probably only temporary. As a result, there has been a concerted effort to find new ways to resolve the problems. One potential "solution" proposed by a number of Nogales, Ariz., residents and officials is a second treatment plant built next to the existing one, so that wastewater received from the two cities can be completely separated. Construction of a second plant would increase overall treatment capacities, but it still would not address excess discharges of nitrogen, heavy metals, and solvents, since these are not substantially affected by treatment processes.

A second plant for Nogales, Ariz., would, however, enable the city to avoid some of its problems with regulators. Not only would contaminants from Mexico no longer be included within their permit, but smaller facilities have to meet less stringent standards than larger facilities. Thus, splitting the treatment plant in two would result in the application of more relaxed standards. The primary disadvantage of a second plant is cost, not only for construction and operation of the new plant but also for construction of a separate sewer trunk line from the border. Construction of a 14.5-kilometer (9-mile) trunk line through the city would be extremely expensive and would also disrupt downtown traffic and commerce. Nogales residents had hoped that the federal government would build a separate plant using federal money, and in fact the budget submitted by President Bush to the U.S. Congress during the election year of 1992 contained $5 million for the design of a new treatment plant and sewer trunk line in Nogales. Congress dashed these hopes when it struck the measure from the budget.

Alternative wastewater treatment proposals have also been under consideration in Nogales, Son. As late as 1987, the Mexican government was still expressing a desire to use treated effluent for irrigation in the Río Magdalena watershed. A plan was devised calling for 7.6 kilometers (4.7 miles) of pressurized pipe to lift the sewage 122 meters (400 feet) in elevation to the watershed boundary. Operations and maintenance costs were projected to be $2.9 million per year—half of it for energy to run the pumps.[35] The idea of constructing a domestic Mexican sewage treatment plant, while made difficult by considerations of geography and topography, apparently remains alive. In 1992 El Colegio de la Frontera Norte (College of the Northern Border; COLEF) proposed that the city of Nogales, Son., design and employ several small treatment systems in order to use treated effluent as a new source of water (COLEF, 1992). Both alternatives are likely to cause great concern to Nogales, Ariz., and IBWC officials, because of potential problems with pump reliability and the collateral reduction in effluent flow from the NIWWTF.

The effect of effluent reduction on the Santa Cruz riparian area. In an interview held in November 1993, Silberio Ruiz, director of COAPAES-Nogales, stated that Mexico does indeed intend to build its own wastewater treatment plant within the next two years, the idea being to return the treated effluent to the Río Magdalena watershed for agricultural use. Figure 3.6 shows the annual percentage contribution of effluent release to the Santa Cruz River's total flow in the upper watershed region and the importance of effluent release on an aggregated monthly basis. Two things are abundantly clear. First, the relative importance of effluent as a percentage of the total annual flow has increased over time, so much so that during particularly dry years the effluent essentially *is* the Santa Cruz River flow in the upper watershed. Second, effluent is particularly important to the riparian area during the premonsoon summer months.

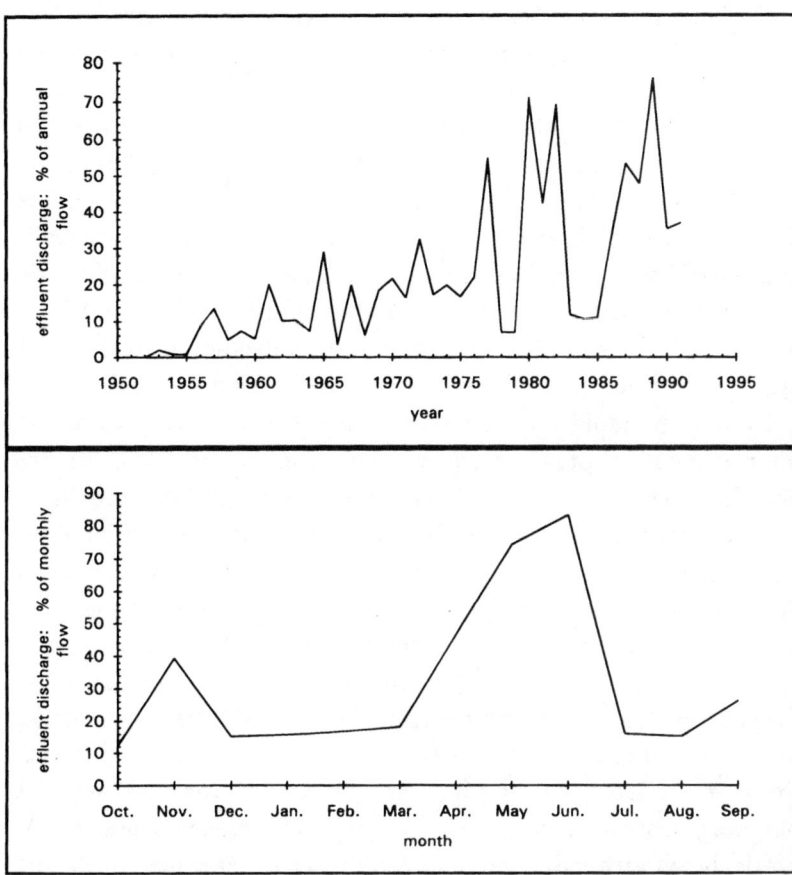

Figure 3.6 *Top*: The annual percentage contribution of effluent release from the NIWWTF to the Santa Cruz River's total flow in the upper watershed region, north of the NIWWTF. Effluent values from 1952 to 1970 are estimates. *Bottom*: The importance of effluent release on an aggregated monthly basis; values are averaged from 1973 to 1992. *Source*: Center for Environmental Studies, Arizona State University, Tempe.

If Mexico were to build its own wastewater treatment plant and direct its effluent to a different watershed, the Santa Cruz riparian area would suffer. Surface water flows may cease entirely during the driest months of the year, and the availability of subsurface water to the ecosystem is then decided in large part by the amount of water withdrawn upstream by Ambos Nogales.

Drainage and flood control systems. Most visitors to Ambos Nogales during the rainy season see large quantities of standing water in city streets, especially downtown and in the *colonias* (squatter settlements). The growth of urban areas in previously undisturbed watersheds does not stop the natural processes of precipitation and runoff. In fact, urban development usually increases runoff because the infiltration capacity diminishes as buildings, streets, parking lots, and other impervious facilities cover the soil and eliminate vegetation. If new land uses are incompatible with preexisting hydrologic processes, then water flowing through or collecting in urban areas can cause serious problems—as is the case in Ambos Nogales.

Despite the rapid population and areal growth, additions to and improvements of the drainage and flood control systems in Ambos Nogales since the 1940s have been quite modest. The covered channels beneath the streets of downtown Ambos Nogales and the lined channels in Nogales, Ariz., continue to be the primary routes of drainage and floodwaters through the city. State and local governments in Sonora have lined portions of Nogales Wash above the inlet to the Nogales Wash Covered Channel, while Santa Cruz County and the U.S. Soil Conservation Service performed some bank-protection work downstream from the lined channels in 1985 and 1987, respectively. In the late 1980s, the U.S. Army Corps of Engineers began a planning process to determine how best to protect certain flood-prone neighborhoods near the confluence of Nogales Wash and Potrero Creek, but for the most part the only other existing drainage routes in the city are the remnants of the preexisting natural drainage channels.

The absence of drainage facilities—whether "improved" natural channels or entirely artificial ones—causes frequent and serious drainage problems in Ambos Nogales. Water runs through the streets and collects in low spots after every major storm, significantly disrupting transportation, commerce, and community affairs. More seriously, some storms have caused extensive property damage and threatened human life and health. Floods in 1977 claimed three lives, inundated more than 40 homes, damaged the NIWWTF, and eroded several acres of land. Flooding in 1983 caused similar damage but no deaths (U.S. Department of the Army, 1987).

The limited utility of existing drainage plans and facilities is due to several factors. First, the facilities were designed and built long before rapid population growth increased runoff, on the one hand, and changed the size and location of areas that require protection, on the other. Second, the Nogales Wash channels possess only a limited number of inlets, so water that once flowed freely into the natural drainage now either collects in pools or must be channeled an additional distance through the city to one of the inlets. Third, much of the new development, especially in Nogales, Son., has occurred without adequate (or any) consideration of drainage needs. Finally, lack of maintenance is another obvious source of problems; in 1987, the U.S. Army Corps of Engineers found that 80 percent of the southern inlet to the Arroyo Boulevard Covered Channel had been plugged by silt and debris (U.S. Department of the Army, 1987).

Drainage problems and flooding are especially severe in the colonias of Nogales, Son., and in downstream Arizona neighborhoods located on the Nogales Wash floodplain. Generally, colonias are situated on terrain that has very poor drainage, and water flowing between houses and through the steep, unpaved streets causes significant erosion and property damage. Floodwaters also mobilize a variety of contaminants, from human wastes to toxic chemicals, that have been disposed of improperly. In Nogales, Ariz., some floodplain neighborhoods are protected by physical barriers such as the canalization mentioned above, or through more recent efforts by the Corps of Engineers.

The corps's 1987 draft feasibility report for new flood control measures in Nogales, Ariz., indirectly points to another problem. Because everything that occurs at a given point in a watershed is the result of all the processes occurring above that point, it is very difficult to design and construct effective drainage and flood control systems without taking into account the hydrologic processes of the entire watershed. Nonetheless, the report indicates that measures to control drainage upstream in Sonora were not even contemplated because the IBWC had told the corps that financial constraints would keep the Mexican government from participating in the project (U.S. Department of the Army, 1987).

Water Quality

The natural water system of the Nogales and Santa Cruz Valleys has been measurably altered in the last century by the development of water resources. Water has been removed from the system at specific locations and then returned, altered in quality and reduced in quantity, at others. Some of the vegetation and habitat changes that have occurred as a result of reduced water flows were described earlier in this chapter, but it is important to realize that changes in water quality also have negative impacts on the area's people.

From the earliest years of the city to the present, the greatest source of water quality problems in Ambos Nogales has been unconfined sewage. To recapitulate the section above, virtually all Nogales, Ariz., households are connected to the public sewer system or to septic tanks, but a sizable number of residents of Nogales, Son., still do not have access to adequate wastewater collection and removal services despite rapid expansions of the sewer system. Much of the wastewater generated in Nogales, Son., never enters the sewer system at all, and a substantial portion of that which does enter escapes through broken or leaky pipes.

The region's topography and shared hydrology dictate that a water quality problem originating in Sonora quickly becomes binational. Unconfined wastewater following the natural contours of the land flows down through neighborhoods and streets toward Arizona and Nogales Wash. In some cases, sewage doesn't have very far to go before it gets to the wash, because primary sewage collector lines, which lie at the lowest points of the sewage system in order to utilize gravity flows, run along both sides of the wash.

It is difficult and expensive to test for and measure all of the biological contaminants that might be present in water, so fecal coliform bacteria are commonly used to indicate the presence of other bacteria, viruses, and pathogenic microorganisms; the existence of fecal coliform bacteria is presumptive evidence of contamination by a variety of pathogens. Fecal coliform concentrations in Nogales Wash are always high, and they become even higher during rain events, which wash surface contaminants into the area's watercourses. Concentrations reach dramatically high levels following breaks in major sewer lines, as has happened on numerous occasions (the history of sewage flows in Nogales Wash and its tributaries is discussed at greater length in Chapter 5).

The IBWC has installed chlorination facilities at the Sonoran inlet to the Nogales Wash Covered Channel to help combat the extreme public health threat arising from sewage flows in the wash. The facility mixes chlorine with water and then automatically dispenses it into the wash. The chlorination facility has generally been effective in killing bacteria, though there have been several breakdowns. The facility is also incapable of handling large flows, such as those that occur after the summer monsoon storms. High flows are still likely to contain elevated levels of biological contaminants, and, more important, many people are exposed to the contaminated water before it ever reaches the chlorination facility.

In addition to potential health problems resulting from direct contact, unconfined sewage has the potential to contaminate public water supplies. The public water supply system in Nogales, Ariz., relies primarily on water from wells in the Santa Cruz Valley and Potrero Canyon, which are not downstream from potentially contaminating urban areas. The NWD chlorinates water at the wellheads, and so far supplies have been free of bacterial contamination. Private wells are generally not chlorinated, however, and they remain susceptible to contamination by sewage. More than 100 private wells along Nogales Wash and the Santa Cruz River downstream from the wash were sampled following a major sewage line break in 1990; 87 were free of contamination, 7 were contaminated, and 6 were possibly contaminated.[36]

The situation is much worse in Nogales, Son., where water supplies frequently are not very well isolated from potential sources of contamination and chlorination is less consistent. Almost all the wells within the city are adjacent to drainages such as the Nogales Wash, and thus are vulnerable to unconfined sewage flows. Water quality sampling in 1990 found bacterial contamination in several wells, including wells used by water delivery trucks and one used by a bottled water plant. The same sampling program found bacterial contamination in several of the city's storage reservoirs (Udall Center, 1993b).

Biological contamination is the most widespread and noticeable water quality problem, but in recent years it has become clear that it is not the only one. Urban residents and especially industries use numerous materials that can contaminate water supplies if not disposed of properly. Chemicals that leak, spill, or are intentionally dumped eventually reach the groundwater table, especially near the Nogales Wash, where the aquifer is closer to the surface. Once in the groundwater, the contamination spreads, moving in the same direction as the groundwater flow. Groundwater sampling in Nogales, Son., has indicated the presence of a variety of toxic volatile organic compounds (VOCs) that are usually associated with industrial solvents. Some of these have been detected in water pumped from water supply wells. Though so far the VOCs have generally been found in concentrations below health guidelines and standards, concentrations of at least one, tetrachloroethylene (PCE), have exceeded those standards (Udall Center, 1993b).

An incident that took place in Tijuana in 1993 illustrates both the urgent need for better regulation of toxic waste disposal and the positive results that can follow when individual citizens concern themselves with environmental safety.

"They have come from all over, saying they are going to invest, that they are going to help us," said Maurilio Sánchez, a community organizer in Ejido Chilpacingo [Tijuana], a dusty sprawl of tarpaper and brick that sits just below a big maquiladora park on the city's outskirts. "But when it comes to complying with the ecological laws, they say they cannot speak Spanish."

For the most part, Mr. Sánchez said, the authorities ignore him. But they have been paying more attention since March 8 [1993], when sewer openings in the neighborhood exploded and he led a clutch of firemen and inspectors to a waste recycling system in the industrial park.

Just as the posse arrived, the company's owner and two workers were pouring barrels of toxic chemicals down a sewer drain. Investigators concluded that they have been doing so for years.

By law, the foreign-owned plants are obliged to ship their hazardous wastes back out of Mexico for disposal. In practice, officials say, there is a flourishing traffic in waste dumping. A United States

Congressional study [1992] found that fewer than one-third of the plants even reported on their wastes as required and that the reports went virtually unchecked.[37]

Cyanide and heavy metals such as mercury and copper have been detected in both surface waters and groundwater. Groundwater moves very slowly, and the contaminants found to date may represent only the tip of the iceberg; problems with contamination by toxic substances will probably continue to worsen. So far, contaminated groundwater has been found primarily in Nogales, Son., but since the contaminant plumes are slowly moving downhill—and northward—the problem poses a binational threat.

Virtually every urban area has experienced water quality problems resulting from "nonpoint," or diffused, sources. Heavy metals and hydrocarbons are ubiquitous in urban watercourses, and their sources are numerous. Road-surface and vehicular pollutants, street litter, and pesticides and fertilizers applied to lawns and gardens are the most frequent sources of the chemical contaminants in urban runoff; and traffic and decomposing pavement and construction materials have been cited as the major sources of metals (Streigl, 1987; Whipple and Hunter, 1979; Duda et al., 1982).

Much of the measured contamination in Nogales, Son., however, is suspected to be from far less diffuse sources. These are readily apparent in a casual stroll along uncovered portions of Nogales Wash. Despite the strong laws barring contamination of the environment, numerous pipes can be spotted that appear to drain directly from industrial and commercial buildings into the wash. Soil is stained red, black, and green along the wash banks where dumps and junkyards are located. A mix of bottles, cans, and other trash is always present within the channel, raising the possibility that paints, solvents, pesticides, and other chemicals are being discarded there. Covered portions of the wash may hide even more contamination sources, but detection is more difficult there because only the IBWC has the jurisdiction to operate within the covered channels, and the IBWC does not enforce water quality laws.

The maquiladoras are another obvious and frequently mentioned source of contaminants. Under the terms of a 1983 treaty, hazardous waste generated by the maquilas is supposed to be returned to the

United States for disposal, but it is a widely acknowledged fact that very little actually leaves Mexico. Numerous critics of the maquila industry, as well as environmentalists and other concerned citizens, charge that the maquilas routinely dump toxic waste into the sewers or pay Mexican firms to take the waste and ask no questions about where it is ultimately dumped. Industry spokespersons typically dispute these allegations, though some will acknowledge that other firms are not very careful or concerned about what happens to the chemicals they use.[38]

Because the chemicals are never inventoried or officially tracked, and since enforcement of hazardous waste laws is spotty at best (see Chapter 5), there is very little hard evidence to support claims that toxic materials are being dumped illegally. Rumors and innuendos abound, however, and circumstantial evidence tends to substantiate the charges. Almost all the VOCs found in the groundwater of Nogales, Son., are derived from solvents used in industry, and the maquilas account for the vast majority of local industry. In 1990, a *New York Times* reporter investigating claims of widespread dumping by the maquilas took water samples from a sewer near a maquiladora industrial park in Nogales. Laboratory analyses of the samples found high levels of various toxic chemicals, including chloroform, benzene, toluene, and PCE. The chloroform and benzene concentrations were double the limits set by the Mexican environmental protection agency, and the toluene concentrations were seven times the limit. That these results seem to have surprised no one affirms the widespread belief that the maquilas are a primary source of the chemicals that are starting to contaminate the city's groundwater.[39]

The development of Ambos Nogales and its associated water resource systems has dramatically affected the shared hydrologic environment. Groundwater levels have fallen in both the Nogales and Santa Cruz Valleys, flows in the Santa Cruz River have diminished, and marshes and wetlands in both valleys have disappeared. A substantial amount of riparian vegetation has been lost, and the only continuous stand of vegetation left in the area exists downstream of the NIWWTF.

Urban water resource systems have developed quite differently on the two sides of the border. Residents of Nogales, Ariz., are able to obtain water in quantities sufficient to sustain substantial rates of consumption and have adequate access to wastewater collection and removal services. Their neighbors in Nogales, Son., are less fortunate; the public water supply system is inefficient and prone to breakdowns, and many or most residents must spend large sums of money and energy to obtain water from alternative sources. Many are also unable to obtain adequate wastewater collection services. Finally, flood protection and drainage problems have been especially severe in Nogales, Son., though they have had significant impacts in Nogales, Ariz., as well.

Both cities are beginning to face additional water problems. The long-term sustainability of water supplies has never been evaluated adequately and could become critical as the population of the valley continues to grow. The cost of securing new water supplies and of collecting and treating wastewater is rising much faster than local financial resources are growing. Both cities face numerous institutional and regulatory problems, particularly in their relationships to state and federal governments. Water quality has been dramatically reduced, and substantial quantities of chlorine must be added to natural waters because it is impossible to adequately capture and treat wastewater flows. There seems to be no end in sight to the city's chronic problems with sewage contamination of neighborhoods and watercourses, and new, potentially more dangerous and more expensive contamination problems are emerging. The loss of cultural, aesthetic, and recreational resources that accompanies the replacement of natural drainage channels with concrete tunnels is also being felt.

Any effort to improve the water resources situation in Ambos Nogales must begin with an understanding of the physical setting and the history and nature of constructed water resource systems. This understanding is critical not only for defining problems but also for formulating solutions, and it is for this reason that we have so carefully described the area's physical water resource systems. However, it would be a mistake to view water in Ambos Nogales only in terms of physical systems. Water resource systems are designed to meet the needs of people, and water and water issues affect the people of Ambos Nogales in many ways. The relationship of the people of Ambos Nogales to their water resources is the subject of the next chapter.

Chapter 4

Divided Neighbors

Water is a fluid resource. It flows from one place to another. Thus, water supply and disposal practices in one location can become water problems further down the water gradient. In many ways, human beings are also a fluid resource. Although we think of them as belonging to one place, it is increasingly true that people move into and out of places, carrying with them their own sets of needs and expectations. Over the years, the population of Ambos Nogales has flowed back and forth across the border, creating important social connections and interrelationships between the cities. Residents of Ambos Nogales who have lived there for generations have deep roots that tie them to the place. But many residents have migrated to Ambos Nogales from the interior of Mexico, from the colder climes of the United States, and from other places around the world. These newcomers bring with them their own concerns and ways of connecting to their environment. An unskilled laborer from Morelia arriving in Nogales, Son., to try to make a new home has a much different set of expectations and needs than an executive from Pittsburgh arriving in Nogales, Ariz., to manage a maquila. But both belong to the mix of people for whom water management programs must be devised and implemented in Ambos Nogales.

As is the case in other cities along the U.S.-Mexico border, the population of Ambos Nogales has grown dramatically in recent years. According to official Mexican sources, which tend to be conservative in their estimates, Nogales, Son., grew at an annual average of 4.8 percent in the 1980s. The city's official population increased from approximately 70,000 in 1980 to almost 110,000 in 1990 (see Chapter 2). The population on the U.S. side of the border has not increased at quite that rate, but there has been a marked influx of businesspeople engaging in trade-related activities and of retirees, particularly in outlying suburban areas such as Rio Rico.

The rich diversity of experiences and perspectives of residents of Ambos Nogales is highlighted in the following stories about four families who live there. Although they are neighbors, their lives have followed distinctly different paths in bringing them to Ambos Nogales. This chapter explores the social and economic factors that divide these neighbors from each other as well as the factors that unite them in spite of the international boundary. With this background, we proceed to examine the attitudes and beliefs that residents of Ambos Nogales hold about water issues.[1]

Four Families

The Sepulvedas of Nogales, Sonora

Arturo and Maria Sepulveda and their four children are third- and fourth-generation Nogales residents. Arturo's grandparents came to the northern province when Mexico began exporting winter fruits and vegetables to the United States in the early 1900s, and the family still owns a profitable export business. Arturo and his family keep close familial and political ties to the Mexico City area, though their relatives and business associates in the capital frequently express skepticism about their living so far away on the northern frontier.

The Sepulvedas are concerned about maintaining their Mexican identity and about the negative influences that their children may be exposed to at the border. At the same time, Arturo and Sylvia like to take advantage of the many opportunities there. Sylvia travels to Tucson at least once a month to shop at a department store, where Spanish-speaking clerks are always available. She or her maid crosses to Nogales, Ariz., several times a week to buy groceries and bottled water. Both of the Sepulvedas have a working knowledge of English, which they use when they must in business exchanges. They are pleased that their children have become fluent in English because bilingualism is thought to be essential for those who want to succeed in modern Mexico.

The Sepulvedas were instrumental in bringing the national symphony to Nogales, and they travel to the capital at least once a year to see relatives, visit museums, and hear the latest political and social gossip. Arturo also goes to Mexico City quite frequently on business, where he meets with government officials to straighten out problems and looks for new business opportunities.

The Sepulvedas' lovely colonial home is located in a well-established, pleasant residential area in the low foothills close to the center of the city. Although the family likes the convenience of being in town, they sometimes think of moving to the newer planned residential community on the outskirts of town where roads and utilities are new and not so frequently in need of repair or out of service. They are connected to the city water system and would have water all day long if not for the fact that pressure in the lines is often low, old pipes in the neighborhood frequently leak, and there are frequent outages for repairs. To compensate, they follow the same practice that their relatives in Mexico City use—they have a water storage tank on their roof. The tank refills automatically from the water line when pressure in the system is high, and a private water company with whom they have a contract also regularly replenishes their supply.

Arturo often says that his family is very fortunate to live on their low hill rather than in the lower-lying areas, which flood during the summer monsoon season. His downtown office is sometimes flooded, and debris and sewage flowing from the uncovered portions of the wash can make other parts of town smelly and unpleasant. The location of their house on a hillside also means that their sewer drains well, although they are concerned about the same sewer line serving new houses further up the hill. The family is very careful about what goes into their drains because the old pipes are prone to clogging. All of this causes Arturo to harbor some suspicions about the quality of water delivered by the city, although he comforts himself that his family uses bottled water from Arizona for drinking and cooking, and the Nogales water is likely no worse than that used by family and friends in other Mexican cities.

The Cadenas in Nogales, Arizona

Robert and Sylvia Cadena have lived in Nogales all their lives. Robert's grandfather immigrated from Hermosillo to Nogales and started a small clothing store on the Arizona side of the line, where he had better access to supplies. The better quality and selection of the American goods he stocks are a draw to his Mexican customers, on whom his business depends almost entirely. At the same time, the Cadenas make use of many services and products that are cheaper in Mexico, including doctors, dentists, and pharmaceuticals. A cleaning woman and a gardener also come to their house once a week from Mexico, luxuries that they certainly could not afford if they had to pay U.S. wages.

Sylvia maintains a close friendship with her sister and several cousins in Nogales, Son., and both of the Cadenas are close to Robert's family in Hermosillo. The Cadenas' children and the children of Sylvia's sister spend considerable time together, frequently staying at one or the other household during weekends and holidays. Once, when her sister's daughter was very sick, the Cadenas brought the girl to Arizona to stay with them for several months so she could receive regular treatments at the local hospital.

Both the Cadenas and their children have been educated in English at school, but with friends and family they tend to speak Spanish interspersed with many English words. Whenever Sylvia speaks with her Mexican cousins about the growing problems with water and other services in Nogales, Son., she is glad to have been born on the U.S. side of the line. Sylvia knows that every time she turns on the tap, limitless clean water will be available. Once in a while the Mexican radio station the Cadenas listen to at the store talks about flooding, or the need to boil water, or other problems related to the contamination of Nogales Wash. But to them, the difficulties seem minor and nothing that city officials cannot handle. Water generally is a subject to be dealt with by experts, and not something they or their relatives personally can do much about.

The Wilsons of Rio Rico, Arizona

Arthur and Sally Wilson investigated a lot of alternatives before deciding to retire in Rio Rico, a well-to-do suburb of Nogales. Arthur spent his career as a machinist in Ohio and his pension is not large, but it is adequate to live well in relatively low-cost southern Arizona. The warm, dry climate is also beneficial for Sally's arthritis. Their son lives in Phoenix, and they considered moving to one of the retirement communities there, but they liked the fact that Rio Rico was less expensive and cooler in the summer. There are many other retired couples in the Wilsons' neighborhood, and they are so surrounded by people like themselves that they sometimes forget that they are so close to Mexico. They enjoy reading about the desert and about the history of the Southwest, but except for occasional quick visits to the tourist areas in Nogales, Son., they don't have much personal experience with Mexico. They don't speak Spanish, and they are uncomfortable with the thought of venturing very far from places where they know that the shopkeepers can speak English. It especially doesn't make much sense to them to go very far into Mexico when there are so many places to explore on the U.S. side of the line. They also are concerned about getting sick in Mexico, because they have heard so many stories about how the air and the water there are not very clean.

Much of what the Wilsons know about daily life in Mexico comes from reading the local newspaper, the *Nogales International*. It seems to the Wilsons that Mexico has a lot of problems. They follow with great interest the stories about fires in the dump on the Sonoran side because the fires have been polluting the air on both sides of the boundary. News about water contamination in Nogales Wash greatly concerns them—both because they enjoy birdwatching in the wooded, cool areas along the Santa Cruz River and because such stories increase their worries about the deteriorating drinking-water quality.

The Wilsons thought little about water problems before they moved to Rio Rico, and their water bill there is no larger than it was in Ohio. However, they were very concerned when Nogales officials started talking about not letting Rio Rico continue to use the sewage treatment plant when the plant was overloaded, because they thought their taxes might go up as a consequence. And since reading all the news about pollution coming from Mexico, they have begun to buy bottled water for drinking, even though the local water company insists that its supplies are safe. On one occasion Mr. Wilson became so concerned about the problems of handling Mexican sewage that he wrote a strong letter to one of Arizona's senators urging federal action to solve the problem, but he feels that despite all the rhetoric, it doesn't look like anybody is going to do anything.

Mercedes Gonzales of Nogales, Sonora

Mercedes Gonzales is the unmarried mother of two small children. She immigrated to Nogales from Morelia in the interior of Mexico, where unemployment was high and the principal industry, agriculture, offered little opportunity. Her mother was concerned about her moving so far away from home at the young age of 17, but she needed money for her children, and her mother also needed the cash income she would be able to send home. Further, she knew could find a place to live with her cousins in one of the many colonias springing up around Nogales.

In the five years Mercedes has been in Nogales, she has managed to build her own small dwelling in a new colonia close to the maquila where she now works, the fourth maquila in which she has been employed. Since her boyfriend left several months ago, she has had difficulty arranging for child care during her 10-hour shift. Too often her little ones run with a pack of others around the neighborhood. Although it will be difficult for her to pay for school clothes and textbooks for her children, she will be grateful when the new school that the colonia has been lobbying for finally opens. She badly misses the emotional support of her extended family and wishes there was a job for her at home.

The biggest day-to-day problem Mercedes has in her life is obtaining sufficient quantities of clean water to meet the needs of her family. There is no running water to her new colonia, although some of her neighbors are trying to tap into a nearby water main. Mercedes uses as little water as she can, but bathing and doing laundry to keep her children presentable and herself attractive requires water. She wishes that her colonia at least had central spigots like some of the other new colonias, but her colonia does not have enough influence with the government to obtain such things. One of her neighbors helped her bring home two 200-liter (55-gallon) metal drums that were discarded by a maquila. She thoroughly cleaned the drums, but she has lingering concerns about what may have been stored in them. She knows that some of the women who work in maquilas have rashes and other skin problems from chemicals stored in such drums. Because of her doubts she always boils the water, and when she can she buys bottled water from the corner store for drinking and cooking.

Because Mercedes lives on a steep hill, the pipa trucks seldom come more than once a week. Even so, she finds it very difficult to pay so much of her income for water. She is grateful during the weeks when the government pipas come and deliver water free of charge, but she never knows when they are coming. Because her house lies at the end of steep, winding, ungraded roads, the truck drivers find many excuses not to come. When the pipas do not show up, she must carry water up her hill from a faucet in the city park.

Socioeconomic Dividing Lines

As these stories demonstrate, there are significant differences in the standard of living enjoyed by residents of Ambos Nogales. Some of the distinctions stem from the disparate levels of economic development of the two countries, although the most dramatic contrasts exist among residents of Nogales, Son. On the average, living conditions in Nogales, Son., are much worse than those in Nogales, Ariz. The minimum wages paid by most of the maquilas and many other employers are not enough to buy even basic goods and services, much less luxury items. Households with two, three, or even four or more working members often are not able to pay rent or house payments and are forced to build homes on land they don't own with whatever materials are at hand (these squatter settlements are discussed in greater detail below). Many residents of Nogales, Son., live in homes that don't have even basic services; 16.5 percent of the households don't have connections to the public water system, and 19 percent are not connected to the sewer system (fig. 4.1). According to Mexican census figures, 13 percent of households don't have electricity. The rudimentary nature of much of the city's housing is indicated by the fact that 12 percent of the homes have dirt floors and 21 percent have roofs made of laminated cardboard. Though almost three quarters of Nogales, Son., households own their own homes, 24 percent of the homes have two or fewer rooms (INEGI, 1990a, 1990b).[2]

Nogales, Son., appears to be a city with more people than there are houses and urban services for. It is difficult, however, to quantify the discrepancy. The 1990 Mexican Census indicated that 107,936 people were living in the municipality of Nogales, Son., but the official figures are not always readily accepted. Unofficial, and common, estimates place the city's population at double or even triple the official figure. Methodological problems, such as flawed data-gathering techniques and the fact that surveyors ask respondents for their primary place of residence rather than where they have been living, make the official figures somewhat questionable. Many residents consider themselves to be visitors, even though they have been living in Nogales for several years (Francisco Lara, COLEF-Nogales, pers. comm., 1993). Most people believe that census data are used to support particular political positions, and the numbers are therefore susceptible to political influence. Understating the population allows politicians to also understate the magnitude of existing problems and unmet needs. Conversely, the size of the population may be overstated by those desiring to dramatize the size of the city's problems and support the case for greater federal and state funding of social programs and infrastructure. The people's skepticism about the population figures is mirrored by their disbelief about the proportion of the city's residents said to have access to basic services.

Though living conditions often appear marginal at best, the standard of living in Nogales is higher than it is in many interior regions of Mexico. Nogalensians have access to a wider range of goods and services because they can shop on both sides of the international boundary. They also have more opportunities to earn "hard" money by working at jobs in the United States, where even minimum wages are much higher than comparable salaries in Mexico. Residents of Nogales, Son., with green cards may cross the border daily to work at jobs in Arizona. Others may find temporary or casual employment, legally or illegally, often utilizing connections with friends and family in Arizona.

There is also substantial disparity in the living conditions experienced by Nogales, Son., residents. While many lack basic services and adequate housing, others live in spacious, comfortable homes and have access to virtually all services, including water 24 hours per day. Nogales, Ariz., neighborhoods show a great deal of uniformity, but the character of Nogales, Son., neighborhoods is much more variable. From an observation point overlooking the city, one can see both neighborhoods dominated by large, well-constructed homes and squatter settlements with tiny, flimsy houses. A low hillside in the west-central area of the city contains houses resembling those found in upscale suburban neighborhoods in the United States. At the far southern end of the valley, near Nogales Pass, is a modern, planned development with houses built to include all utility services. On the hillsides east and west of the city are sprawling, unplanned communities that often are not even served by roads, let alone electricity, water, and sewage utilities. Some residents, typified by the Sepulvedas described above, live lives of relative comfort. Others struggle every day just to obtain the bare necessities.

Though not unique to Nogales, the colonias are perhaps more shocking there because they occur in such close proximity to the much different conditions across the border. Colonia Buenos Aires, a squatter settlement situated next to the international boundary in the hills east of downtown, can easily be viewed from a Nogales, Ariz., neighborhood filled with comfortable, well-maintained homes typical of any suburban U.S. community. Buenos Aires homes, in contrast, are conglomerations of scavenged materials including wooden pallets, cardboard, blankets, tarpaper, and plastic. An occasional home has a tin or plywood roof. Many homes are attached to partially built rooms made of cinder block, because their owners are slowly and incrementally building more solid structures as they are able to afford or find the necessary materials. Several houses perch precariously on the steep hillsides; some are surrounded by earth-filled tires acting as berms that the residents hope will control erosion.

Residents of Buenos Aires do much of their living outdoors, because the houses are too small and too dark to live and work in comfortably. Looking across the border from Arizona, one can see people cooking and washing clothes outside their homes, carrying water in plastic milk jugs known as *galones*, and moving back and forth between their homes and the outhouses and makeshift showers that substitute for indoor plumbing. Smoke rises in the air from fires used to cook food, heat homes and water, and burn garbage. There are no power lines or gas pipes because the colonia does not have any utilities. The few roads are unpaved, dusty, and severely eroded. There are no facilities for disposing of wastewater, so water used for cooking, washing clothes, and bathing ends up on the ground, where it creates permanent mud puddles. During storms, the mud and water mix with garbage and sewage leaking from the outhouses, and the mixture runs down the hillside and through the neighborhood. It eventually drains into Cerro Pelon Wash, which runs across the border, through a Nogales, Ariz., neighborhood, and past an elementary school before reaching Nogales Wash. To combat the health hazard the IBWC has installed a rudimentary chlorination station on the Arizona side of the border. Bags of chlorine are placed into a small concrete box, and the water running through the box contacts and dissolves the chlorine. Disinfection measures even this primitive are not available in Buenos Aires, where the contaminated water is more widely dispersed and the potential for disease is therefore far more serious.

The squatter settlements vary in their sites and in their access to urban services. Some settlements are on flatter ground and are closer to the center of the valley than is Buenos Aires. Some have roads, some have electricity, and some have access to water, sewage, and garbage collection services. But the conditions in all the colonias make their residents' lives uniformly difficult, as we explain below.

A striking feature of many colonias is the number of single mothers and their children who live there. In part this is because some colonia organizations give preference to single mothers when accepting petitions for new residents.[3] Parents of young children face special difficulties because there are no schools in many of the colonias. Some maquila employees have access to child-care services at work, but others are forced to make other arrangements or leave their children to their own devices during the day.

Transportation to, from, and within the squatter settlements is usually by foot. Residents of the more distant settlements may have to walk several miles up and down steep hills to reach bus lines. Transportation therefore requires substantial time and energy, and this in turn often limits the amount of food, fuel, water, and other goods that can be brought home. Some residents have access to private automobiles, and they carpool to work and stores over the dusty, rutted roads that run through some of the settlements.

The lack of utilities in most settlements means that residents swelter in the heat of summer, when temperatures sometimes exceed 38°C (100°F), and shiver in the cold of winter, when temperatures can be well below freezing and it sometimes snows. Few houses provide significant insulation from the weather; many have leaky roofs and walls that allow the wind to blow right through.

Some of the settlements have electricity to run lights, refrigerators, heaters, and stoves, but many do not. Food often has to be obtained daily because it spoils quickly without refrigeration. Televisions are rare, but battery-driven portable and car radios are often heard and are the primary source of news and information. As described in Chapter 3, obtaining water can be difficult even in the best of situations, since residents must make arrangements to be home when it is delivered or physically carry it, often over long distances.

Health fears are widespread and real in the squatter settlements. The lack of heating and cooling, clean water, wastewater disposal facilities, and garbage collection greatly increases residents' exposure and susceptibility to a wide range of bacterial, viral, and parasitic infections. In 1991 the chief of preventive medicine at the Instituto Mexicano de Salud stated that the constant stream of immigrants and the lack of sanitary water and wastewater facilities made Nogales susceptible to a cholera epidemic.[4] Even if residents have the money to pay for medical treatment, health-care facilities are virtually nonexistent in the settlements.

The threat of fire is also a concern because of the widespread use of open fires and the prevalence of closely spaced wooden houses. Even a small fire could spread rapidly throughout an entire neighborhood because there are no pressurized water sources and little, if any, access for mobile firefighting equipment.

Leisure time is perhaps the scarcest resource in the squatter communities because so much time and effort must be expended to secure basic amenities in addition to the time spent working and raising families. Adults may spend nine or more hours at work every day of the week except one, plus another hour or two per day in transit. They must procure food, water, fuel, and anything else needed by their households on an almost daily basis, and often must carry their purchases home on foot. Children must be taken care of and houses must be repaired and kept clean. Small household tasks become major chores when utilities are not available with the flip of a switch or the turn of a faucet; meals must be prepared over open fires, water for drinking must be boiled, clothes must be washed by hand. Something as simple as taking a shower requires extra water, which must be obtained, heated, and then carried to a makeshift shower. Life in the colonias requires an enormous amount of work in extremely trying conditions and places a premium on coordination of activities and cooperation among residents.

The residents of Nogales, Ariz., enjoy a much higher standard of living. Obvious signs of poverty are infrequent. Nogales appears to be an economically well-integrated community. With the exception of a few small areas of low-income housing, it is difficult to identify significant socioeconomic differences between neighborhoods. Homes are generally well maintained, and residents have access to basic household goods. The 1991 Udall Center survey found that 83 percent of the population lives in single-family homes, and 78 percent are homeowners. According to data collected by the 1990 U.S. Census, Nogales housing units have a median of 2.5 bedrooms, and only 1.7 percent of them lack complete plumbing facilities. More than 90 percent of water department customers reported having washing machines at home, 71 percent have evaporative coolers, and 47 percent have lawns or gardens extensive enough to require frequent watering; homes have, on average, two bathrooms. Yet it is important to point out that Nogales, Ariz., is a poor community compared with the rest of Arizona. Data from the 1990 U.S. Census indicate that the unemployment rate in Santa Cruz County is higher than in the rest of the state (10.4 percent vs. 7.2 percent), and the income per capita is much lower ($9,007 vs. $13,461). The same data

116   Divided Waters

also indicate that Nogalensians have less formal education than other Arizonans; only 57 percent have high school diplomas, and 11 percent have a bachelor's degree or higher, compared with 79 percent and 20 percent, respectively, for the state as a whole. Their relative lack of formal education may make it more difficult for residents of Nogales to adjust to changing patterns of employment and economic disruptions. The median household income is lower in Santa Cruz County than in the state as a whole ($22,066 vs. $27,540 per year), and one-fourth of the county's residents live below the U.S. poverty level.

Perceptions and Attitudes about Water

Despite the relative poverty of Nogales, Ariz., compared with the rest of the state, the city's water and sewer systems are in line with U.S. standards. Residents of Nogales, Son., even those with considerable personal wealth, must endure a public water and sewer system that is grossly inadequate. It is hardly surprising, then, that the attitudes and perceptions of residents of the two cities are quite distinct. North of the border, where everyone has access to the same high-quality water service, concerns focus on water quality and environmental contamination. South of the border, residents of Nogales, Son., tend to think more about improving the quantity of water available and the accessibility of water services.

Sonorans' Attitudes Concerning Water

Nogales, Son., residents' perceptions and attitudes are shaped largely by their individual situations. Though 83.5 percent of residents are connected to the public water supply system, the proportion varies widely in different parts of the city. Analysts at the Colegio de la Frontera Norte divided the city into seven separate zones (fig. 4.1, top) based on topography and socioeconomic characteristics. As figure 4.1 (bottom) shows, almost none of the residents in the higher-income zones (zones 5 and 7) are without connections to the system, but up to one-third of the residents in the hillside areas that have many squatter settlements (zones 3, 4, and 6) are not connected. Topography also plays a role in the distribution of services, as

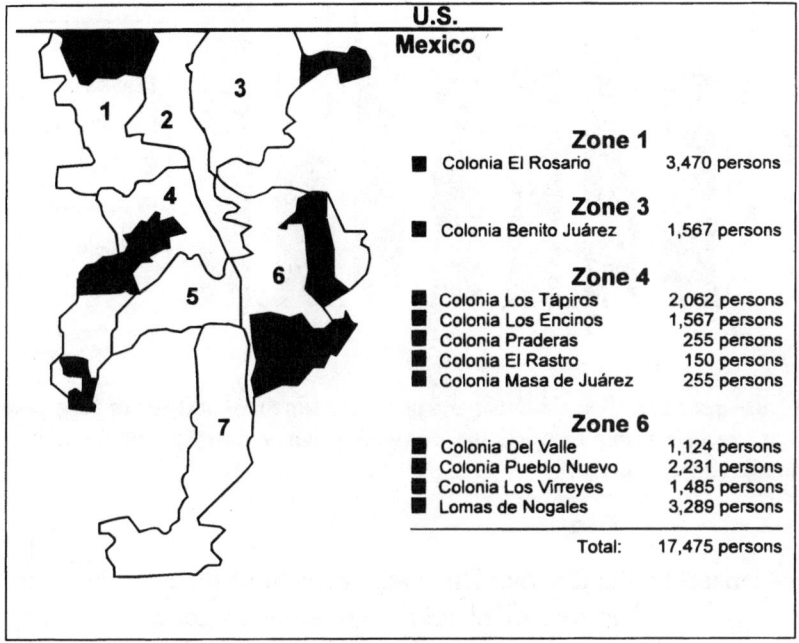

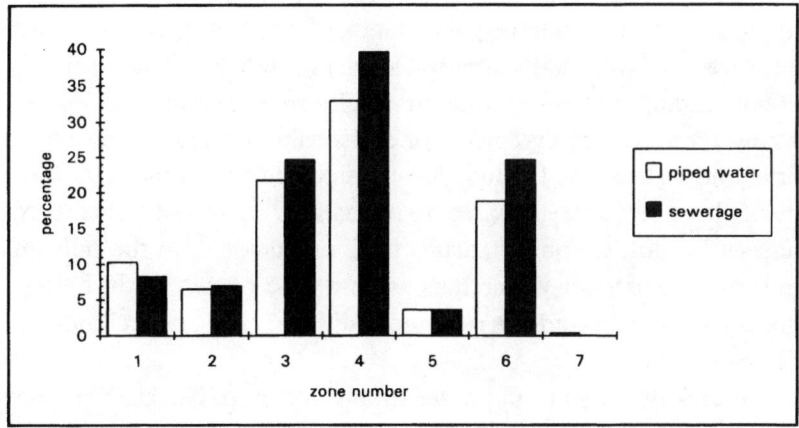

Figure 4.1 *Top*: Zones supplied with potable water by pipas in Nogales, Son. *Bottom*: Percentage of residents (by zone) of Nogales, Son., who do not have access to public water supply or sewer systems. *Source*: COLEF, 1992.

118   Divided Waters

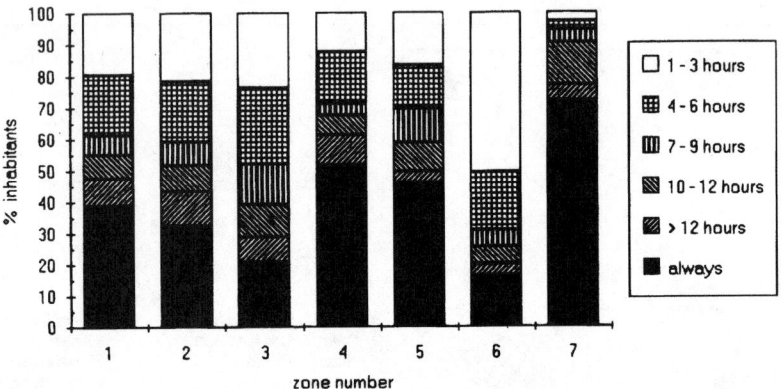

Figure 4.2   Number of hours per day during which inhabitants of Nogales, Son., receive water through the COAPAES water supply system, by zone. *Source:* COLEF, 1992.

evidenced by the fact that less than 7 percent of the households in the three zones located on or near the valley floor (zones 2, 5, and 7) are not connected to the system. The situation is similar with respect to the availability of sewage systems. From 25 to 40 percent of the residents in the hillside neighborhoods of zones 3, 4, and 6 do not have access to wastewater removal services, while less than 8 percent of households in all other zones of the city are not connected. Aggregating these figures by entire zones probably obscures even more dramatic differences, because most residents in the squatter settlements have few if any services. In a small survey of the residents in one settlement, Colonia Articulo 27 Constitucional, in the hills on the west side of town, researchers found that 62 percent of the households had latrines and the remainder did not have any facilities for disposing of wastes.[5]

The lack of access to the water supply system in Nogales's poorer communities is aggravated by the fact that those who *are* connected receive water much less frequently than do residents of other neighborhoods. Only one-fifth or less of the households in zones 3 and 6 have water 24 hours per day, while almost three-fourths of the residents in zone 7 enjoy that luxury (fig. 4.2).

Perceptions of health risks also vary between the zones (fig. 4.3).

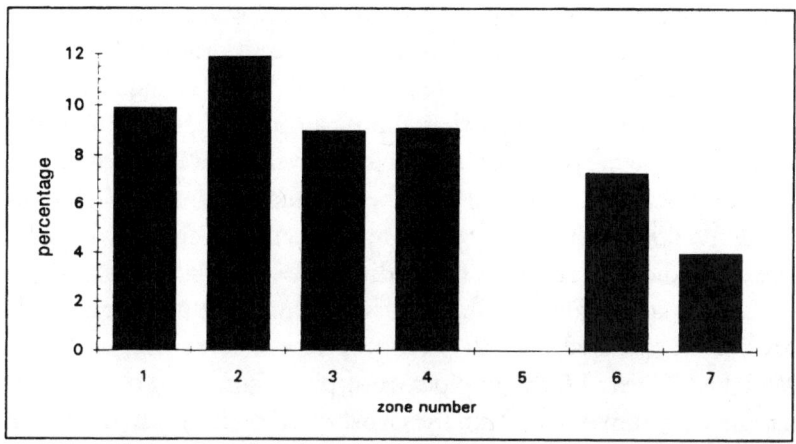

Figure 4.3 Percentage (by zone) of residents of Nogales, Son., who believe that adverse health effects occur as a consequence of drinking or coming into contact with contaminated water. *Source*: COLEF, 1992.

Around 10 percent of the residents in zones 1–4 believe that their health has been adversely affected by the ingestion of contaminated water or by contact with untreated sewage. About 7 percent of the residents of zone 6, 4 percent of the residents of zone 7, and none of the residents of zone 5 think that their health has been affected. This finding emphasizes the importance of geography when considering water issues in Nogales. Their geographic setting—on low hills with no sources of contamination above them—largely insulates zones 5 and 7 from contamination, while the other zones are either on steep hillsides or on the valley floor. Neighborhoods in the steep hills have less access to sewage services, and the pipes that are there are prone to leak. Valley floor neighborhoods are susceptible because storm water and leaked water collect in the lower elevations. Residents of zone 2, the downtown area, which has the oldest infrastructure and the lowest elevation, were the most likely to believe that their health had been affected by bad water (12 percent). Once again, the aggregation by broad zones may obscure even larger differences. An overwhelming 97 percent of the residents of Colonia Articulo 27 Constitucional felt that the health of someone in their family might be affected by a disease caused by contaminated water.[6]

Perceptions of water quality. When asked to rate the quality of water delivered to their homes, 46 percent of Nogales, Son., residents said the quality was "good." Another 42 percent thought it was "acceptable," and only 12 percent felt that it had been "getting worse" in the last five years. The fact that almost 90 percent found the water quality acceptable or better is surprising given the water contamination in Nogales (Chapter 3) and the fact that 9 percent of Nogales residents think that bad water has made them ill. Mortality data for the city indicate that two of the leading causes of death among those under the age of four are intestinal infections and parasites, which are often associated with the consumption of contaminated water. Whether delivered through pipes or by pipas, almost all of the water originating from wells within the city showed signs of contamination by fecal coliform bacteria, volatile organic chemicals, or both when sampled and analyzed in 1991, and the piped-water supply well (the COAPAES well) had the highest level of bacterial contamination. Even bottled water obtained from the local bottling plant was contaminated by industrial solvents, and yet 82 percent of the respondents felt that the quality of bottled water was good while only 1 percent thought it was poor.

There are several possible explanations for these survey results. One is that people don't expect water delivered to their homes to be free of contamination. Most residents of the United States expect that the water running through their faucets, showers, hoses, and even toilets will be uncontaminated, and it virtually always is. But in most of the developing world, the purity of water cannot be taken for granted, and virtually all water intended for direct consumption must first be boiled or otherwise treated in the home. Boiling water that is to be consumed directly and buying bottled water are common activities throughout most of Mexico, and residents of Nogales, Son., are likely to feel that, at least relative to their friends and family in other Mexican cities, their water quality really isn't that bad.

Another possibility is that residents do not know that their water is contaminated. The existence of pathogens and contaminants in city water supplies has not been well publicized, and residents are unlikely to discover the contamination on their own. The concentrations at which most organic solvents and other synthetic chemicals are considered to be health threats are so low that contamination at those levels is not likely to be detected outside a laboratory. Moreover, the primary health threat of such chemicals, at least in the relatively low levels found in Nogales, Son., is cancer, which often takes years to develop. Even bacterial, viral, and parasitic infections do not show up instantaneously following consumption, making it difficult or impossible to determine their true causes, especially in the presence of other potential causes such as raw sewage, insects, and uncollected waste. Residents may sometimes suspect that their water is contaminated but be unable to rule out other causes of disease. Furthermore, illness does not invariably result from the consumption of contaminated water, so residents may not suspect something that "usually" does not make them sick. Official pronouncements appearing in the local media may also confuse the issue. Examples include the April 16, 1991, issue of *Imparcial*, which quotes the mayor of Nogales, Son., as saying that Nogales Wash is not contaminated; and the May 12, 1991, issue of *La Voz del Norte*, which quotes the director of COAPAES in Nogales as saying that COAPAES employs a strict system of chlorination throughout its distribution area, even though bacterial levels indicate otherwise.

Confidence in water service providers. Only 46 percent of Nogales, Son., residents felt that the quality of service delivered by the public water company COAPAES is "good," but there are indications that progress is being made. Though 38 percent of residents reported no change in quality over the last five years, twice as many respondents felt there had been improvements than felt that the quality of service had worsened. As was true with respect to people's feelings about basic access to services, these proportions varied within different zones of the city, but everywhere except zone 3, residents reported greater improvements than declines. It is interesting to note, however, that the proportion reporting that the quality of water service was good (46 percent) is substantially greater than the proportion reporting that they received water 24 hours per day (32 percent), indicating that, as with water quality, residents may be satisfied with a lower level of service than exists throughout most of the United States.

Nogales residents are in a good position to judge the quality of their own water service but may find it difficult to determine what is happening in other parts of the city. Official pronouncements in the media often offer a much more positive view of the city's water situation than is apparent to individual residents. Perhaps the leading case in point is the long series of newspaper articles that preceded completion of Los Alisos, the city's latest major water project. Typical of the optimism that surrounded that project is the editorial that appeared in the March 13, 1991, edition of *La Voz del Norte*, which said that the new water project would completely eliminate the water availability problem in Nogales for the next 30 years. Three months later (June 6), following the symbolic completion of the project, which was attended by an array of luminaries and officials, including the president of Mexico, the same newspaper quoted the director of COAPAES-Sonora as saying that Los Alisos had solved the water shortage and that 95 percent of the demand for potable water in Nogales was now being met. Many residents find it difficult to reconcile these pronouncements with actual conditions.[7] Just as with population data, many people assume that what they hear about the water situation from government officials has been manipulated to achieve political goals. When problems recur, residents become cynical, like the one who compared the government to "a Mafia. They use the money for everything they need but the people's needs, the town's needs."[8] Following the January 1993 floods that destroyed large portions of the city's water supply and distribution system, COAPAES's overly optimistic reports on their progress in restoring service met with great disdain and were widely disregarded.[9]

Officials' failure to acknowledge the city's water problems provides abundant material for their political opponents. Three months after the completion of Los Alisos, an opposition party mayoral candidate was quoted in *La Voz del Norte* as saying that the water situation continued to be among the most serious of the city's problems. The candidate added that a study done by honest and capable people was needed as a first step to ensure that everyone in Nogales could eventually have access to potable water.[10] Even ruling party officials sometimes find it difficult to maintain that problems are being solved. The ruling party's candidate for the legislature indirectly acknowledged the city's problems when he told a convention of architects and engineers that their support and commitment would be needed to solve problems with the city's water distribution system.[11]

Community groups. Residents of Nogales, Son., gain access to municipal water systems in many ways. Half of those surveyed received services simply by applying to COAPAES for a connection to the system. An additional third received services when they purchased a home from a developer who had installed infrastructure and connected it to the municipal grid as part of the construction and permitting process. Many other residents cannot secure services so easily. For instance, only 31 percent of those without connections to the municipal sewerage system even bothered to apply for service, either because they couldn't afford the installation and service fees or because they thought there was no chance that COAPAES would fulfill their request. Continuing problems in securing access to water services have led to the development of numerous alternative coping strategies among residents. Many strategies—like buying bottled water, carrying water, installing household storage tanks, and arranging for pipa deliveries—are undertaken individually (see Chapter 3), but many residents unable to gain access to essential public services band together to acquire them by forming community groups.

Community groups are important social and political actors in most Latin American societies. In contrast with more broadly based political movements and parties, community groups generally form to work on issues within a single small geographic area or neighborhood. Often neighborhood boundaries serve as the boundaries of membership, with those living inside the boundaries automatically included as members of the group. At least 80 community groups have formed in Nogales, Son., in response to the lack of urban services, and 40 percent of them have as a primary goal the introduction of water and sewerage services into their communities. Political pressure is one avenue that community groups use to try to secure services. Community groups organize demonstrations, call in to radio talk shows, write letters, and support—or threaten to support—candidates from opposition parties. They visit government agencies and officials in Nogales and in the state and federal capitals. One community group successfully pressured the government into providing services in their neighborhood by blocking a major commercial thoroughfare and stalling traffic, and then threatening to repeat the activity until they received the services.

Community groups sometimes ally themselves directly with individual politicians or the governing political party in order to secure services. The community groups form a base of support for the politicians; they turn out for political rallies and trade their votes for promises to secure government services. The groups are rewarded when the newly elected government officials are able to secure funding for public works projects in the neighborhood. In some cases, community group leaders, who often work full time as a kind of informal level of local government, are supported financially by the governing political party in return for their activities and support.

Community groups pressure the government for services in other ways as well. The most common form of intervention is to negotiate directly with COAPAES on behalf of the entire membership rather than having members apply individually for services. Community groups also solicit the city government for free pipa deliveries and solicit COAPAES to provide public water taps in poor neighborhoods. Other community group activities designed to secure water services are more direct. Some groups acquire and lay their own water supply and sewage pipes, then connect them, with or without authorization, to the existing municipal water system. Community groups also hold fundraisers and collect money, install water storage tanks, distribute 55-gallon drums that can be used by households for on-site water storage, and build latrines in neighborhoods without access to municipal water systems.

The self-help activities of community groups may be successful in acquiring services for their own members, but often it is at the expense of the quality of the service provided to the entire population. New infrastructure added as the result of political pressure or direct action is not usually accompanied by additional resources for operating and maintaining the system. Politically driven development does not occur in response to a comprehensive planning process that has balanced community needs, priorities, and resources. Building new distribution systems without additional water supplies mean that more customers are competing for the same quantity of water. And new development without consideration of the region's long-term sustainable yield and anticipated needs can handicap future opportunities for growth.

The benefits of planned growth. One does not have to leave Mexico—or even Nogales—to find an example of an effective way to provide urban water services. At the southern end of Nogales, beyond one of the city's two industrial parks and not far below Nogales Pass, are two relatively new neighborhoods, Villa Sonora and Nuevo Nogales, that were constructed as planned communities to house members of the middle class. Houses there are much more spacious, secure, and comfortable than those found in the colonias, although not as luxurious as those found in some other parts of the city. The roads in the two neighborhoods were laid out before the houses were constructed, as were utilities such as water lines, sewers, and electricity. Though other characteristics also distinguish the two neighborhoods from much of the rest of the city, it is the absence of water problems that makes them particularly notable.

Villa Sonora and Nuevo Nogales, which together constitute zone 7 in the COLEF survey, consistently stand out from the other zones of the city in the survey results. Virtually all households in these two neighborhoods have water and sewer connections; citywide, the comparable figures are 84 and 81 percent, respectively. Only one-third of city residents reported having water available 24 hours per day, while more than two-thirds of Villa Sonora and Nuevo Nogales residents reported constant availability. Just over three-fourths of zone 7 residents rated the water quality as "good," compared with less than half citywide. Better access to water and improved quality are also evident in the fact that only 28 percent of the residents buy bottled water, compared with 39 percent citywide. And only 5 percent of residents in the two neighborhoods felt that their health had been affected by contaminated water, compared with an average of 11 percent citywide. The two neighborhoods' locations near the top of the watershed provide some advantages, primarily with respect to water quality, because there are no potential sources of contamination above them. But location alone cannot account for these survey results, especially those related to water and sewer availability. Villa Sonora and Nuevo Nogales are proof that improvement in the city's water supply services is possible given enough resources and

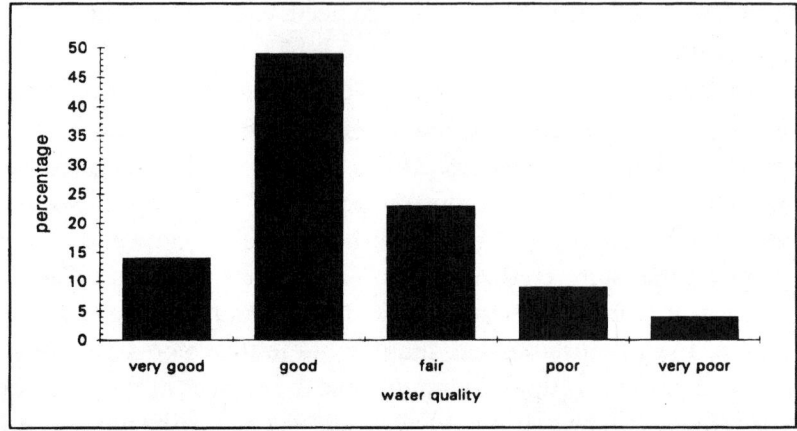

Figure 4.4 Residents' perceptions of water quality in Nogales, Ariz. *Source*: Udall Center, 1993c.

adequate planning, and that there is nothing inherently unimaginable about the concept of providing adequate water services within the city of Nogales.

Arizonans' Attitudes Concerning Water

In contrast with their neighbors across the line, residents of Nogales, Ariz., are much more concerned about water quality than about water supply and delivery issues. Nationwide, most Americans believe that water quality problems are serious and growing worse. However, they also feel that water quality is not actually a problem in their own communities; that is, they think that their own water quality is fine, but that problems exist somewhere else (O'Connor et al., 1994). This was the attitude of most of the residents of Nogales, Ariz., contacted in the Udall Center survey, who thought that the water they received in their homes was of good quality. More than 60 percent of the residents felt it was "good" or "very good," and most of the rest thought it was "fair" (fig. 4.4).

Arizonans are much more concerned about water quality problems in their environment than they are about their tap water. Problems with sewage flows across the border and with the contamina-

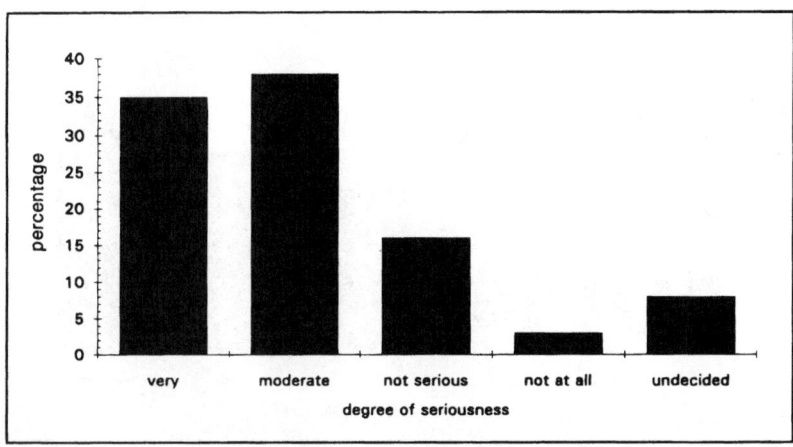

Figure 4.5 Residents' perceptions of the degree of seriousness of water contamination in Nogales, Ariz. *Source*: Udall Center, 1993c.

tion of the Nogales Wash have been very well publicized, and very few of the people surveyed did not believe that environmental water quality is a serious problem in the community (fig. 4.5).

More than three quarters of Nogales residents reported that they were also "very" or "moderately" concerned about the quality of water in the Santa Cruz River, into which Nogales Wash flows, but the immediacy of water contamination problems in Nogales is perhaps most readily reflected by the fact that more than 10 percent of Nogales residents felt that the health of someone in their family had been affected by contamination in the Nogales Wash. Not surprisingly, many survey respondents had strong feelings about the contamination and its sources, as illustrated by the comments below:

> My daughter had leukemia because of hazardous waste in the Nogales Wash—I sold my house at a loss and moved from the area because I believe my well water was contaminated from [a specific Nogales, Ariz., industrial source]. My other daughter had hepatitis at the same house. I will try to influence people to realize how bad our water really is—and what they can do to help clean it up.

> I strongly believe that for a community of this size, cancer is a very big part of our health problems, and I can't but think that all the waste from the maquilas drains into our water supplies and

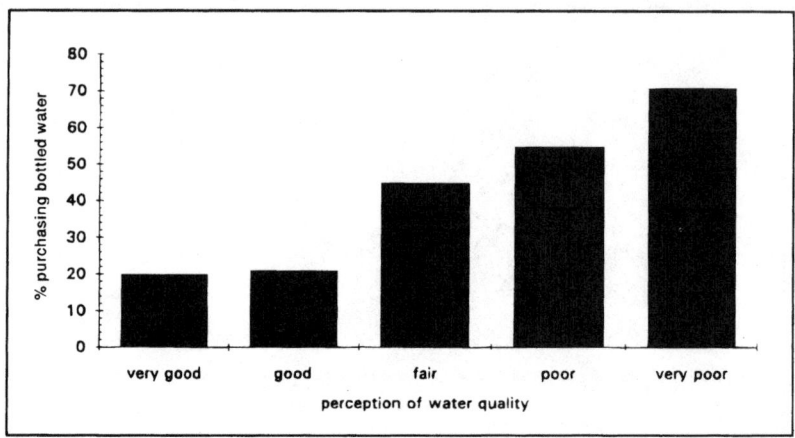

Figure 4.6 Increased purchases of bottled water in response to perceived worsening of water quality in Nogales, Ariz. *Source:* Udall Center, 1993c.

makes this more possible. Just in the past two years I have had either die or been diagnosed many people with pancreatic cancer in this area. I am very, very concerned.

Our water cannot improve until raw sewage from the hills in Mexico stops washing into our waterways! Do we get contaminated? You bet we do![12]

People's methods of coping with the water quality and contamination problems in Nogales vary. Some take individual action, such as buying bottled water. Almost a third of Nogales, Ariz., residents buy bottled water, including some who think the water they receive in their homes is of good quality, but buying bottled water is especially popular among those who have less favorable perceptions about water quality (fig. 4.6).

Other people participate in activities designed to stimulate government action to solve the problem. Twenty percent of residents reported that they had supported a political candidate for his or her stand on water issues, 10 percent had contacted an official about a governmental decision related to water, and 10 percent had signed a petition. Smaller percentages had joined groups in order to influence water policy or had written letters to newspapers or magazines. The officials targeted by these actions are usually chosen largely on the basis of the level of government residents feel should be held responsible for water management in Nogales. About two-thirds of the Nogalensians surveyed believed that local (i.e., city or county) government is most responsible, even though the origin of the problem may transcend local political boundaries. The following comment from a Nogales resident may be typical:

> In my opinion, more government tests should be taken to assure water consumers of water quality. The future trade with Mexico will bring more factories to the Nogales, Son., area creating more contamination of toxic chemicals to the Nogales Wash. It is common knowledge that Mexican environmental policies are very lenient and may very well increase contamination of our water supply in the future. More effort should be taken to protect our water supply. If we can show our concerns today, perhaps we can help shape future actions by city officials.

The remaining one-third of Nogales, Ariz., residents was evenly divided between those who felt that the federal government should be most responsible for the water situation in Nogales and those who thought it the state's responsibility. Some felt that all levels are responsible, such as the resident who commented, "The problem is born on the Mexico side and it will continue to exist if the government of the USA or state and local authorities and politicians continue to tolerate and be indifferent as they are today."[13]

Social and Economic Linkages Across the Border

The discussion up to this point has emphasized the differences, both socioeconomic and attitudinal, among residents of Ambos Nogales. But there are also many factors that link residents of the two border communities. An important common denominator shared by most residents of Ambos Nogales is their Hispanic heritage. Even on the U.S. side of the border, more than 90 percent of the residents of Nogales are of Hispanic origin. Data from the 1990 U.S. Census indicate that 75 percent of the residents of Santa Cruz County speak

Spanish in preference to English at home. As is true in other U.S. border cities, Hispanic residents of Nogales often have strong social and cultural ties to Mexico and actively maintain their ties through frequent visits across the border. At least one study has noted that Hispanic families in U.S. border cities often have members living on the Mexican side of the border (Martinez, 1988), and a 1991 survey of customers of the Nogales, Ariz., Water Department found that three quarters of the respondents had occasion to visit family or friends in Sonora. Many U.S. Hispanics also visit Mexico to participate in Mexican national, religious, and cultural celebrations. Given that half of Santa Cruz County's residents who speak Spanish at home don't feel that they speak English "very well" (U.S. Census, 1990), a good many residents of Nogales, Ariz., probably feel more attuned to the culture and customs of Mexico than to those of the United States.

Many Arizona residents also visit Mexico to purchase items that are cheaper or more easily available there or simply because it is more convenient. The 1991 Udall Center survey found that 57 percent of the customers of the Nogales, Ariz., Water Department visited Nogales, Son., to buy pharmaceuticals, more than 50 percent went there to eat at a restaurant, more than 40 percent to buy groceries, and smaller percentages to visit doctors and dentists, buy newspapers, have their cars repaired, or purchase other services. In addition to facilitating cultural ties and giving shoppers access to a wider range of affordable goods and services, these activities also bind the economies of the two cities. In parallel, having family members on the U.S. side of the border provides many advantages to residents of Sonora. One study of Tijuana (Baja California) families found that the family members living in Mexico visited their U.S.-dwelling relatives to look for work and for financial gain, to take advantage of educational opportunities, to obtain health care, and, lastly, to see their relatives (Anderson and de la Rosa, 1991). Sometimes these temporary sojourns in the United States become permanent residence, but most visitors find ample reasons to return to their homes in Mexico. The incentives for returning are primarily of a social, cultural, and/or personal nature.

Nogales, Son., residents continue to rely on American goods and services, often bought directly in the United States, where stores stock an array of goods not commonly found in Mexico; and some items are cheaper in the United States than they are at home.[14] The ability to stretch incomes by comparative shopping for basic goods on both sides of the border is reflected by the fact that purchases at department and grocery stores, rather than at specialty stores and restaurants, account for most Mexican purchases in Arizona (Hopkins, 1992).

In fiscal years 1992 and 1993, 17,063,681 and 15,844,215 people, respectively, legally crossed into the United States from Mexico at official Nogales border crossings, an average of 45,080 crossings daily.[15] These figures do not include unofficial crossings through the numerous holes in the border fence.[16] A 1991 survey indicated that 80 percent of the people who crossed the border at Nogales never traveled beyond the limits of Nogales, Ariz., so it is evident that the true daily population of Nogales, Ariz., is much larger than its official population. Some Mexican residents shop daily in Arizona, but the average expenditure in Nogales per party crossing the border in 1991 was $121.86, a relatively large sum that indicates that shopping trips are usually less frequent, at least among the survey participants, all of whom had crossed legally (Hopkins, 1992). There can be no doubt, however, that Nogales, Son., residents spend a large proportion of their earnings in Arizona. A 1972 survey indicated that Nogales maquiladora workers spent an average of 50 percent of their wages in Arizona (Ayer and Layton, 1974), while a 1988 survey, made after repeated peso devaluations had diminished the purchasing power of Mexican currency, indicated that the figure was closer to 30 percent (Pavlakovic and Kim, 1991). The latter survey also indicated that lower-income workers spent most of their money on clothing, while higher-income technical and administrative maquiladora workers were more likely to purchase food in Arizona (Chapter 2 addresses the overall economic importance of purchases made by Sonorans in Arizona). Operation Blockade, initiated in September 1993 in El Paso, Texas, by the U.S. Border Patrol to stop illegal border crossings, showed the adverse economic impacts that occur when Mexicans stop shopping in the United States. The dialogue below, taken from National Public Radio's Morning Edition, October 20, 1993, describes how some El Paso merchants have been hurt by Operation Blockade.

Neal Conan: In El Paso, Texas, businesses are feeling the impact of a Border Patrol crackdown originally known as "Operation Blockade." The operation, which began last month, is supposed to deter illegal immigration into the United States from Mexico. It's expected to continue indefinitely, and that's bad news for downtown merchants who rely heavily on shoppers from across the border. From El Paso, Louie Saenz has this report.

Louie Saenz, reporter: As one strolls through downtown El Paso, music can be heard blaring from different storefronts. There are also racks of clothes and other goods laid on tables for customers to go through. A man stands on the corner selling sodas, chips, and ice cream. Next to him is an elderly woman holding a pair of pants which she got from a rack in front of a clothing store. Aside from this, there is not much else happening on this particular block of businesses, which is about a mile away from a bridge linking El Paso and Juarez, Mexico.

Grace: It's a—it's a ghost town. It's a ghost town. It's very bad. We've been like this for almost, what, three weeks, so it is affecting everybody in downtown. All the merchants here are very upset. I mean, what's gonna happen?

Saenz: Grace runs a beauty supply store. She says 99 percent of her clientele is from Mexico. However, since the Border Patrol launched Operation Blockade last month, the money just isn't coming in.

Grace: Every minute, you could hear the money, you know, every second. You could have lines right here, and now nothing, it's dead.

Saenz: Next door to Grace's shop is a women's clothing store. The owner says her business has dropped so much she's had to lay off three workers.

Women's clothing store owner: Even though we have sales, we have no people, no people on the streets, so what can we do? Nothing. Maybe we want to have a meeting, all the merchants, but we don't know—I don't know what to do.

Saenz: El Paso is a city of half a million people. It sits on the border, and downtown is within easy walking distance of Ciudad Juarez, Mexico. For years, people from both cities have crossed the border to transact business, creating jobs for people in both countries. According to the Immigration Service, more than 100,000 people a day cross into El Paso from Mexico legally. For almost a century, people have been crossing the border illegally, many of them waiting to cross the Rio Grande. It was not uncommon for the Border Patrol to arrest as many as 1,000 illegal immigrants a day. The district director of the Immigration Service is Al Jeune. He says Mexicans coming into this country to work make five times as much money as they do in Mexico.

Al Jeune, district director, Immigration Service: The vast majority of the individuals who are attempting to enter the United States illegally are persons who are seeking employment here or already have a job as a maid. Others are attempting to enter to obtain day work such as rock wall contractors, roofing contractors, etc.

Saenz: Last month, the U.S. Border Patrol started Operation Blockade as an effort to fight illegal immigration. The operation is made up of hundreds of Border Patrol agents who are lining a 20-mile stretch of the Rio Grande along the border, sometimes as close as 50 yards apart. Border Patrol chief Sylvester Raes says the operation is in direct response to an increasing and dramatic surge of illegal immigrant crossings and crime along the border.

Sylvester Raes, Border Patrol chief: The first thing that people want to do, particularly in this community, is blame undocumented workers, illegal aliens, for all the troubles of the community. This will give us a good, solid gauge to judge that.

Saenz: El Paso police say that since Operation Blockade was initiated, some crime has gone down, but they say you can't blame all of the city's crime on illegal immigrants. Some El Pasoans say it's easy to blame crime and other border problems on undocumented workers rather than to admit the problems are homegrown. Martin Sanchez of the Border Rights Coalition says the blockade does nothing but hurt relations between both countries.

Martin Sanchez, Border Rights Coalition: The blocking of the border has created an ambience of terror, I think, in some people's minds, particularly people who work on this side of the border, and also we have no idea what kind of long-term impact it will have on the economy of the small businesses that operate downtown who cater to people who cross over and spend a dollar or two dollars to buy bread, to buy spark plugs. The people who planned this did not figure that into their long-range plan, the impact, the economic impact on the community. (From KTEP Radio, University of Texas at El Paso)

The easy movement of people back and forth across the border is aided by the widespread use of English and Spanish on both sides. The majority of Nogales, Ariz., residents speak Spanish, and English is common in Nogales, Son., though it is not usually spoken at home or as a native tongue. English-language signs and advertisements are common in Nogales, Son., and English is frequently heard in Sonoran businesses and classrooms. English proficiency varies; some street vendors and shopkeepers speak just enough to make sales to American tourists, while businesspeople, students, and those who frequently work across the border may be fluent.

Transboundary Linkages:
The View from Nogales, Arizona

The various social and economic factors that bind the residents of Ambos Nogales to each other point to the possibility that there may be cross-border attitudinal linkages as well. In fact, when the survey responses of Nogales, Ariz., residents were analyzed for related "binational" attributes and to determine whether those attributes correlated with certain attitudes toward water, some interesting trends emerged. It is clear that a more sophisticated analysis of the determinants of attitudes about water is required than can be provided by looking merely at residence in Arizona or Sonora. The language preference of respondents emerged as an important explanatory variable

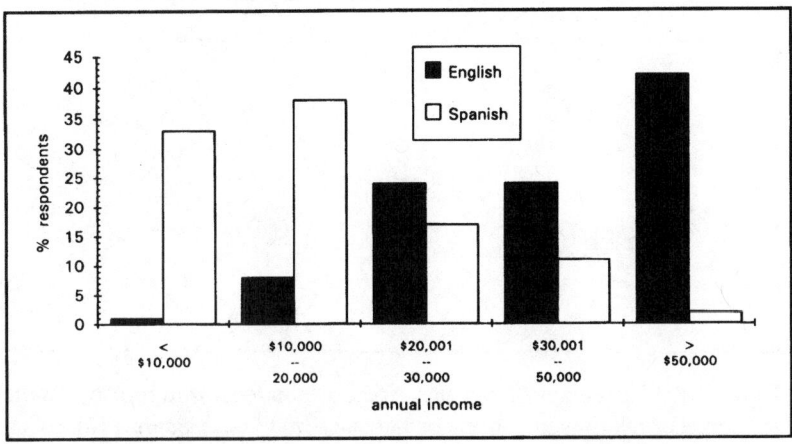

Figure 4.7 Household income according to language preference of respondents aged 25–59, Nogales, Ariz. *Source*: Udall Center, 1993c.

related to other binational characteristics. Respondents were given the choice of answering the Udall Center survey in either English or Spanish. Some respondents switched back and forth between the languages after starting the survey, but initially 57 percent chose to answer the questionnaire in Spanish and 43 percent chose to answer in English. Respondents who answered the survey in Spanish had dramatically lower incomes than those who responded in English. This is most evident among respondents in the highest-income working years (25–59), as figure 4.7 shows.

Almost three-quarters of the Spanish respondents had annual household incomes below $20,000, while two-thirds of the English-speaking respondents had annual household incomes above $30,000. Almost all respondents who reported household incomes above $50,000 answered the survey in English, while almost all who reported household incomes below $10,000 responded in Spanish. English respondents also tended to be older than Spanish respondents. Almost twice as many English respondents (40.8 percent) as Spanish respondents (24.2 percent) reported their age as 60 or above, probably a reflection of the influx of retirees from other areas of the United States. Analyses of survey results also indicated, sometimes indirectly, striking differences between the two language groups in

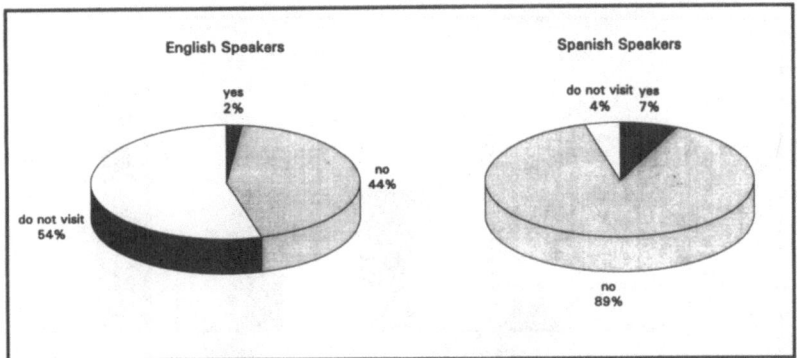

Figure 4.8 Percentage of Nogales, Ariz., respondents who transport water to friends or relatives in Sonora, by language preference. *Source*: Udall Center, 1993c.

the amount of their regular contact with Mexico. One survey question asked respondents whether or not they brought water with them when visiting friends or family in Nogales, Son. The English respondents were much more likely to answer "not applicable/do not visit" than were the Spanish respondents (fig. 4.8).

Spanish-speaking respondents were also much more likely to shop for groceries, newspapers, and medical or dental services in Sonora, and somewhat more likely to buy pharmaceuticals and obtain car repairs there (fig. 4.9). Food ("dining out") was the only commodity that English respondents were more likely to seek in Sonora than Spanish respondents. More than 1.5 times as many Spanish respondents (68 percent) as English respondents (40 percent) reported that they regularly shopped for one or more items and spent at least $20 per month in Nogales, Son.

A picture emerges of a subset of Nogales, Ariz., residents who are more comfortable speaking Spanish than English, relatively younger than other city residents, less well-off financially, and who maintain close social and economic ties across the border in Mexico. These people can be viewed as *binational* in orientation. At the other extreme is a distinct subset of Nogales, Ariz., residents who speak English and have higher incomes, and whose contacts across the line are limited to occasional dining or shopping excursions. The orientation of this group can be characterized as *national*.

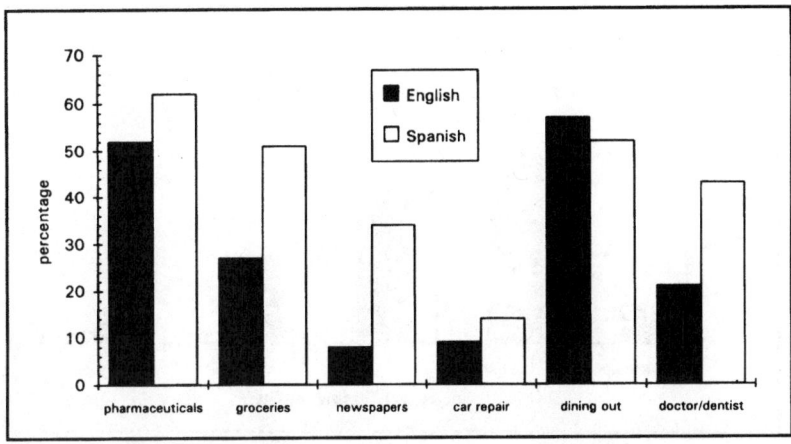

Figure 4.9 Goods and services purchased in Nogales, Son., by residents of Nogales, Ariz., by respondents' language preference. *Source*: Udall Center, 1993c.

Differing Perceptions of Water Issues in Nogales, Arizona

Not surprisingly, the differences between the binational and national groups extended to their perceptions about water and water issues. For example, respondents who answered in Spanish had much more favorable perceptions of the quality of the water delivered to their homes. The proportion of Spanish respondents who thought the quality of the water was "good" or "very good" was much higher than the proportion of English respondents with similar perceptions (fig. 4.10).

In the same vein, English-speaking respondents were somewhat more likely to express strong feelings about the contamination of Nogales Wash. Large majorities of all respondents thought that contamination is a serious problem, but English respondents generally felt that the contamination is "very" serious, while Spanish respondents tended to feel that it is "moderately" serious (fig. 4.11).

Sources of Information

Large differences separated the two language preference groups in their perceptions about the adequacy of information about water.

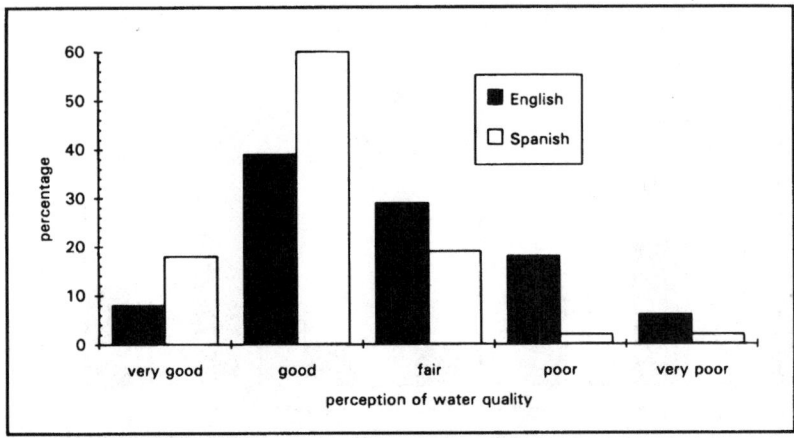

Figure 4.10 Nogales, Ariz., respondents' perceptions of NWD-delivered water quality, by language preference. *Source*: Udall Center, 1993c.

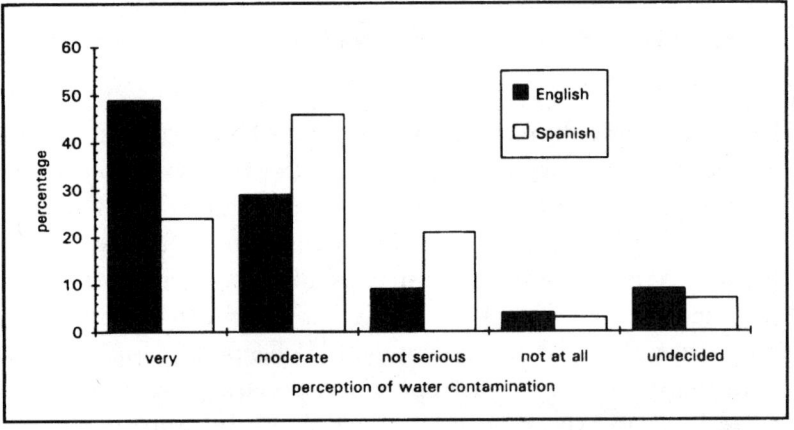

Figure 4.11 Nogales, Ariz., residents' perceptions of water contamination, by respondents' language preference. *Source*: Udall Center, 1993c.

Three quarters of the Spanish respondents felt that they received adequate information about water issues, but fewer than half of the English respondents believed that. Some of this difference may be the result of differences in the information sources the two groups preferred. Newspapers were the primary source of information about water for both groups, but especially the English respondents.

Three quarters of the English respondents cited newspapers as their primary source of information about water issues, compared with only half of the Spanish respondents. Radio was a far more common source of information among Spanish respondents than among English respondents. The two language-preference groups were approximately equal in their reliance on television and word of mouth for receiving information about water issues, but both of those sources were cited less frequently than newspapers or radio as a primary source of information about water. Ambos Nogales has no local television stations, so television news is usually dominated by coverage of events occurring in Hermosillo or Tucson.

Coping Strategies

We stated earlier that about a third of Nogales, Ariz., residents buy bottled water on a regular basis, and that the proportion of residents buying bottled water is higher among those who perceive that the quality of water delivered to their homes is inadequate. Given the generally higher evaluations of water quality by Spanish respondents, it should not be surprising that a lower proportion of Spanish respondents (26 percent) than English respondents (38 percent) said they bought bottled water. A comparable disparity occurs with respect to efforts to cope with water problems by exerting pressure on government officials. Supporting political candidates, contacting officials directly, and signing petitions are the three most common methods used by Nogales residents to influence government officials about water problems. English respondents to our survey were 3 times as likely to support a candidate for his or her stand on water issues, 10 times as likely to sign petitions, and 20 times as likely to contact government officials as Spanish respondents were (fig. 4.12).

English-language preference accounted for only 43 percent of all completed questionnaires received—but 70 percent of all respondents who supported candidates, 89 percent of those who had signed petitions, and 94 percent of those who had contacted government officials! The relative lack of political activity on the part of Spanish respondents may be due in part to the fact that many of them think "water experts" rather than government officials or other interest

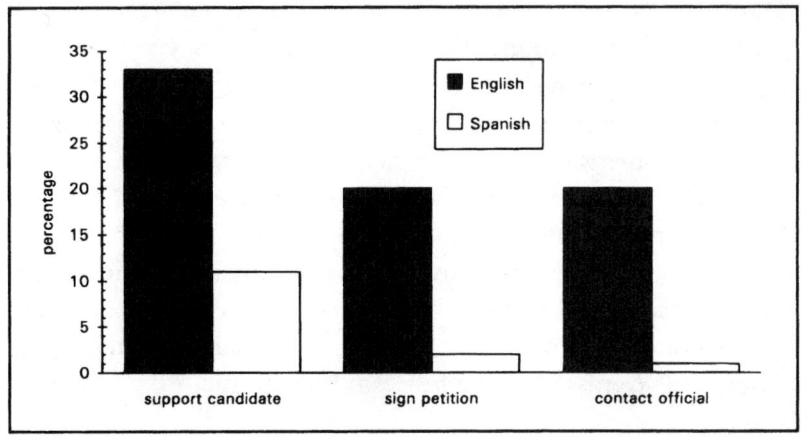

Figure 4.12 Nogales, Ariz., respondents' political actions in response to water problems, by language preference. *Source*: Udall Center, 1993c.

groups have the most influence over water policy. Forty-two percent of Spanish respondents said that water experts have the most influence, while less than half as many cited government officials or other interest groups (such as community groups, environmentalists, and developers) as having the most influence. In contrast, only 22 percent of English respondents said that "water experts" have the most influence; most believed that government officials and other interest groups wield influence. It is also interesting to note similarities and differences between Spanish and English respondents in the level of government held to be most responsible for water policy in Nogales. City government was the most popular choice for both language preference groups, in approximately equal proportions, but English respondents were more likely to look to the federal government, and less likely to look to county government, than were Spanish respondents (fig. 4.13).

National Versus Binational Orientation

In earlier chapters we stated that residents of the U.S.-Mexico border region have developed unique characteristics and lifestyles that are simultaneously related to and separate from the cultures of the two

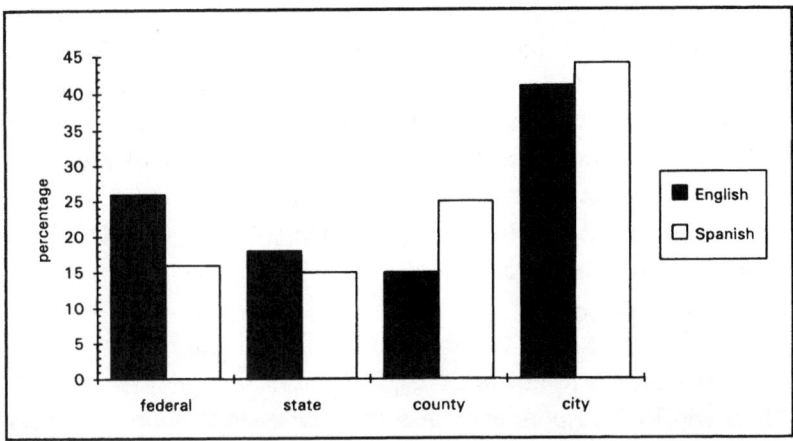

Figure 4.13 Nogales, Ariz., respondents' perceptions of the level of government most responsible for water policy, by language preference. *Source*: Udall Center, 1993c.

nations. The data obtained in the Udall Center survey make it clear that not all residents of Nogales, Ariz., participate equally in this unique border culture. Some residents have substantial contacts and common interests with their neighbors across the line, while others have very little in common with their Mexican neighbors. As we discuss above, the orientation of the former group can be characterized as binational, while the latter group's orientation may be dubbed national.

Residents of Nogales, Ariz., whose orientation tends to be national generally speak English, have higher incomes, rely on English-language newspapers for their information about water, and have the fewest ties to Mexico. They are also associated with more pessimistic assessments of water quality, both as delivered to their homes and in the environment, and are less satisfied with the adequacy of information concerning water issues. They have a greater tendency to think that government officials rather than water experts have the most influence over water decisions, and they believe that the federal government is most responsible for water management in Nogales. They also participate more frequently in efforts to make government officials respond to the city's water problems. In contrast, residents whose orientation is binational are more comfortable speaking Spanish, have lower incomes, use the radio as well as newspapers as their primary information sources, and have stronger ties to Mexico. These traits are associated with positive assessments of water quality, greater satisfaction with the information received about water, and a greater tendency to think that water experts have the most influence over water decisions. Perhaps the most striking characteristic is that binational residents are not very politically active, at least with respect to water issues.

The differences between national and binational orientations are evident in survey results from Nogales and its well-to-do suburb, Rio Rico. Rio Rico respondents answered the questionnaire in English much more frequently (86 percent) than did Nogales respondents (43 percent), and they had much higher incomes. When asked if they take water along when visiting family or friends in Sonora, two-thirds of the Rio Rico respondents replied that they "do not visit," compared with only a quarter of the respondents in Nogales who gave the same answer. Rio Ricans also perceived water quality and water issues much differently than their neighbors in Nogales. They perceived the quality of the water they currently receive in their homes to be much lower, and they were more likely to say that water contamination is "very" serious. A much higher proportion of Rio Rico respondents had visited the Santa Cruz River in the last year, and their concern for the quality of the Santa Cruz as riparian habitat was much stronger.

Rio Ricans were much less likely to believe that they receive adequate information about water issues than were residents of Nogales. They were more likely to believe that government officials, community groups, and environmentalists have the most influence over water decisions, and less likely to believe that water experts have such influence. Perhaps most striking, compared with residents of Nogales, the residents of Rio Rico were much less likely to believe that city government is the level of government most responsible for water management, and much more likely to believe that federal and state levels of government are most responsible (fig. 4.14).

Although the survey conducted in Nogales, Son., by COLEF does not permit the same kind of analysis of binational versus national

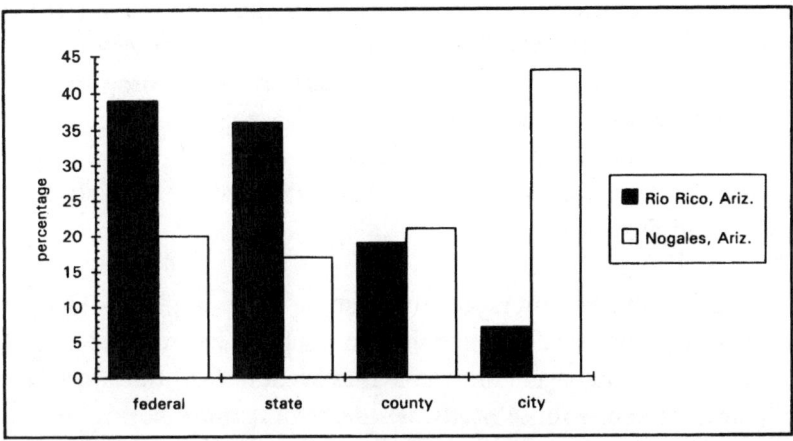

Figure 4.14 "National" versus "binational" orientations in Rio Rico and Nogales, Ariz., respondents' perceptions of the level of government most responsible for water policy. *Source*: Udall Center, 1993c.

orientations, it is reasonable to expect similar results for residents of Nogales, Son. Earlier generalizations about cross-border visits and cultural interaction should not be permitted to mask the existence of important variations in the degree to which residents of Nogales, Son., participate in the binational border culture. Consistent with our categorization of the orientation of Arizona border residents as binational and national, one study divided Mexican border residents into *national fronterizos* and *transnational fronterizos*. National fronterizos are

> people who, while subject to foreign economic and cultural influences, have minimal or superficial contact with the United States owing to their indifference to their next-door neighbors or their unwillingness or inability to function in any substantive way in another society. Transnational fronterizos, on the other hand, are individuals who maintain significant ties with the U.S. side; they seek to overcome obstacles that impede such contact and take advantage of every opportunity to visit, shop, work or live in the United States. Thus their lifestyles reflect foreign influence. (Martinez, 1990, p. 70)

The same study also estimated that more than half of all residents in Mexican border communities are transnational fronterizos; however, it is not possible to know with certainty what proportion of residents in a specific town actually fit this category. The important point is that there are people on both sides of the border who share a binational orientation, while there are others whose focus does not transcend the border.

If scarce water resources are to be successfully managed, the real needs and concerns of the people who use the water must be considered, and the managers must take into account how the consumers themselves define those needs. Residents of Ambos Nogales receive very different water services on the two sides of the international line, and not surprisingly, the issues they find relevant and the ways they seek to address them are often just as different.

In Nogales, Son., many residents are preoccupied with their private or neighborhood efforts to secure basic and reliable water supply and wastewater removal services. They have very little faith in the ability of local agencies to provide these services. Those who can afford to take measures on their own, or who have the power to bring political pressure to bear in the furtherance of their own self-interests, do so. These selfish activities often weaken the ability of local agencies to improve services for the entire community.

In Nogales, Ariz., residents are concerned about water quality and environmental degradation. There is strong support for local action to deal with perceived problems, but perceptions about the ability of individuals and institutions to deal with these problems vary. The residents most concerned about water quality problems tend to be the ones least likely to work for change at the local level and most likely to appeal for federal relief. Appeals from local residents for federal action have the potential to be as destructive to local efforts to resolve problems as the selfish coping mechanisms employed by their Sonoran neighbors.

The binational orientation described in this chapter provides a promising starting point for future efforts to achieve transnational solutions to the water problems of Ambos Nogales. This orientation builds on the shared history and cultural roots of the border communities. The commonalities in life experiences and outlooks of binationally oriented residents on both sides of the border provide fertile ground for cooperative action. At the same time, individuals with a binational orientation tend to adopt individual coping solutions rather than encouraging larger political or institutional solutions to shared problems. This is reinforced by the sources of information relied on by binationally oriented residents. Effective strategies for improved binational water management will need to tap into, and expand on, these traditional sources of information with new information about risks and opportunities in water resources management.

The discussion in this chapter also points to the need to increase the binational awareness of many residents of Ambos Nogales who now have a national orientation. A greater appreciation of the shared culture, economy, and water resources of border communities might make border residents more receptive to joint solutions for their common water problems. If ignorance breeds distrust and suspicion, then perhaps more information may lay the foundations for future cooperative action. Institutional strategies for binational management of border water resources ultimately can be effective only if the people affected allow them to be. It is to institutional issues that we turn our attention in Chapter 5.

Chapter 5

Stranded Communities and Failed Crossings

Laws and institutions establish the jurisdictional boundaries of authority. The jurisdiction over many public policy issues, including water resources management, is divided among a number of different agencies and officials within both Mexico and the United States. For example, U.S. water contamination standards are set by federal agencies and enforced at the state level, while water service responsibilities lie with local utilities but are regulated at the state level. The regulation of land use, which is closely related to both water quality and supply issues, is largely under the jurisdiction of local planning and zoning agencies. In Mexico, the federal government plays the dominant role in water resources regulation, allocation, and financing. Certain limited responsibilities have been delegated to state and local agencies by the Mexican federal government, and greater decentralization is promised for the future.

For local officials along the U.S.-Mexico border, the difficulties associated with these jurisdictional divisions are compounded by the international boundary. The border creates a dividing line where issues of national sovereignty take precedence over common interests and shared resources. Local agencies within either country cannot take cross-border actions without the permission of their respective national governments. Yet these local officials must be able to jointly manage shared transboundary resources as well as respond to the pressures created by increasing industrialization and population growth along the border.

To illustrate the legal and institutional difficulties faced by local officials in border communities, this chapter begins with the story of one such official on the U.S. side. This story, based on a personal interview and told from the perspective of the official himself, is intended to bring a human dimension to our analysis of jurisdictional divisions in border communities. The specific laws, regulations, and agency mandates that govern water resources management in Mexico and the United States change frequently, but certain themes remain constant. A good place to begin an analysis of those themes is by looking through the eyes of one person trying to do his job across agency and international boundaries.

Who Is Responsible for Sewage in Nogales Wash?

It was 1989, and Patrick Zurick was ready to assume his new position as deputy director of the Santa Cruz County Health Department. After several years of working on health issues for the city of Phoenix and serving as environmental health director for Greenlee County in eastern Arizona, he had decided to accept the position in Nogales. Initially, Zurick had been reluctant to make the move. It was common knowledge in the state's public health circles that Nogales was a tough place to work. The problems were substantial, and the support was not there to deal with them. However, Dr. Charles Hott, the part-time public health director for Santa Cruz County, had been persistent in his recruitment of Zurick. Hott himself had only recently been recruited to his position after opening a medical practice in Nogales. During his brief tenure as public health director, Hott had come to understand that the health department faced major issues and problems, and he was looking for a full-time deputy director with the expertise to deal with them.

Zurick decided to accept the position in Nogales after Hott repeatedly assured him that he would get the support necessary to improve the Santa Cruz County Health Department. Zurick told himself that he would take the job for a year but would start looking for another position after that. How bad could it be, he asked himself, when the entire population of Santa Cruz County was only 30,000, compared with almost 2 million residents in Maricopa County, where he had worked before? Enforcing health regulations in a county that small seemed like a manageable task, even if the international border did present special challenges.

The first shock Zurick experienced when he came to Nogales was the condition of the Santa Cruz County Health Department, which had been neglected by county officials for years. When Zurick arrived, the entire staff of the department consisted of a part-time director (Dr. Hott), one secretary, one food inspector, and one septic tank inspector. Staffing had been at that same level for at least five years, in spite of the noticeable growth in Nogales's population and commercial activities.

Zurick set to work with Hott to reorganize the small staff to make it more effective. They decided to establish priorities for their activities in order to have the greatest impact with their limited resources. In view of the department's mandate to protect the public health, they wanted to focus on the issues that posed the most significant threats to the health of the people of Nogales and for which there were clear guidelines and regulations. After reviewing the limited information available, Zurick and Hott decided to concentrate the department's short-term efforts on inspecting food establishments and sampling water quality.

When they implemented the stepped-up inspection program for food establishments, some of the affected businesspeople in Nogales grumbled. The standards were too strict and expensive to comply with, they said. But when the county health department officials made it clear that they would shut down any business that did not meet food-handling and other regulations, the businesses took immediate steps to comply. Although meeting the stricter standards was inconvenient and costly for many establishments, the expenses of temporary closures and negative publicity were much greater. Gradually, under the health department's new program of regular inspections and enforced sanctions, health and safety violations in local food establishments began to decrease.

This relatively positive experience in implementing the new food inspection program did not prepare Zurick for the exasperating problems he would encounter when the health department began to systematically sample water in Nogales. The decision to undertake the sampling program was based on some unsettling pieces of information that had come to Zurick's attention about water quality problems in Nogales Wash. While perusing the shelves in his new office shortly after assuming his post, Zurick came across a 1990 report prepared by Earth Technology Corporation for the Arizona

Department of Environmental Quality that showed the existence of volatile organic compound contaminants in groundwater samples from a number of wells in the vicinity of Nogales Wash.[1] Zurick also learned about several ad hoc water-sampling studies conducted by researchers at the University of Arizona that had raised real concerns about possibly significant contamination problems.

Although Zurick had not previously worked in the water quality area, he was aware of the standards for drinking water quality, and he recognized that a sampling program had to be systematic and analytical in order to determine actual levels and sources of contaminants. Zurick believed that ensuring that the people of Nogales had clean water was obviously important, a goal that the community would support. Who could argue with the need to protect the public from unsafe drinking water?

Zurick began a weekly sampling program in Nogales Wash, limited to the Arizona side of the border, in the summer of 1990. From the beginning the laboratory results were distressing. Of particular concern were high levels of fecal coliform, a bacteria found in the feces of animals that can cause a variety of intestinal and other ailments in humans. Arizona's maximum allowable standard for fecal coliform in surface flows is 4,000 CFU/100 ml.[2] A July 9 sample had a coliform count twice that amount. Then, on August 15, a sample taken from the same location had more than 1.6 million CFU/100 ml, 400 times the allowable limit. Zurick learned that a sewer line in Nogales, Son., had recently ruptured, spilling raw sewage into Nogales Wash.

Zurick and Hott were greatly concerned about the safety of people coming into direct contact with the contaminated water in the wash. The playground of a local elementary school was bounded on one side by Cerro Pelon Wash, a drainage to Nogales Wash, and children often played in Cerro Pelon Wash.[3] A school bus stop was located along Trickey Wash, another drainage to Nogales Wash, and children played in the wash while waiting for the bus.[4] Further downstream, the beach areas along Nogales Wash are popular recreational spots for families with young children and for teenagers.[5] A number of grocery stores and restaurants are located adjacent to Nogales Wash, and food deliveries and other activities take place right along its banks. Zurick was also concerned that surface flows in Nogales Wash might contaminate the shallower private wells located nearby. A number of produce warehouses that ship produce from Mexico throughout North America have private wells along Nogales Wash. Zurick had also observed that the Nogales Wash tunnels under the border were entryways for undocumented Mexican nationals crossing into the United States. Anyone using these routes must walk alongside and in the water.[6]

The first step Zurick and his colleagues at the health department took in response to these alarming findings was to issue public notices to advise people of the hazard. They also sent notices and background information to the local news media. These actions attracted the attention of a local reporter, Kathy Vandervoet of the *Nogales International*, who questioned Zurick and, later, members of the county board of supervisors about what would be done to solve the problem. The dozens of articles written by Vandervoet over the next two years became an important source of public information and criticism about the handling of the Nogales Wash sewage situation.

Most of the Nogales community, however, seemed unmoved by the test results. Zurick was frustrated by repeated comments that such problems have always existed and that prevailing health standards do not really apply to border communities such as Nogales. Instead of supporting his efforts to protect water quality, many business leaders and city officials expressed anger at Zurick's actions, which, they feared, would disrupt tourism and damage the local economy.

Nevertheless, on September 13, at Zurick's urging, the Santa Cruz County Board of Supervisors passed a resolution expressing its concern about the sewage contamination from Nogales, Son. The board also sent letters of concern to a number of state and federal agencies and officials, including the governor, the Arizona Department of Environmental Quality (ADEQ), the Arizona Department of Health Services, the U.S. Environmental Protection Agency (EPA), the International Boundary and Water Commission (IBWC), and members of the Arizona congressional delegation. Not one of the officials or agencies contacted by the county officials responded promptly.

On September 26, a sample taken at one of the sampling locations in Nogales Wash had a fecal coliform count of 16 million cfu/100 ml—4,000 times the allowable limit! Zurick determined that these (and even much lower) levels of fecal coliform constituted levels of contamination that could be classified as a "public nuisance." The county health department was empowered to deal with public nuisances by issuing cease-and-desist orders to stop the activities that were creating the nuisance, but because the sewage was originating in another country, local officials had no enforcement means available to them.

Zurick was providing weekly updates of the sampling results to the board of supervisors, but he was frustrated that the county did not have the ability or jurisdiction to solve the contamination problems. They still had not received any substantive response to their many communications to state and federal officials. Exasperated with this lack of response, in early October, Hott formally declared that Nogales Wash was a public nuisance and a danger to public health. The county's emergency services coordinator said there was nothing he could do locally about it, so he asked the board of supervisors to declare a state of emergency in order to involve the state. The board declared a state of emergency on October 3, 1990. But still nothing happened. When Zurick called and spoke with a field manager from ADEQ about the situation, he was told, "You've had the problem for years, why should we all of a sudden get excited about it?"

Two days after the county declared a state of emergency, the city of Nogales followed suit. Finally, Governor Rose Mofford was prompted to sign a state declaration of emergency that allocated $50,000 of the state's emergency funds to build a temporary dam. Departing from past practices, the governor appointed ADEQ rather than the Arizona Department of Emergency Services to investigate the matter. ADEQ's expertise, however, was in long-term projects rather than emergency response, for which they had neither resources nor background. Moreover, the field representatives sent to Nogales appeared to be receiving little support from higher administrative levels. In Zurick's estimation, the field representatives' role seemed to be aimed more at placating the local populace than at addressing the threat to the public health. After two weeks of waiting for the state to take corrective action, Zurick and the county emergency coordinator, Mac McWilliams, decided to take things into their own hands again. McWilliams sent an official emergency alert to the ADEQ emergency response team for hazardous spills. The team came down from Phoenix within hours and went into high gear. They decided to treat the situation as if it were a hazardous waste spill, allowing them to use private cleanup companies under contract to the state. In less than a week they had set up three 190-cubic-meter (50,000-gallon) chlorine tanks along Nogales Wash, with sandbags channeling the water through the chlorine stations. Within a couple of weeks, more than $250,000 had been spent on these mitigation activities.

In addition to summoning the state emergency response team, Zurick and McWilliams also collected the fax numbers of every news organization they could think of and began faxing press releases on the declaration of emergency and copies of the letters that had been sent earlier to the various officials. They had finally succeeded in getting attention for Nogales's problems, but whether solutions would follow remained to be seen.

Their communications to the IBWC still had received no response. By now Congressman Jim Kolbe and Senator John McCain of Arizona were both involved, and they urged the IBWC to take action. A meeting in late October called by Governor Mofford was attended by her, her top aides and those of Kolbe and McCain, members of the Santa Cruz County Board of Supervisors, and other local officials. Commissioner Narendra Gunaji of the IBWC reluctantly attended, presumably at the strong request of the congressmen. Zurick was amazed at his demeanor. Rather than being mild and diplomatic, as Zurick had expected, Gunaji was very combative, stating openly that he had come only because he had been told to, and that Nogales's problems were less severe than those elsewhere on the border. Gunaji later issued a statement in which he maintained that his response to "this highly publicized problem has been low-key because of sensitivities on the treaty matter with Mexico."[7]

Having so recently come from Phoenix, where health emergencies were taken very seriously and acted on quickly, Zurick had expected equally prompt official action regarding the Nogales Wash sewage problems. He soon found out, however, that there were no protocols or procedures in place for dealing with a transboundary environmental emergency. The EPA did not want to get involved; it had neither met with any county officials nor sent a representative to Nogales to review the situation. The EPA's sole communication with the county had been a letter disclaiming jurisdiction over the problem.

The EPA continued to maintain that the IBWC had sole jurisdiction over transboundary pollution, while the IBWC asserted that the problem became the EPA's once the sewage crossed the U.S. border. For Zurick, the underlying message communicated by all these agencies was, If you live on the border, you should expect this kind of problem—it goes with the territory; these problems have occurred in the past and they will again in the future. Zurick's response was to ask why Nogales residents should be treated differently from people in Phoenix. When an ADEQ official was asked what would happen if a tanker of water from Nogales Wash was brought to Phoenix and dumped into the Salt River, he responded that the perpetrator would be cited for violations of state and federal pollution laws.

A few weeks after the meeting called by the governor at which Commissioner Gunaji had appeared so openly hostile, Zurick was surprised by a dramatic turnaround in the commissioner's attitude. The change was rumored to have been caused by pressure from influential senators and important players in the U.S. State Department. Suddenly, the IBWC found $500,000 to put a pumping station in Nogales Wash and replace the existing state-funded chlorine stations. The federal government assumed payments for the chlorine, which cost $500–$600 a day. Zurick and other county officials began to receive weekly reports from the IBWC, and one of the commission's representatives started to make regular appearances before the board of supervisors. This turnaround was all the more unexpected because the IBWC had never before made any effort to interact with local officials and the community. In fact, Zurick had been struck by how many longtime local residents had never even heard of the IBWC.

The media blitz and letter-writing campaign orchestrated by Zurick were facilitated by the efforts of private groups concerned about public health and the border environment. In particular, the Border

Ecology Project (BEP), headed by Dick Kamp, was an effective advocate for the message Zurick was trying to disseminate. Zurick would send information and data regarding water quality problems to Kamp, who would forward it to his wide array of media and nongovernmental organization (NGO) contacts.

As a government official, Zurick faced many more constraints on using the information available to him than a private group like the Border Ecology Project did. For example, the chlorination program implemented by the IBWC in 1990–91 included chlorination stations that extended upstream 1.6 kilometers (1 mile) into Mexico. With these new stations, the ongoing water-sampling program now included samples from a prechlorinated site in Mexico, a site at the border, and a site downstream, in order to demonstrate the effectiveness of the chlorination program. The samples showed fecal coliform counts in the millions before chlorination and within acceptable limits after chlorination. Zurick presented the sample results at board of supervisors meetings every week during a period in 1991–92 and distributed them on request. One day, more than a year after he had begun reporting these results, members of the Mexican news media happened to be visiting Zurick at his office, and he invited them to attend that week's board meeting. When they left, the Mexican reporters took with them copies of Zurick's weekly report of sampling results and published them in the local Sonora newspaper. In their articles they also quoted Mexican governmental officials as saying that there was no problem with sewage contamination in Nogales, Son. Within two days Zurick was informed by the IBWC that the results of the water testing could no longer be made public. Zurick refused to accept the data under that limitation, and the IBWC stopped providing the Mexico water sample results to the county.

The combined efforts to gain recognition for Nogales's situation achieved results, beginning with the IBWC commissioner's startling reversal. Not only did the IBWC become an active presence in efforts to deal with the sewerage problem, but the EPA also became more involved in local issues. Several local officials, including Zurick, were invited by the EPA to attend a working-group meeting on hazardous waste in El Paso, Texas. Although a number of such working groups had been set up by the EPA since 1983, pursuant to the agency's border environmental responsibilities under the La Paz Agreement, nobody in the Santa Cruz County government had ever been invited to attend one of their meetings. When Zurick expressed chagrin that no local officials had ever been asked for input or ideas about the environmental problems the communities were experiencing, he was told that *states* had only recently been represented in the working groups.

In the summer of 1991 Zurick was invited to testify before the U.S. Senate Subcommittee on Environmental Protection. The Nogales situation was widely discussed at national and regional meetings, and the EPA made many promises at a meeting of the national coordinators' working groups from the EPA and the Secretaría de Desarrollo Social (Ministry for Social Development, SEDESOL) held in Santa Fe, New Mexico, in June 1992.[8] The EPA told Zurick that it would commission a hazardous waste inventory for Nogales that would serve as a model for other areas of the border and committed itself to assigning a full-time employee for two or three years to work on joint inspections on the two sides of the border. These inspections would attempt to document the wastes generated by the maquiladora factories operating in Nogales, Son. The EPA also promised an extensive groundwater-monitoring program to determine what pollutants were actually reaching the aquifer. A binational air-sampling program also was discussed, and Nogales was selected by the EPA as one of two sites for a border pollution prevention program. Needless to say, Zurick and his local colleagues were pleased.

Two years later, almost none of the promises had been kept. The EPA hazardous waste specialist never arrived. The hazardous waste inventory was reduced to plans for a limited mail survey rather than inspections by a hired contractor. Zurick dismisses the validity of such an inventory, pointing out that he has never had a restaurant write and tell him "I'm dirty, come and inspect me," even though he often finds deplorable conditions in restaurants. A model based on mail surveys will be worthless, Zurick believes, particularly when what is desperately needed are live inspectors to get the attention of maquila owners and managers.

The groundwater study had not yet begun in 1993, and posturing between the IBWC and the EPA appeared to have scuttled it as well.

What was to have been a million-dollar, several-year study was downsized and delayed. According to Zurick, the study was based on an IBWC proposal for a study under the commission's control. The EPA criticized the IBWC's proposal and asserted that it would not contribute financially to the study unless it also shared in the control. In the meantime, national and state attention to the Nogales Wash situation receded. The IBWC and the EPA shifted their attention and activities to other areas, and county officials once again found themselves on their own in dealing with water contamination problems in Nogales Wash.

Zurick became the director of the health department in January 1993. Lacking jurisdiction to establish formal ties with local officials in Nogales, Son., Zurick has instead developed informal cooperative strategies. He looks for opportunities to acquire funds that can be spent on both sides of the border—something that cannot be done with state or local money. The health department obtained a grant from the Office of International Health, funded through the Pan American Health Organization, to conduct a binational environmental education program. Although the grant provides only $30,000, the fact that it funds activities in Mexico makes it very valuable. Zurick has worked with his Nogales counterpart on the Sonora side, Dr. Enrique Davis, to get information to women in Sonora about how to safely chlorinate their drinking water and to encourage them to use pickle barrels in place of the hazardous solvent drums often used by colonia residents to store their household water (see Chapter 3). Zurick developed these amicable, informal relationships across the line on his own, with no assistance from the IBWC; in fact, his experiences have shown that IBWC involvement impairs his ability to establish working relationships in Sonora.

Zurick tries not to get involved in Mexican politics, but he does look for ways to share information and ideas with his neighbors across the line. Formal binational channels are difficult to establish. In order for Zurick to set up an official binational meeting on water quality with his Mexican counterpart, Dr. Davis, both must get the approval of their bosses and clearance from the IBWC, the body with official jurisdiction over border water matters. Sometimes these formal routes cannot be avoided, such as when Zurick wanted to get federal funding to support the water-sampling program in 1991 and he was told that Mexico could not be formally involved unless the IBWC ran the program.

Zurick's best working relationships with Mexican officials have come from contacts he has made outside official county health department business. He has found attendance at binational meetings set up by other organizations to be particularly valuable. For example, a binational primary-health-care project under the auspices of the University of Arizona's Rural Health Office, COLEF, and El Colegio de Sonora includes a number of binational meetings that Zurick tries to attend whenever he can. The advantage for him is that he can attend as a committee member rather than in his official capacity as county health director. This allows him to get to know people in Mexico with common interests and to share information informally in a nonthreatening context.

Zurick has found NGOs to be valuable partners in some of the things he is trying to accomplish locally. He is working with a community group, the Friends of the Santa Cruz River, to expand the water-sampling program downstream, north of Nogales. Members of the Friends have trained with ADEQ and are certified to conduct water sampling. The county bought $2,000 worth of testing equipment for the group so it could begin an official monthly sampling program. ADEQ pays for the laboratory work and considers the results to be official governmental data. Zurick is encouraged by this kind of public-private partnership and wishes he could see more of it. He and the Friends of the Santa Cruz River also worked together to organize a binational meeting on the subject of the river.

Zurick thinks these local partnerships are important because he is skeptical about the kind of support Nogales realistically can expect from the EPA, the IBWC, and other national agencies with regard to local environmental and health problems. Although he is quick to point out that local EPA and ADEQ personnel with whom he has worked are competent, well-intentioned people, they are technicians, not policymakers. In Zurick's view, support for border programs does not exist at higher levels. And even the EPA border office employees have responsibilities that extend well beyond the border's environment. Zurick recalls that in January 1993 he conducted a tour for a visiting EPA emergency response coordinator. The coordinator was amazed at what he saw, exclaiming that it was much different (and worse) than he had anticipated. The coordinator also mentioned that this was the first time that anyone from the EPA emergency response office had ever made an official visit to the border—the entire U.S.-Mexico border!

It has been Zurick's experience that state and federal agency representatives are never assigned to work solely on border matters. He has met a few officials who became interested in border issues and had to find funds in their limited travel budgets to visit the border to see things firsthand. Once there, these officials found themselves in the difficult position of explaining to local representatives why decisions affecting the border are made in Washington and San Francisco.[9] Local officials who do not agree with those decisions (or the lack of decisions) are forced to go around the agency representatives to try to get the attention of the politicians and policymakers in Washington. Sometimes the local agency representatives take it personally when Zurick publicizes an issue, but he explains that he is trying to build political support so that they will be able to take stronger action.

Zurick is encouraged that his department's efforts to educate local residents about environmental health risks are paying off. Many of the people and businesses who in 1990 were strong opponents of the water-sampling program are now its most forceful advocates. As long as people in the community were convinced that nothing could be done about the sewage, they did not want to know the unpleasant facts. But when Zurick was able to link water quality issues to documented health risks, and then to create pressure for state and federal assistance to solve the problem, many skeptics changed their minds. Although he entered as an outsider, Zurick has won the respect and support of many local residents. He now proudly points to local people who have of their own volition helped in areas where his department does not have the time or resources to work. For example, several individuals are spearheading a research project to document incidences of cancer deaths and lupus in Nogales to determine if "clusters" exist that may be attributable to TCE in the water supply.[10] To lend scientific credibility to the project, the Mariposa Community

Health Center in Nogales and the University of Arizona (Tucson) are also involved in the study. Zurick believes that the study will make an important contribution to the information base needed by policymakers and the public in Nogales.

Zurick is not as optimistic, however, about his department's or the local government's ability to meaningfully address the staggering problems Nogales faces. State and federal assistance to the county is based on its population of 30,000, which puts Santa Cruz County on a par with sparsely populated Graham County in eastern Arizona. Although both are classified as rural counties, the only thing that sleepy Graham County and burgeoning Santa Cruz County have in common is their "official" populations. Nogales, Ariz., may have only 20,000 residents, but Ambos Nogales has a population of more than 150,000, all in need of clean water and air, sewage treatment, solid waste disposal, roads, and other infrastructure.

From Zurick's perspective, Nogales suffers from all the problems created by the industrialization of the border—increased traffic, increased population, increased pollution, increased crime—while enjoying none of the benefits that industrialization is supposed to bring. The maquiladoras in Sonora do not contribute to Santa Cruz County's tax base, nor do they pay customs fees that could be used by local governments to mitigate the damage caused by some of their activities. Zurick points to the incredible levels of traffic that pass through the Port of Nogales—600 to 700 produce trucks every day, for example. The existing roads cannot support that level of traffic, and the congestion is horrific, but there is no money to build new roads. There is also a high volume of train activity right through the heart of Nogales carrying materials to and from factories and maquiladoras. In the future, Guaymas, Son., is expected to become a major port for containers that now go to ports on the California coast. Spills of hazardous substances from tractor trailers and railroad cars are becoming more commonplace, but the closest emergency response team is 280 kilometers (175 miles) away in Phoenix. Zurick wants to have a hazardous materials team available locally, but it costs $250,000 to train and equip a four-person team.

There are many programs that Zurick would like to implement in his department, but he knows he cannot expect greater financial support from an already overextended county. For example, the county jail is on the brink of bankruptcy because drug smugglers have evidently instructed their operatives that if they are arrested they should demand a jury trial and a public defender. In 1990, the county spent $100,000 on public defenders, and in 1993 they were expecting to spend $300,000.[11] The jail has three times as many prisoners as it was built to hold, and both Santa Cruz County and a local judge have begun to make public pleas for help. The money to deal with international drug smuggling must come out of the same limited county funds that support needed infrastructure improvements, planning, resource management, police, fire services, and so on. Zurick maintains that a tax base of 30,000 people cannot pay for the problems created by the international border at Nogales, and he is pessimistic about the future.

Postscript. Somewhat belatedly, a Border Health Task Force was created by Governor Fife Symington on December 2, 1993, six weeks after national media attention focused on alleged cancer and lupus clusters in Nogales, Ariz.—clusters that residents attribute to groundwater chemical contamination.[12]

Lessons from Nogales

Nogales is only one among many border communities, and Pat Zurick is but one local official, but his story illustrates many of the important issues facing communities all along the U.S.-Mexico border. Periodic crises, whether sewage spills in Tijuana and Nogales, toxic waste contamination in El Paso/Ciudad Juarez, or pollution of the Rio Grande/Río Bravo, focus national attention on the border. But the limelight soon fades, and the border communities are left once again to cope largely on their own with the significant day-to-day problems engendered by their special status as gateways between two sovereign nations. Border communities are the most directly affected by the negative impacts of increased trade activities, migration of low-wage workers, and border industrialization. They must confront resulting overuse and contamination of water supplies, inadequate water and sewage transport systems and other infrastructure, and the concomitant uncertainties about what the future holds for their communities.

Local government officials are charged with providing their constituents with adequate potable water and other essential services. But local officials are largely powerless to prevent or combat the environmental problems their communities now face. They often lack both legal jurisdiction over the problems and the resources necessary to take meaningful action. Legal jurisdiction establishes who has the authority to make decisions and sets limits on the available choices. Beyond that, the decision-making institution must have the financial and administrative capacity to implement and enforce the policies that are legally within its authority to set. The rights to regulate the use of groundwater, control sources of contamination, manage effluent, and finance and construct delivery systems in Ambos Nogales and other border communities are divided among a number of different federal, state, and local agencies and institutions. Local officials have neither the authority to make many critical decisions about their communities' water resources nor the financial resources to implement those decisions.

The many jurisdictional boundaries that divide Ambos Nogales work against the unifying themes of shared resources, common history, and joint destiny. The officials and agencies empowered to make crucial decisions about water management in these border cities are far removed from the local scene and answer to different constituencies. The relatively small populations and low economic importance of these communities disadvantage them in larger national and state political arenas; while border communities directly experience problems with water resources, for example, they have very little say in the solutions that are proposed and implemented.

The most obvious and troubling—but not the only—jurisdictional dividing line in Ambos Nogales is the international border. This fundamental boundary separates the two communities, legally binding them to separate sovereign nations. Notwithstanding their many shared problems, the two Nogaleses lack the authority to formally reach across the border to cooperate in solving problems. Instead, they must look to Washington and Mexico City to devise, negotiate, approve, and finance international solutions to their joint local water problems. In addition to dealing with the divisions occasioned by the international boundary, these border cities also must contend with different institutions and agencies within their respective countries that have jurisdiction over various aspects of water management. The mandates, priorities, and support structures of these institutions make them largely insensitive to the special needs of binational border communities. On the U.S. side, water resources are primarily regulated by state agencies, which tend to serve the needs of population centers, where political and economic influence is greatest. In Mexico, the political agenda of the federal government tends to be the driving force behind water resources regulation. In neither country do border communities have adequate jurisdiction or the institutional capabilities to manage their own water regimes, much less transboundary problems.

As Santa Cruz County health director, Pat Zurick is responsible for protecting the public from known health risks in its water supplies. But as a local official in a border community, he is faced with jurisdictional barriers at every turn. His first, and perhaps most difficult, hurdle was the pervasive U.S. attitude that border communities ought to expect fewer amenities and be willing to accept greater environmental degradation and health risks than their interior counterparts. Simply put, different standards apply in border areas. This tendency to tolerate unacceptable conditions when they affect only certain disadvantaged groups is not limited to border communities; it also exists on Native American reservations, in urban ghettos, and in many poor rural areas that have been bypassed by economic development. Border areas, despite their increasing economic development, continue to be only marginally important in the minds of many people. Ironically, this attitude exists even among some border business and government leaders, who fear adverse public reaction to a full airing of the border's environmental problems. This double standard also suffuses much of the political debate at the state and national levels on border matters.

In many cases, this tendency toward differential treatment of border communities may be exacerbated by a lack of good information and planning capabilities at the local level. Officials in border communities often do not have access to reliable, comprehensive data about shared transboundary resources and resource problems; nor do local officials generally have the staff and internal capability to attempt effective planning and resource management. In the face of the lack of data and planning capabilities, it is difficult for these localities to call attention to their special environmental problems and to effectively compete for scarce state and federal funds or other external assistance.

The existence of so many local, state, and federal institutions and agencies, each with limited jurisdiction over border resources and environmental matters, might lead one to conclude that local officials have many avenues of relief and assistance available to them. On the contrary, Zurick's experience points instead to the lack of accountability and responsibility fostered by conflicting and inadequate jurisdictional mandates. Agencies possessing limited resources and trying to contend with problems that have joint or overlapping authority are much more likely to avoid action than to work cooperatively to find solutions. Incentives for action by any one agency are lacking when overall coordination, accountability, and financial remuneration do not exist.

This fragmentation and lack of accountability are exacerbated by the presence of the international boundary, which superimposes questions of national sovereignty and self-determination on the already crowded mix of agency mandates and missions. Official agency actions that require recognition of rights or expenditure of funds across the international border must have the special approval of the respective federal governments, thus placing what would otherwise be local issues into a national or international context. Although the result may be greater federal attention and funding for certain local issues that involve national security or trade balances, the presence of the border works against comprehensive, implementable policies. International diplomatic arrangements may end up bearing little relation to the solutions that border communities themselves would implement if they had the authority and resources.

Despite their lack of authority and jurisdiction, however, local governments in border communities such as Nogales have substantial obligations in water matters. They are largely responsible for operating the water utilities that provide water to residents and for disposing of locally generated sewage and hazardous materials created within their communities. Most Mexican communities, including

Nogales, Son., have a woefully inadequate infrastructure for water delivery and sewage transport and little prospect of acquiring the financial means to improve the deficit. In addition, federal and state mandates in pollution control are expanding in both countries, causing paperwork compliance headaches for already overburdened local governments.

Taking advantage of their position as "outsiders" independent of official hierarchies and prerogatives, NGOs are becoming increasingly important players in border environmental matters. They are frequently in a better position to publicize problems and direct media attention to border issues than are local governmental officials. Unofficial data can be disseminated by an NGO in circumstances where it would be too risky or controversial for a government official to do so. Local and regional NGOs tend to form around particular issues and localized problems. A good example is the Border Ecology Project, which was originally organized to combat air-polluting emissions from copper smelters in southern Arizona and northern Sonora. BEP has been active in disseminating information about toxic substances and water quality issues in Ambos Nogales.[13] NGOs with state and national ties may bring a broader perspective and larger constituencies to border issues than would otherwise exist, although their emphasis has tended to be on national environmental standards and enforcement rather than border environmental issues. While generally united in their criticisms of national border environmental policy, grassroots groups on the two sides of the border tend to have different agendas. Groups in the United States tend to focus on pollution, while those based in Mexico or with ties in Mexico are more concerned about water supply and occupational health.

But no matter how effective and valuable NGOs may be within their areas of activity, the management of water resources along the border remains essentially the government's responsibility. Pat Zurick's experiences highlight some of the pitfalls as well as the avenues of cooperation that exist for local U.S. officials trying to work in a border community. The following discussion focuses on the legal and regulatory context through which local Mexican officials must act.

The Mexican Perspective

The hierarchy of Mexican political institutions contains no equivalent to U.S. county-level government. But there is a direct counterpart in Nogales, Son., to Pat Zurick. Authority for public health matters is vested in Dr. Enrique Davis Ramirez, a Nogales, Son.–born gynecologist who accepted his current position in March 1992 and works out of an office at the Hospital Básico. In a fall 1993 interview, Davis described himself as in charge of *community* health rather than public health. This distinction may explain some of the differences in the ways the two officials perceive the magnitude of the threats to the public health.

Davis's focus is on prevention and extension services, with special emphasis on education and immunization programs. He believes that great progress has been made in the public health sphere over the past several years, and he sees a general lack of funding as the limiting factor in his work. Davis views himself as a member of a team, as someone joining others from different state and federal agencies in a combined effort. He contrasts this with the situation in the United States, where he sees disparate groups addressing public health issues without working together.

Davis does not place great priority on waterborne diseases—he cites statistics indicating that diarrhea-induced mortality is not one of the top 10 causes of death in Nogales, Son.[14]—but he does concede that water issues are a major concern. As part of the task of controlling waterborne pathogens, Davis enforces sanitary regulations. He attempts to identify the main health problems, and having done so, responds primarily with educational outreach. He focuses on water treatment and food handling at the household level and has produced a one-page illustrated information sheet that describes both how to boil water and how to treat it with iodine to destroy any pathogens it might contain. The educational outreach program is primed to control outbreaks of diarrhea and explains the use of oral rehydration therapy when outbreaks do occur. Another goal of the outreach program is to educate people in the proper construction of adequate latrines; in this case, a longer illustrated pamphlet is distributed to households. Outreach is accomplished through these

166   Divided Waters

informational pamphlets and also through the radio, television, and newspaper media.

Davis blames the general lack of education of the populace as the root cause both of health problems and of people's reluctance to seek treatment from the nationalized Mexican health services system. Primary health care is available free of charge to all Mexican citizens.

Davis perceives no health problems derivable from leaking sewerage in Nogales, Son. He feels that Nogales, Ariz., is overblowing the issue of Mexican sewage, particularly since the sewage stream is now chlorinated while it is still in Mexico, and he says that chemical contamination of water is outside his jurisdiction. While he contends that there is no cholera in Nogales, he does not deny the existence of various committees that target specific health problems such as cholera. Honorary members of the committees include the mayor of Nogales and the governor of Sonora.

Davis believes that the most critical issue in Nogales, Son., is economic development, through which more and better services will be provided to the population. As an example, he cites the increase in surgeons from 4 in 1980 to 22 in 1993.

Differing Perceptions of Public Health and Environmental Issues

A number of articles with environmental themes were published in Ambos Nogales newspapers between October 1990 and October 1991. Figure 5.1 expresses the relative importance of the themes on the two sides of the international border. The category "Nogales Wash and Tributaries" obviously encompasses public health issues because of the association of public health with the contaminated water in the wash. Figure 5.2 shows the various sources of the articles during the same period. The most frequent source of health-related articles in the Nogales, Ariz., press was the Santa Cruz County Health Department—Pat Zurick's domain—which generated more than twice as many articles as did the top two Mexican protagonists combined: SEDUE (a federal institution) and academics (persons at COLEF, Colegio de Sonora, and Instituto Tecnológico de Sonora). The press is the only investigative segment of the media in Nogales, Son.; by and

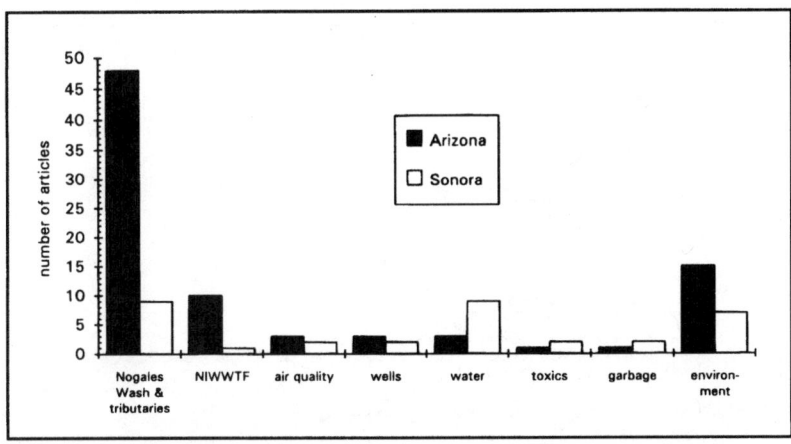

Figure 5.1 Environmental themes appearing in Ambos Nogales newspapers by category, October 1990–October 1991. *Source*: COLEF, Sistema de Información Fronteriza.

large, public service announcements on radio stations tend to be exhortative rather than expostulative. For example, a public service announcement may exhort people to boil water, but radio programming fails to follow up with information on why this is necessary.

Changing Times in Mexican Water Regulation

The highly centralized Mexican regulatory system vests both jurisdictional and fiscal authority in the federal government. Regulatory action and funding for projects often depend on political decisions made by remote federal officials. A border city such as Nogales is not only geographically distant from the national capital but also politically remote from the center of decision making. That isolation is reinforced by the tendency of the Mexican administrative system to base policymaking on personal relationships and political power.

Mexico's political system has remained remarkably stable over the last 50 years. Mexico is the only Latin American nation that has not experienced a political coup in the era since World War II. Even more remarkably, and unlike events in the United States, every president elected since 1934 has survived his six-year term to peacefully relinquish office to his successor. (During that same period, three of the

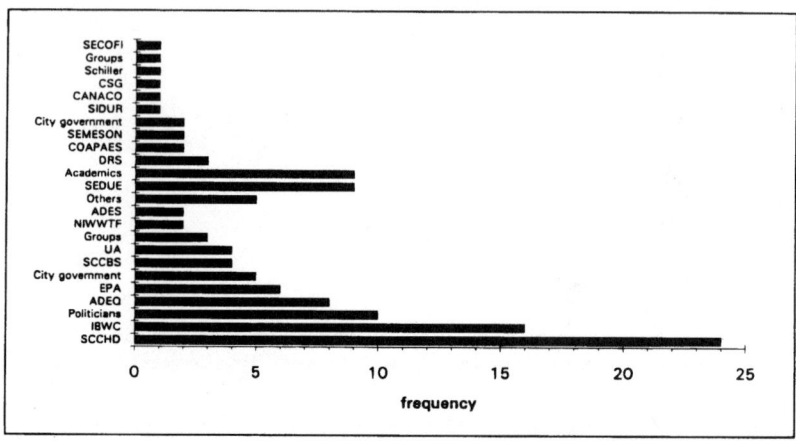

Figure 5.2 Sources of information for articles on the environment appearing in Ambos Nogales newspapers. *For Sonora*: SECOFI = Secretaría de Comercio y Fomento Industrial, a federal agency; Groups = Grupo Ecologista Independiente de Nogales, Grupo Dignidad, Grupos de Colonos, Border Ecology Project; Schiller = Instituto Schiller, a religious organization; CSG = President Carlos Salinas de Gortari; CANACO = Cámaro Nacional de Comercio (National Chamber of Commerce); SIDUR = Secretaría de Infraestructura y Desarrollo Urbano y Rural, a federal agency; SEMESON = Servicios Médicos de Sonora, a state agency; COAPAES = Comisión de Agua Potable y Alcantarillado del Estado de Sonora, a state agency; DRS = Dirección de Regulación Sanitaria, a state agency; Academics = El Colegio de la Frontera Norte, Colegio de Sonora, and Instituto Tecnológico de Sonora; SEDUE = Secretaría de Desarrollo Urbano y Ecología, a federal agency. *For Arizona*: ADES = Arizona Department of Economic Security; NIWWTF = Nogales International Wastewater Treatment Facility; Groups = Border Ecology Project and Friends of the Santa Cruz River; UA = Udall Center for Studies in Public Policy and the University of Arizona; SCCBS = Santa Cruz County Board of Supervisors; EPA = U.S. Environmental Protection Agency; ADEQ = Arizona Department of Environmental Quality; IBWC = International Boundary and Water Commission; SCCHD = Santa Cruz County Health Department. *Source*: COLEF, Sistema de Información Fronteriza.

nine elected presidents of the United States did not complete their terms.) The one-party regime of the PRI has lasted since 1929, although recent elections have seen significant challenges to its dominance.

The centralized political and legal authority of the federal government is concentrated in the presidency. The president of Mexico possesses very broad powers to create and realign departments within the federal government, and he can appoint and dismiss agency officials as he chooses. The president selects his successor from among his cabinet members. The strong presidency in turn confers broad powers on the cabinet members and their ministries. Although Mexico has a federal congress modeled on the U.S. Congress, that body is not an effective check or balance to the exercise of presidential power. Most legislation is initiated by the president, and the legislature serves essentially as a rubber stamp for his programs.

Neither does the Mexican judiciary play a very effective balancing role, primarily because of the nature of the Mexican legal system, which is based on a civil-law tradition rather than the common-law tradition of the United States. The enforcement of legal rights in Mexico thus depends primarily on administrative proceedings rather than on litigation. Disputes are resolved by administrative agencies rather than in the courts, and agencies and presidential appointees have the power to resolve most issues without meaningful review by the courts. A significant amount of political decision making in Mexico is based on demands presented by petitioners to agencies of the federal government, to local and state governments, and even to the president (Levy and Székely, 1987). The law is interpreted by the agency to whom the petition is made, so the practice of reinterpreting written law occurs at all administrative levels of government. The president, not the judiciary, is the ultimate authority in interpreting federal law. The power of the judiciary is further weakened by its close political ties to the president and the ruling party. Since 1929, all Supreme Court justices, who are appointed by the president and confirmed by the Senate, have been members of the PRI. Although in theory appointed for life, in practice justices usually resign at the beginning of each new presidential term. Together, these factors result in a much less important role for the Mexican judiciary compared with the functions of the U.S. judiciary.

The legal regime governing water resources in Mexico follows the same centralized federal structure, with ultimate authority vested in the president. The Mexican Constitution of 1917, Article 27, establishes that ownership of all water resources within the borders of Mexico is vested in the nation, and the government is the trustee for the people. It is a commonly held belief among Mexican people that as the beneficiaries of this resource, they should not have to pay for it (Dumars et al., 1993). This view of an inherent right to free water is reinforced by many traditional practices of government-operated water utilities, which often fail to collect fees from users and take no action against illegal connections to water lines and unauthorized wells.

The federal government, the ultimate legal authority over the nation's water resources, has passed on the responsibility for issuing water use permits and for managing the day-to-day operations of water utilities to state governments while maintaining control over the fees collected and most of the infrastructure investment. Under federal water law, private individuals and organizations are not permitted to own the water resource itself and must obtain permits for the right to gain access to and use the water.

Like other aspects of the federal government, the institutional structure governing water resources in Mexico is characterized by an emphasis on the formalities of agency authority and jurisdiction. As problems emerge onto the national political agenda, the president creates agencies and metes out responsibilities. These institutional arrangements tend to continue until new problems emerge or old problems assume greater importance within the political scene and agency structures and areas of responsibility are reorganized to meet the new crisis. Because these reorganizations are the president's prerogative, they can occur quickly and with little input from the public or from agencies within the government. Often, changes are made primarily for their symbolic political value, and little thought is given to the substantive effects on agencies, programs, and the people served. While such reorganizations may create the appearance of action, they are costly in terms of efficiency and efficacy. Changes in the lines of authority and agency mandates interrupt the implementation of programs and retard the development of needed expertise. Regular transfers of officials and areas of authority in and out of agencies may serve the political needs of the president, but they do little to strengthen the agencies themselves.

Governmental efforts to regulate water in Mexico began with the creation of the National Irrigation Commission in 1926. The Ministry of Water Resources was formed in 1946, and among its duties was the development of regional water plans for various areas of the country. These plans were integrated into the first National Water Plan in 1975. The reorganization of the federal government that took place in 1976 resulted in the amalgamation of the Ministries of Water Resources and Agriculture into the single Ministry of Agriculture and Water Resources (Secretaría de Agricultura y Recursos Hidráulicos, SARH). SARH was charged with solving the water problems facing the agricultural sector and was also accorded responsibility for planning, designing, and constructing the infrastructure to deliver municipal and industrial water supplies. The government decentralized the regulation of urban water supplies, assigning that task to the states, but without providing authority or funding mechanisms for the necessary infrastructure. As a result, planning and implementation activities assumed a regional focus and there was no overall federal coordination of efforts and management.

The lack of a coordinated approach to solving problems of water scarcity and conflicting uses caused growing concern, and in 1989, at the request of the president, the Mexican Congress created a new agency to coordinate water allocation activities. The National Water Commission (Comisión Nacional del Agua, CNA) became an autonomous agency, but its jurisdiction overlapped with that of SARH and other agencies. The CNA is responsible for defining the country's water policies; formulating and monitoring implementation of the National Water Plan; regulating water use and issuing the necessary licenses and permits to use water; planning, designing, and constructing federal waterworks; and providing technical assistance and defining and implementing the financing mechanisms for supporting water development and necessary infrastructure (Comisión Nacional del Agua, 1990).

Since it was established in 1988, the Secretaría de Desarrollo Urbano y Ecología (Ministry of Urban Development and Ecology,

SEDUE) had been the federal agency primarily responsible for pollution issues. As such, it was charged with enforcing the comprehensive 1988 General Law of Ecological Equilibrium (General Ecology Law),[15] which is similar in many respects to U.S. environmental statutes, although it does not encompass a superfund or regulate underground storage tanks. The General Ecology Law covers pollution control, natural resource conservation, environmental impacts, and risk assessment. It provides general criteria for developing regulatory standards but allows wide administrative discretion for developing environmental programs through regulations and technical standards. Under a federal reorganization in 1992, SEDUE was dismantled and its functions transferred to a new superagency, the Secretaría de Desarrollo Social (Ministry of Social Development, SEDESOL). This new ministry is responsible for overseeing public housing, the antipoverty public works program (Solidaridad), urban planning, forestry and land use management, promotion of indigenous rights, and education, in addition to the environmental issues and enforcement previously handled by SEDUE.

Whatever agency is in charge, it is in the enforcement of regulatory requirements rather than the requirements themselves that Mexico differs substantially from the United States. Even more so than the EPA, SEDESOL is grossly understaffed and underfunded, and thus unable to perform its enforcement functions effectively. Enforcement activities in Mexico tend to focus on administrative tools such as plant closings (which may be no more than brief "paper closures" to allow companies to get their papers in order), fines, or voluntary compliance agreements. Criminal prosecution for environmental violations is extremely rare in Mexico, and civil lawsuits, a common enforcement tool in the United States, are not an option in Mexico (EPA, 1991).

The Trend Toward Decentralization

Two important processes now under way in Mexico may loosen formal federal control over water resources management. The first is the political trend away from the absolute dominance of the PRI in Mexican political life. In his now famous 1987 speech in Hermosillo,

Son., presidential candidate Carlos Salinas de Gortari chastised his party for electoral fraud and called on PRI leaders to "recognize and accept" that "in some states of the north of Mexico . . . we have come out of the electoral process bruised. Modern politics requires clean elections as well as the rejection of the old thesis of *carro completo*"[16] (in Cornelius, 1988, p. 15). The 1988 election results created, for the first time in Mexican history, the conditions for vigorous multiparty competition within the Congress and between the Congress and the president (Cornelius et al., 1988).

The surge of regional political opposition in the 1980s can be at least partly explained by the emergence of regional economic-technical-administrative structures in the Mexican states linked to the oil industry, prosperous irrigation districts, the maquiladoras, major industrial firms, and centers of tourism (Cornelius et al., 1988). These sectors, which function as regional power structures, are closely tied to the specific economic activities of their regions and are therefore less dependent on federal largess and political favors. Due particularly to the financial malaise of the national government over the last decade, these and other regional forces may be well positioned to step in when the federal government appears unable to address problems.

Another important development leading to greater decentralization is the difficult political and financial realities faced by the federal government in its attempts to manage the nation's water resources. As discussed above, the CNA was created in 1989 to coordinate the federal response to the nation's growing water problems. The focus of the CNA since its creation has been to take steps to lessen the paternalistic role of the federal government as supplier, donor, and benefactor of the country's water resources. Toward that end, the agency is proposing a much stronger role for water utilities based on cost-of-service fees and on the establishment of a single fund for water development combining federal, state, municipal, private, and foreign sources of revenue. The development fund is to be a decentralized system; funds will be disbursed at the state level, but coordination will be at the federal level to ensure "compliance with national standards, policies and objectives" (Comisión Nacional del Agua, 1990).

Under the CNA's proposed restructuring of water resources management, the states will plan and budget the development of water supply and sewerage services in their respective territories. In addition, they will provide technical assistance and support services to water utilities and other local organizations. The CNA produced a state water plan for Sonora in 1990. The plan provides a detailed listing of applicable laws and agencies, and describes Sonora's various water users by category. The plan is less forthcoming in discussing means of implementing the cost-of-service fees, expanding the available infrastructure, and empowering local water utilities. These shortcomings are particularly problematic given the strong tradition in Mexico of viewing water as a basic human right not tied to market considerations. Water use in Nogales is largely unmetered, and the local agencies have difficulty collecting payments for water service (see Chapter 3). Substantial infrastructure improvements, as well as consumer education, will be needed to implement an effective cost-of-service system.

An important presidential decree issued July 14, 1992, provides insight into these implementation questions. The decree establishes a new water commission for Mexico City mandated to optimize efficiency in the allocation of water, sewage treatment, and effluent reuse through the eventual privatization of existing water and sewage distribution systems. Private-sector entities will be encouraged to assume responsibility for maintaining the existing infrastructure, modernizing it, and improving its efficiency. Central to this plan is the private entities' ability to fix leaks, install meters, and successfully collect fees from users. Competition among private providers is to be based on least-cost service, with the more efficient operations winning the right to operate the system. The CNA anticipates that under this new structure it will receive higher payments for bulk water supplies, and the public will receive better service.

This market approach to water resources management is further emphasized by the national groundwater law published in 1992 and first implemented in 1993. Under this new law, the CNA must determine whether a groundwater basin is fully appropriated; if it is, no new permits can be issued. Instead, new users are required to buy already issued permits from existing users. This change in the law, which superimposes a market system over the complex permit system that has long existed under Mexican water law, will take many years and much administrative effort to fully implement.

It is difficult to foresee where the trend toward decentralization of water management in Mexico will end, or how decentralization will be implemented. It is clear, however, that the time has arrived to empower state (or possibly even newly created local) agencies to manage water resources more effectively and efficiently. With greater administrative latitude and new authority to assess, impose, and keep utility fee revenues, nonfederal agencies will have a real opportunity to improve water management in their communities.

In Sonora, water and sewerage services are provided by COAPAES, a state-level organization that receives "subsidies" from the CNA, an arm of the federal government. In actuality, the operation is somewhat more labyrinthine than this simple statement implies. The CNA gives permission to COAPAES to drill and operate wellfields. COAPAES produces the water and delivers it in bulk to municipalities. The price of the water is based on the cost of the infrastructure used for delivery, infrastructure that has most likely been subsidized by CNA loans. COAPAES passes this price on to the municipalities, which in turn pass on the cost to rate payers, who pay at COAPAES offices. Since little revenue is actually collected—many rate payers simply do not pay their bills—the municipalities, COAPAES, and the CNA negotiate to set future water prices.[17] Because water was until recently considered a right in Mexico, nonpayers could not be cut off; the worst sanction that could be applied was a reduction in the flow to nonpayers' dwellings (Irasema Coronado, COLEF-Nogales, pers. comm., 1993).

Operations within Nogales are controlled by a local affiliated office that retains the revenues collected but is directed from Hermosillo. Whether decentralization trends ultimately result in analogues to the Nogales, Ariz., Water Department (an independent municipal utility) or a private water supply–sewerage company (or companies) in line with the New Privatization Decree of July 14, 1992, for Mexico City (discussed above) remains to be seen. Whichever route is chosen, the salient point is that jurisdiction over the water supply and sewerage systems should devolve from federal- and state-level institutions to the local level and to local utilities.

The View from COAPAES, Nogales

Silberio Ruiz is the administrator of the Nogales office of COAPAES. He strongly believes that COAPAES is doing the best it can under difficult, perhaps impossible circumstances. In an interview, Ruiz outlined his thoughts and perceptions concerning the problems with which COAPAES has had to contend.

Rapid growth is occurring all along the northern border of Mexico, especially in Nogales, and current estimates project that the population of Nogales will reach 220,000 by the year 2012. During a shorter span, from 1970 to 1974, the Nogales population grew from 50,000 to almost 100,000 inhabitants. Naturally, the explosive growth affected all the municipal public services, including water and sewage. Government officials strove year after year to contend with such fast growth, but ultimately this proved impossible. When COAPAES examined its position, it found itself facing a very serious credibility problem and a vicious circle. People who were not supplied with adequate water refused to pay their bills, but the resultant lack of revenue prevented COAPAES from extending its services. Faced with those circumstances, COAPAES opted to communicate with the whole community, asking individuals to pay their debts. Through almost daily communication COAPAES was able to break the circle. More payments were made, more water was supplied, more income was derived, more sewage was generated, more teams were created to help communities, and more leaks were repaired. Now, for the first time in Ruiz's memory, Nogales has enough water for all. "But of course, the water problem is very complex. Today, we have the water, but not what's next: conduction, distribution, storage, etc. We are working on that. And I can tell you that now, even though there are deficiencies, we are getting the water to almost the whole town."

The available statistics appear to substantially support this statement. In 1992, 80 percent of the total population was supplied; this had increased to 85 percent in 1993. In 1990 the supply rate was 90 liters per second; in 1991, after state elections when new management took charge, the supply rate improved to 490 liters per second; in 1993, the supply rate increased to more than 700 liters per second. In 1991 there were 14,000 metered users; by late 1993 this number had increased to 22,000. The number of hours per day that water is supplied has also increased. Ruiz believes that the main sewage collector network is spatially adequate but concedes that parts of the system need to be replaced. Currently the thrust is to connect households to these collectors. The other major change involves legislation passed in September 1993 that permits COAPAES to completely shut off the water to households that refuse to pay their water bills.

Ruiz, like Dr. Enrique Davis, believes that Nogales, Ariz., is overstating the amount of sewage emanating from Mexico: "What's been happening is that those who want to set up borders, barriers, lines, bridges, fences, between one individual and another, between one country and another, between one world and another, do not know yet how to erect barriers across the environment, and do not recognize that ecological and environmental issues are common problems." He blames the chemical contamination in Nogales Wash on the U.S. producers who ship the material to Mexico and says it is shortsighted to then place all the blame on Mexico, although he "supposes" that the maquiladoras discharge chemicals directly into the wash ("out of 74 maquiladoras, there are 49 that could be contaminating"). COAPAES has initiated a program to inventory all industries and all possible sources of contaminants and is in the process of compiling a list of all industrial establishments that might be sources of contamination, classifying them, and plotting them on a city map. The goal is to get individual establishments to pretreat their own discharge before it reaches the sewage system. For maquilas specifically, the goal is removal of toxic substances such as mercury and chrome from the waste stream.

Addressing income and financing, Ruiz stated that COAPAES now collects enough revenue to operate the water supply system. The state government has lent equipment and provided economic resources to augment the water supply. The water supply and wastewater systems need reorganization, but there are insufficient local or state funds for that, so COAPAES must seek bank credits for all the required services. With the state government's intervention, the bank credits are usually acquired. Although COAPAES collects sufficient revenue to operate the water supply system, it is currently unable to cover its monthly loan payments to the banks.

Ruiz claims that COAPAES's relationship with SEDESOL is very good and that they are in constant contact. SEDESOL, from its own resources, invests capital in water supply and sewage treatment. Ideally, COAPAES and SEDESOL should work on common problems cooperatively. In the state government, COAPAES works with the office of the Secretary of Urban Infrastructure and Ecology, both for investments and for ecological problems. Ruiz characterizes the relationship as very good and believes that without this state-level support he would not have been able to achieve the radical changes that have occurred in Nogales. "Excuse me if I say this, but the change is noticeable. And we are still not satisfied."

The Path toward Decentralization and Shared Goals

In order to take full advantage of the decentralization trends in federal water management in Mexico, local communities will need special help, both in developing administrative capabilities and in making essential infrastructure improvements. The federal government cannot be expected to provide adequate funds to local utilities to make them more effective. With the existing substantial deficits in infrastructure, privatization of the utilities will be a slow and arduous process. Border communities, with their special international status and closeness to their more prosperous U.S. neighbors, may be better positioned to take advantage of trends toward decentralization than cities in the interior of Mexico.

Major improvements in the water system would bring water service in border communities like Nogales, Son., closer to the standards of their U.S. neighbors across the line, but still not to parity. It is clearly in the interests of both sides to narrow the existing gap in quality of water service and sewage disposal. A more reliable water service would greatly enhance the quality of life for Sonoran residents. For residents of Arizona, better water delivery and sewage retrieval systems in Sonora would make it easier to control contaminants flowing into the United States, an issue of great concern to Arizonans (see Chapter 4). Future water supplies are also a matter of concern to residents on both sides of the border. Both communities are sinking new wells and moving into new areas to acquire water supplies; neither coordinates these activities with its sister city, although they share the same resource. Nogales, Ariz., must try to plan its own future water supplies without knowing what its much larger neighbor to the south will be doing to meet its water needs. Better management and information exchange would make it easier for both communities to plan for the future.

These shared goals and common interests cannot result in joint action and formal cooperation, however, without an effective binational institution that has jurisdiction on both sides of the border. In the absence of a binational institution, joint actions must either remain informal (nongovernmental) or pass through formal federal diplomatic channels, both of which have obvious limitations. In order to be able to share information, distribute funds, and plan jointly across the border, the two sovereign nations must cede jurisdiction to a binational body.

Two formal agreements between Mexico and the United States authorize certain kinds of joint action along the U.S.-Mexico border. The first is the treaty and related law creating the International Boundary and Water Commission (IBWC). The commission, formed of U.S. and Mexican sections (the Mexican arm is the Comisión Internacional de Limites y Aguas, CILA), has jurisdiction over boundary waters and related issues. The IBWC traditionally has had a central role in U.S.-Mexico border water resource matters, including the negotiations relating to the establishment of the international wastewater treatment facility in Nogales, Ariz. The other existing binational agreement between Mexico and the United States is the La Paz Agreement of 1983, also known as the Reagan–de la Madrid Accord. The La Paz Agreement focuses on a broader area than the IBWC; it extends to *all* border environmental issues. Unlike the IBWC, which was created by a formal treaty between the two countries, the La Paz Agreement is only an executive agreement between presidents. The La Paz Agreement designates the U.S. EPA and the Mexican Ministry for Social Development, SEDESOL, as the coordinating agencies for the two countries in implementing the agreement.[18]

The following discussions of the IBWC and the La Paz Agreement analyze these border institutions from the perspective of Ambos

Nogales. We will consider the legal mandates and past performances of these institutions in handling water and environmental issues in Ambos Nogales and other border communities. Our objective is to assess the future efficacy of these institutions in addressing the water and other environmental issues now facing the U.S.-Mexico border region. In so doing, we will bear in mind the needs of local officials such as Pat Zurick, who must cope with the complex problems associated with international trade, border industrialization, and rapid population growth.

The IBWC:
Hope for the Future or Outdated Institution?

The IBWC has a 50-year history in water management along the U.S.-Mexico border. Its institutional predecessor, the International Boundary Commission (IBC), was created by the Convention of 1889 to delineate the boundary between Mexico and the United States. The IBC was involved in water matters from the beginning because nearly two-thirds of the boundary between the two countries was defined by the Rio Grande/Río Bravo and the Colorado River, whose courses and banks have shifted over time. With the Water Treaty of 1944, the newly created IBWC's primary mandate became water management, including water allocation and flood control responsibilities for the boundary waters of the Rio Grande and the Colorado River.

The IBWC is an institution designed to facilitate joint action while protecting national sovereignty. It has two national sections, each with a commissioner (who must be an engineer), a chief engineer, legal counsel, and a secretary. Each section represents its own country and is responsible to its own government. The treaty gives each section of the IBWC jurisdiction only within its respective country and subjects any action by the IBWC to the concurrence of both governments. The U.S. section operates as part of the State Department, and the Mexican section is part of the Mexican Foreign Ministry. In essence, each section operates as technical adviser on border water problems and as operational field agent for the construction and management of water-related projects for their respective federal governments.

Although the two sections of the IBWC act jointly, each develops its negotiating position through the political processes of its own country. The IBWC thus facilitates parallel national action on water-related problems between Mexico and the United States. Although different from (and preferable to) unilateral action in response to shared problems, the parallel national actions undertaken by the IBWC do not constitute true binationalism.

Nevertheless, the IBWC has acquired a reputation as an effective diplomatic and administrative agency in a world with few examples of institutionalized transboundary cooperation. The IBWC and its predecessor have officiated for more than a century over the peaceful settlement of boundary and water disputes between Mexico and the United States. Much of the commission's success has derived from its low visibility; it is an institution that usually operates at elite governmental levels far from the public limelight.

In the United States, the IBWC has served the constituency needs of members of Congress by constructing projects that are visible symbols of the member's ability to "bring home the bacon" from Washington. The IBWC has insulated itself from political controversy by interpreting its jurisdiction narrowly and sharply delimiting its formal functions (Mumme, 1984). Further, the IBWC has always emphasized the technical aspects of its mission. It has enjoyed a virtual monopoly over border resources data acquisition and planning through its role, under the 1944 treaty, as the formal conduit of information for communicating the desires and intentions of each country with respect to border water problems. Its special relationship with Congress has enabled the IBWC to remain quasi independent of the State Department.

CILA, the Mexican section of the IBWC, has tended to be much more closely aligned with the Mexican Foreign Ministry (Secretaría de Relaciones Exteriores) than the U.S. section is with the State Department. As such, it has been insulated from political constituency pressures in the border region as well as pressure from other federal and state agencies (Sánchez, 1993). Although CILA also has a very technical, engineering focus, it is even more constrained than the U.S. section to follow formal diplomatic channels in defining its role and permissible actions.

In recent years, both sections of the IBWC have been criticized for their failure to address problems proactively (before they become critical), for their conservatism in responding to environmental issues, and for the closed nature of their planning, operational, and information-gathering functions (Mumme, 1992; Sánchez, 1993). The reluctance of both sections of the IBWC to allow the public, NGOs, and state and local governments to participate in their decision-making processes has occasioned strong criticism from scholars and activists (Mumme, 1992; Sánchez, 1993). Pat Zurick's experience with the IBWC at the outset of the 1990 Nogales sewage crisis was consistent with these criticisms, although the IBWC did eventually become actively and publicly involved in remediating the Nogales Wash sewage situation.

Ambos Nogales and the IBWC

The sewage crisis of 1990, however, was only one in an extended series of water "crises" that have plagued this border community. In fact, for more than 50 years the city of Nogales, Ariz., has looked to the IBWC and to its congressional delegation to solve its flooding, drainage, and wastewater problems. In 1931, for example, in response to fatal damaging floods, the mayor of Nogales wrote to Congressman Lewis Douglas and Senator Carl Hayden asking that the governments of the United States and Mexico take steps to eliminate the flood hazard facing the two cities.[19] In turn, the Arizona members of Congress contacted Secretary of State H. L. Stimson, who replied that U.S. Commissioner Lawson would visit Ambos Nogales soon with his Mexican counterpart and suggested that the congressmen advise Arizona's governor of the impending IBWC investigative trip.[20] The eventual results of this and other meetings were a series of storm drains, channels, and flood control conduits aimed at keeping the water within its banks on both sides of the border. But these measures had an unintended consequence: the storm water collectors and channels facilitated the flow of water—and contaminants— across the boundary even during normal flow conditions. Flood hazards were mitigated, but the stage was set for a new kind of crisis: cross-border sewage contamination.

During the following decade, sewage problems did indeed become a priority for Nogales officials, as demonstrated by the papers of Senator Carl Hayden. Nogales city officials contacted their congressional delegation and the U.S. commissioner directly, and state officials became involved only when they were asked to provide supporting documentation. A sanitary engineer at the Arizona Department of Health hurriedly prepared a report on sanitary problems in response to a telegram signed by the entire Arizona congressional delegation and submitted the report directly to the U.S. commissioner. Because the situation the engineer observed in 1946 so closely parallels the state of affairs experienced in 1990 by Pat Zurick, it is useful to quote at length from his report:

> The twin cities of Nogales, Arizona and Nogales, Sonora should be considered, from a public health standpoint, as a single community, for the only line of demarcation between the two communities is the international boundary line. Nogales, therefore, for the purpose of this report, has an over-all population of 30,000. Imports, exports, and tourists are the principal industries of this community. As far as the boundary line is concerned, the local population goes back and forth routinely. Food is purchased from sources on both sides of the line for use in either one or the other or both communities. . . . Of this population of approximately 30,000 only 25% is sewered, and this chiefly in Nogales, Arizona, with only a few down town business houses in Nogales, Sonora connected to a short special sewer line which terminates in the Nogales, Arizona system. Nogales, Arizona, considered by itself is practically 100% sewered. Considering Nogales, Sonora, disposal in this community is chiefly by means of insanitary outdoor privies. . . . Occasionally in the past it has been noted by local health authorities that domestic sewage has been drained directly into the international storm drain. . . . The situation then is this, that the sewage disposal south of the border is on top of an impervious rock foundation permitting, during the rainy season at least, drainage of contaminating material to the storm drain, and down the streets on both sides of the line toward the Santa Cruz River. This, of course, creates a definite public health hazard to the popu-

lation on both sides of the line of this important community....
The principal source of water for both sides of the line has been
the Nogales, Arizona water plant and system which has a pumping
rate of approximately 750 gallons per minute. The majority of this
water is used on the United States side of the line. South of the
line, water service lines are not extensive. The consumption of
water in Nogales, Sonora is at the present time at a minimum
because of the lack of adequate water service systems at all homes.
Here again the down town business houses are the principal consumers. The majority of the public obtain their water for domestic
use in buckets. The picture, however, will change, for the water
project south of the line [which included several wells and the
original infiltration gallery at the Santa Cruz River] is at this writing 50% completed.... Here again a sanitary problem will be aggravated in that water consumption will be definitely increased
because of the installation of water facilities, resulting in the production of a tremendous amount of liquid waste in comparison
to that in existence up to now. (Arizona Department of Health,
"Report: Sanitary Sewage Disposal Problem," pp. 1–5)

The state engineer further pointed to the adverse health effects
these sanitary problems were having in 1946. Several cases of typhoid
and dysentery had been reported in Santa Cruz County, and the
numbers of such illnesses rose during the rainy season. The report
included a statement that the Arizona Department of Health had for
some years been advocating "a single sewerage system and disposal
plant [for the entire town] which would most efficiently and economically handle the situation." The report concluded, "[It] is ur-
gently recommended that since this apparently is an international
problem as well, that adequate means be provided to effectively solve
the situation."[21]

The strength of the ties between the congressional delegation,
local officials, and the U.S. section is illustrated vividly by the state
sanitary engineer's report. Clearly, the state was being asked to provide reasons for something that the congressional delegation and the
U.S. section of the IBWC had already decided to support. Through its
reference to the situation as an "international problem," the letter

also helps to explain why local officials sought aid through the congressional–U.S. section connection.

The 1946 report said that for most purposes, Ambos Nogales should be considered a single community with open communication. And while the IBWC had previously been asked to help with flood control, the two communities had jointly solved a number of other water-related issues without outside help. As the letter indicates, at the time the two communities had a single water supply system serving downtown businesses and other residents. Further, many of these same businesses were connected to the Nogales, Ariz., wastewater treatment plant. These modes seem to have been worked out without resort to international decision making and without seeking the permission of higher authorities. In sum, then, there have been instances when the existence of an international boundary has not prevented the implementation of binational responses forged at the local level.

Representing community water issues as international issues provided advantages far beyond the facilitation of cooperation and agreement, which the Nogales community appeared quite capable of forging on its own. The involvement of the IBWC and U.S. congressional appropriations committees generated a direct pipeline of funds running from the U.S. Treasury to Ambos Nogales. The availability of federal funds meant that the city of Nogales, Ariz., did not need to compete with other Arizona communities for scarce wastewater treatment project funding. The funds also made it possible to deflect a large portion of the costs to U.S. taxpayers. A 1949 letter from the commissioner of the U.S. section of the IBWC to Senator Hayden after U.S. funding for the proposed wastewater treatment project had been secured acknowledges the roles of Congress, Nogales, Ariz., and the IBWC in the funding process:

> My Dear Carl:
> You will recall that through your good offices there was set up an item in the Boundary Commission appropriations for what is known as the Nogales Sanitation Project, located in Nogales, Arizona and Nogales, Sonora.
> The project consists of the building of an outfall sewer ex-

tending from a point in Mexico to a point in the United States about two miles north of the boundary line, and a disposal plant located in the United States at the northerly end of the outfall line. The sewerage from both of the collecting lines to be built in Mexico and from the existing collecting lines with the United States will enter the outfall sewer and be conveyed to the disposal plant. The slope of the topography is from Mexico to the United States, and therefore the outfall line and treating plant must be located in the United States. It is estimated that the total cost of the works will be around $400,000, of which fifty percent will be allocated to each nation. . . .

You may be interested I am sure, of the official notice that we have received from the Mexican Section of this Commission, that arrangements have been completed whereby funds needed for Mexico's contribution have been made available for this Section of the Commission. Accordingly, I have instructed the engineers of this Section to complete the plans for the project in order that construction may be begun at an early date. . . .

You and all concerned, including the Arizona delegation in Congress as well as the officials of the City of Nogales, are to be congratulated for making funds available to this Section for the successful working out of this problem, the solution of which is so necessary to the health of both cities of Nogales.[22]

The U.S. Congress–U.S. section funding conduit was to prove valuable for more than just the construction phase of the wastewater treatment project. The costs of operation and maintenance were originally to be a local obligation split between the cities of Nogales, Ariz., and Nogales, Son., in proportion to each city's share of the effluent. Even before the new plant became operational in 1951, the mayor of Nogales, Ariz., urged Senator Hayden to find some means to help the city defray its operating costs. An arrangement for partial federal funding of local operation and maintenance obligations had previously been worked out by Senator Hayden and the IBWC for a wastewater treatment project in the nearby border cities of Douglas, Ariz., and Agua Prieta, Son., and Senator Hayden was able to push similar legislation through Congress for the benefit of Nogales, Ariz.

The solutions offered by the IBWC and funded by Congress were structural, engineering ones. The U.S. commissioner explained to Senator Hayden that the commission "is now and has been for some time, set up on an engineering basis. This is necessary since the problems which are encountered along the international border require engineering solutions."[23] The engineering solutions offered by the IBWC were employed by the city of Nogales again and again, as mounting problems regularly outstripped previous solutions.

By 1958, just seven years after the first international wastewater treatment facility was completed, raw sewage was again common in Nogales Wash. At first the contamination was the result of the infiltration of groundwater into leaky sewer pipes rather than sewage generated in excess of plant design. The severity of the crisis varied according to rainfall. By 1963, following increased population growth and attendant increases in the amount of sewage produced by the two cities, the plant's design capacity was being continuously exceeded and raw sewage was being bypassed into Nogales Wash. The IBWC recommended constructing a new, larger wastewater treatment facility farther north of the border, as requested by the city of Nogales, Ariz.

Negotiations for the new facility were prolonged, and the U.S. section was slow to act despite prodding from Arizona's congressional delegation. While the city's past successes in obtaining help from the IBWC held open the possibility of both action and funding, neither came easily. In 1966, eight years after the first reports of sewage being bypassed by the treatment plant, a state health official informed the Federal Water Pollution Control Administration that such reports had become increasingly frequent and that there had been no indication from the IBWC as to when concrete action would be taken: "We recently requested the International Boundary and Water Commission to provide facilities to at least chlorinate the raw sewage when it is bypassed until new facilities are provided. We have just received a reply from Mr. Friedkin [U.S. commissioner] stating they have no funds which can be expended for this purpose, and it is the responsibility of the City of Nogales, Arizona to provide this treatment." The health official expressed frustration that he could not deal directly with his Sonoran counterparts and asked that the

Federal Water Pollution Control Administration either use its influence with the State Department or take action itself. Things, he said, were very frustrating because everything had to be routed through the IBWC.[24]

Mexico and the United States finally reached an agreement in 1967. IBWC Minute 227 provided for construction of an enlarged international wastewater treatment plant 14.5 kilometers (9 miles) north of the border, together with a new trunk line to carry the sewage the additional distance. Sixty percent of the new plant's capacity was allocated to Mexico, but Mexico was asked to pay only the amount that would have been necessary to expand the plant at the existing site, which amounted to 29 percent of the total cost of the project. Forty-six percent of the cost was borne by the IBWC's U.S. section, 17 percent by the city of Nogales, Ariz., and 8 percent came from other U.S. federal funds.

The new facility was completed in 1971. By 1976, the need for further expansion was already evident, and again the planning, design, and negotiations for enlarging the facility were lengthy and tortuous. In 1986, the U.S. section made a formal proposal to the Mexican commissioner suggesting that both countries expand the plant. The Mexican section replied that it preferred to use its money to build a new plant on its own side of the border. U.S. interests were very much opposed to that idea because of concerns about delays in such construction and the manner in which the plant would be operated. In 1988, the Mexican section was convinced to sign IBWC Minute 276, which required Mexico to repair leaking sewer lines and build new lines on its side of the border, and to join the United States in paying for another expansion of the international wastewater treatment plant. Mexico agreed to pay $1 million for plant expansion in 10 equal annual installments; Nogales, Ariz., agreed to pay more than $3 million, the U.S. section of the IBWC agreed to pay $5.9 million, and the EPA agreed to pay $1.7 million.

The expansion began in 1989, but history repeated itself as the rapidly expanding waste stream exceeded the capacity of the enlarged plant even before the facility became fully operational. In addition, the treated effluent from the plant was not meeting Arizona water quality standards due to high levels of mercury, cyanide, and other pollutants that were presumably present because local industries were not pretreating their wastes. The future growth of Nogales, Ariz., was threatened when this failure to meet standards resulted in state action to suspend new sewer connections in the city, and plans to expand the facility by 10 percent were made almost immediately.

Now, however, the influence of the Arizona congressional delegation, which might be used to bring federal agency attention and federal funding to Nogales, is clearly on the decline. Democrats with seniority and the power gained through long tenure, such as Representative Morris K. Udall and Senator Dennis DeConcini, have chosen to leave the Congress. Republicans, including Representative Jim Kolbe and Senator John McCain, are as yet too junior to have much control over legislation and funding. Further, even if the delegation had influence, there is little reason to suppose the border would have a high priority. No single member of the House of Representatives has complete jurisdiction over the entire border region. For both Representative Ed Pastor, who replaced Congressman Udall and is a Democrat serving his second term, and Congressman Kolbe, the border is only a small part of their districts' geographical reach. While Congressman Kolbe has indicated great interest in some border matters, his major concern has been free trade.

The IBWC's involvement in the water supply problems of Ambos Nogales has not been as extensive as its participation in the areas of flooding, drainage, and sewage. In the 1950s, the IBWC did become marginally involved in water supply issues in Nogales when Mexico constructed municipal waterworks that Nogales, Ariz., feared would threaten its own water supplies. At that time, a number of Nogales-area interests asked the IBWC's U.S. section to investigate the possibility of negotiating an allocation agreement for the waters of the Santa Cruz River that would be similar to agreements dividing the flows of other transboundary rivers. The IBWC was reluctant to open such negotiations, for reasons made clear in a frank letter from the U.S. commissioner to Senator Hayden. The commissioner indicated that the United States was already using more than half of all the water derived from the joint U.S.-Mexico portion of the Santa Cruz River watershed, despite the fact that only 34 percent of the drainage area contributing that water is in U.S. territory. The commissioner felt that Arizona should be very careful about engaging in negotiations on the subject since the stronger legal arguments for increasing allocation levels were on the Mexican side.[25] In 1954, the U.S. commissioner's office issued a report urging that every effort be made to find a solution to the supply problem that could be implemented without an international agreement. Among the suggested possibilities were a pipeline to draw water from the Santa Cruz River before it first crossed into Mexico and a dam on the U.S. side near Nogales to catch and store the river's flood flows.[26]

Unlike the U.S. commissioner, local interests in Nogales, Ariz., expressed great interest in working out a binational solution between the two federal governments. At a high-level meeting in the offices of the Arizona Interstate Stream Commission that was attended by the U.S. commissioner, the chair of the Santa Cruz Water Users Association put forth the local view: "We also feel that it might be possible for our State Department to negotiate some sort of treaty with Mexico to put in a common water supply system for both cities . . . a common system of withdrawing and distributing the water, much as they have handled the sewage and flood control system which has worked fairly satisfactorily."[27]

To document similar Mexican interest, the chair of the association introduced a letter from the mayor of Nogales, Son., to the chairman of the Santa Cruz River Committee, which stated in part: "During my incumbency as Mayor of Nogales, Sonora, and in my present capacity, the future of our city's water supply has been and is one of my primary concerns. On many different occasions this matter has been the subject of informal exploratory discussions with interested friends in Nogales, Arizona. We have always agreed that the problem is a joint international one and that a joint solution between our respective federal governments would provide the most favorable solution."[28]

Despite the support of local interests, however, the international negotiations did not occur, for reasons aptly expressed by Governor Ernest McFarland of Arizona in the minutes of the same meeting: "When it comes to negotiating a treaty, it becomes a Federal and not a State matter. [U.S. section commissioner] Colonel Hewitt . . . gave us the definite impression that if we entered into a treaty we would get less than we now have.... If we're going to go into a general proposition whereby the Federal Government is going to give up something, it wouldn't be very good for Arizona."[29]

While no other serious attempts to allocate surface or groundwater supplies for Ambos Nogales have been recorded, water supply problems, especially in Mexico, have by no means abated. For example, control of the treated effluent that emerges from the Nogales International Waste Water Treatment Facility (NIWWTF), most of which is generated in Mexico, has become a more important issue with each enlargement of the plant. To Sonorans, the treated effluent represents a potential source of water for industrial processes and irrigation (COLEF, 1992). Across the border, Arizonans see the effluent flowing into the Santa Cruz River from the wastewater treatment plant as the sole source of water for a thriving riparian area. The water provides both an important habitat for wildlife and many recreational opportunities.

Since at least the early 1960s, the Mexican section of the IBWC has favored the idea of building a facility on its own side of the border to treat Sonoran wastewater. The idea is attractive to the Mexicans because the construction funds for such a project would be spent on their own side of the border, and siting the plant in Sonora would enhance opportunities to reuse the treated water in Mexico.[30] The U.S. section has strongly opposed these plans, which is one reason why negotiations between the two sections of the IBWC concerning wastewater issues in Ambos Nogales have taken so long. The U.S. section opposes a plant in Mexico in part for health considerations, because the slope of the valley, from south to north, would require the sewage to be pumped a considerable distance uphill to the proposed treatment plant. Breakdowns in the pumping plants, like those that occur frequently in the Sonoran water supply system, could lead to spills and renegade sewage flows across the border.[31] There are other reasons for the U.S. opposition as well: the U.S. section has argued in the past that "the enlarged plant constructed, operated and maintained in this country to provide complete secondary treatment and disposal in accord with the standards of the State of Arizona, would assure for the United States interests satisfactory solution of the serious border sanitation problem. An incidental advantage would be the retention of the treated sewage effluent in the United States for possible utilization."[32]

So far, the U.S. section has been successful in its ad hoc efforts to convince the Mexican section not to build a separate treatment plant, even though IBWC Minute 227 specified that Mexico is the owner of effluent generated from water south of the border. Should the Mexicans renew their efforts to reclaim the water instead of allowing it to flow to Arizona, the vital riparian habitat below the NIWWTF would be threatened. As of November 1993, the IBWC had not taken any initiative to negotiate a long-term agreement concerning water supplies.

The IBWC's Effectiveness in Ambos Nogales

It is clear that even after 50 years of trying, Ambos Nogales has been unable to transcend the problems dictated by its topography. Water continues to obey the law of gravity and run downhill, and in Ambos Nogales this results in contamination. The construction of wastewater treatment facilities consistently lags behind demand and is increasingly expensive. The depletion of the transboundary aquifer may eventually bring water shortages to Arizona as well as to Sonora. Should the Mexicans choose to reclaim their wastewater, a valuable riparian habitat will be lost. There is also evidence that the problems are worsening. Recent tests suggest the existence of a plume of chemical contaminants moving north from Sonora in the shallow and shared aquifer underlying Nogales Wash (Udall Center, 1993b).

Despite the broad jurisdiction of the IBWC, nothing approximating comprehensive, anticipatory water management has occurred in Ambos Nogales. The commission's solutions to problems have been engineering responses, and these have been implemented only after problems arise, not before. These remedial responses have not been sufficiently sensitive to the dynamics of economic and demographic change in the border region. The IBWC has not correctly anticipated the water and sewer needs of Ambos Nogales because it has not participated in the community's planning processes.

The advantages of locating the IBWC at the federal level where national economic planning and policy is made have not been fully realized. There is scant evidence that the IBWC has participated in water-related decision making; for example, it has not had the foresight to recognize the implications of the trade and industrialization policies that have attracted many Mexican workers to the border region. The IBWC is not a "team player" with other agencies in issues that have direct and important implications for water management in Ambos Nogales and elsewhere along the border.

Furthermore, the IBWC discourages grassroots, binational responses to shared problems. The natural tendency of the residents of Ambos Nogales to collaborate on important decisions is seldom either appreciated or reinforced by a federal agency that takes formalistic stands and keeps neighbors at arms' length. The two cities collaborate informally to fight droughts and fires, but when matters reach the federal level, the position of the U.S. section of the IBWC is aimed toward maximizing U.S. benefits, even if this undercuts Mexican interests. Often, as in the division of Santa Cruz River water described above, the U.S. federal position puts the Mexicans at a severe disadvantage.

It can be argued that the IBWC should at least try to build support and consensus for peaceful international solutions to problems. For this to occur, however, the agency must demonstrate public relations skills, environmental sensitivity, and openness to public participation. The 1990 sewage crisis in Nogales suggests that the IBWC is coming up short on all counts.

The IBWC responded to the 1990 events in Nogales very much as it had reacted in the past, despite the fact that the general public has become much more aware of and concerned about the environmental and health effects of water contamination. While the press and local officials recognized this rise in public consciousness and reacted appropriately, the IBWC appeared to be both deaf and blind. The members of Arizona's congressional delegation withdrew their support from the IBWC and instead involved themselves directly in the situation, often taking a more binational perspective than that espoused by the commission. They communicated with Mexican officials outside the IBWC framework. Senator John McCain, for example, wrote directly to President Carlos Salinas de Gortari of Mexico to appeal for his help. All of Arizona's congressional delegates took positions in favor of greater U.S. government involvement in preserving a clean border environment.

This increased congressional activism is not difficult to explain. The number of influential NGOs interested in the border and its environment has increased, partly as a result of the debate over the North American Free Trade Agreement, and legislators do not want their environmental records to be based on what they can accomplish through the usual channels with the IBWC. Further, congressional action on border projects has become politicized. Instead of being a typical pork-barrel constituency service, new wastewater treatment projects have become entwined in the free trade versus environment debate. The IBWC's reputation for nonpolitical professionalism turned out to have little practical value in securing funding for the proposed expansion of the NIWWTF in 1991.

The IBWC is impeded from displaying greater environmental sensitivity by the narrow definition of its mission. It appears doubtful that regulatory solutions and planning can be avoided if border environmental health is to be protected, and yet it seems that the U.S. section is unlikely to rise to the challenge. Unfortunately for the IBWC, the Ambos Nogales experience suggests that merely adhering to standard operating procedures is no longer sufficient to deflect criticism. If flexibility, sensitivity to public relations, and heightened environmental consciousness are the qualities that will be necessary to address border water problems in the future, then the U.S. section's recent responses to the problems in Ambos Nogales indicate that the agency will continue to fail to respond appropriately. This should not be surprising; established bureaucracies do not easily or quickly change their organizational perspectives and standard operating procedures (Hogwood and Peters, 1985).

The La Paz Agreement: Adequate Basis for Binational Action?

As the inadequacies of the IBWC have come to light, border scholars and activists have paid increasing attention to the La Paz Agreement. Formally designated the Agreement Between the United States of America and the United Mexican States on Cooperation for the Protection and Improvement of the Environment in the Border Area, the La Paz Agreement was signed by Presidents Ronald Reagan and Miguel de la Madrid in 1983 and is therefore also known as the Reagan–de la Madrid Accord. The La Paz Agreement was negotiated in response to enhanced public attention to and concern over the significant environmental problems resulting from the rapid industrialization and urbanization of the border region and the perception that these problems were not being adequately addressed by either government.

The La Paz Agreement is largely symbolic and aspirational rather than substantive and institutional. Executive-level agreements such as this one, unlike treaties, do not require the U.S. Senate's approval and do not have the same force of law as treaties. The agreement calls for cooperation between the countries to solve environmental problems of mutual concern in the border area. Suggested methods for cooperating and linking the countries' efforts include the coordination of national programs, scientific and educational exchanges, environmental monitoring and impact assessment, and periodic exchanges of information and data on sources of pollution. The La Paz Agreement has no timetables for action, commits no funds, and delegates no power to permit binational action or enforcement. Nor does it create an institutional structure to implement its terms other than to designate the EPA and SEDUE (since replaced by SEDESOL) the national coordinators responsible for monitoring implementation. The two agencies are further mandated to hold at least one meeting each year to review implementation of the agreement, and they are permitted to convene meetings of experts to provide technical assistance. Each agency is also permitted, but not required, to include representatives of state and local governments in their meetings; and each is "responsible for informing its border states and for consulting them in accordance with their respective constitutional systems."

The La Paz Agreement provides for separate annexes to be negotiated in connection with specific common problems. To date, five annexes have been signed. Annex I, signed in 1985, required the IBWC to negotiate a solution to the Tijuana/San Diego sewage problems. It ultimately resulted in an agreement to construct an international wastewater treatment plant. Annex II, also signed in 1985, created the Joint Contingency Response Plan to manage the discharges of hazardous substances and oil spills across the border. Annex III, signed in 1986, established a framework for the regulation of transboundary shipment of hazardous substances. Annex IV, signed in 1987, limited the sulfur dioxide emissions from the Phelps Dodge copper-smelting plant in Douglas, Ariz., and the Mexican Cobre de Caridad copper smelter in Nacozari, Son. Annex V, signed in 1989, provided for coordinated evaluation and monitoring of air pollution sources in certain border cities.

These annexes, and the La Paz Agreement itself, have done little to foster binational action. They generally provide for consultation, notification, exchange of information, or other "coordinated" actions that are parallel and separate rather than binational in character. Deadlines, specific standards, and other leverage points that could have been built into the agreement to foster joint action were not included. Rather than resulting in a comprehensive set of commitments for addressing the full spectrum of binational environmental issues, then, the agreement and its annexes instead established a noncomprehensive, incremental approach to dealing with discrete problems (Mumme, 1992). The poor enforcement of the terms of the annexes has led many environmentalists to openly criticize the accord, further weakening its effectiveness. For example, although Annex III requires all industries importing chemicals to Mexico to ship back to the originating country any resulting chemical wastes, fewer than 1 percent of maquiladoras reported sending hazardous wastes back to the United States in 1988.[33] Border residents and environmentalists are particularly critical of the general lack of public representation and participation in the EPA's planning and decision-making activities under the agreement, and they oppose the restrictions placed on public access to information generated under the agreement (discussed below; see Mumme, 1992). Although the agreement provides for public participation and consultation with local border officials, it is permissive rather than mandatory. In practice, the EPA has a poor record when it comes to including representatives of state and local governments and NGOs in the various working groups that it has set up under the La Paz

Agreement (Richard Kamp, director, BEP, pers. comm., 1994). During the entire period between 1983 and 1990, no state or local officials were appointed to any of the working groups. In 1991 and 1992, with the emergence of NAFTA as a driving political force, the EPA appointed several state and local officials to the working groups, but NGO representatives still were not included. In addition to being limited in membership, the working groups' operation has tended to be formalistic and protocol-driven, offering little opportunity for public input (Richard Kamp, pers. comm., 1994).

Public participation is further limited by Article 16 of the La Paz Agreement, which provides that the United States and Mexico must mutually agree to the release to third parties of all technical information obtained through implementation of the agreement. This has substantially limited the availability of the technical information generated by the EPA and SEDUE/SEDESOL (Kelly, 1991). It is impossible for an effective clearinghouse of border information to be developed when either country can unilaterally and without limitation prevent the dissemination of joint technical data.

Ambos Nogales and the EPA

Unlike the IBWC, neither the EPA nor SEDESOL has a long history of involvement in the environmental problems of Ambos Nogales. The EPA has not been a presence in Nogales, and in fact has been reluctant to become involved in transboundary environmental problems in the border community even when directly implored to do so. During the 1990 sewage crisis, Pat Zurick and his colleagues wrote letters to the EPA requesting assistance with Nogales's transboundary pollution problems. Zurick waited weeks for a response; when it finally arrived, it was a letter disclaiming the agency's jurisdiction over the problem.[34]

Although seven years earlier, in 1983, the EPA had been designated the coordinating U.S. agency for border environmental problems, it had done little in the years since to establish an institutional presence on the border. There were no EPA representatives on the border, certainly not in Nogales. The agency never took steps to cultivate local contacts in Nogales, nor had it involved Nogales officials in any of its working groups or other activities conducted under the La Paz Agreement. When the EPA was asked to assist Nogales with water pollution problems in 1990, it had neither a plan for action nor the means to implement any solution. Under these circumstances, it was predictable that the EPA would avoid involvement.

When the neighboring, nonborder town of Patagonia objected to the EPA's seemingly hypocritical enforcement against it for much less egregious pollution discharges than those occurring in Nogales, Ariz., the EPA backed away from its tough stance against Patagonia. It is apparent, then, that the EPA had an effective, rigorous pollution enforcement program for nonborder communities but was not prepared to apply the same standards—or any standards—to border communities.

The difficulties associated with placing the responsibility for border environmental problems in a national regulatory agency became evident during the development of the Integrated Environmental Plan for the Mexico–United States Border Area (IBEP). The plan was developed in 1990–91 by the EPA in response to concerns about the presumed adverse environmental consequences of the proposed North American Free Trade Agreement. In order to dispel growing criticism of NAFTA by environmental groups, in late 1990 Presidents Bush and Salinas instructed their respective environmental agencies, EPA and SEDUE, to draft a joint plan for addressing environmental problems on the U.S.-Mexico border.

When the EPA released a preliminary plan some 10 months later, the agency was severely criticized on both procedural and substantive grounds. Procedurally, the EPA was chastised for its secrecy and aloofness in developing the plan, which was purportedly written by a consulting firm in Massachusetts under contract to the EPA.[35] Although the report was ostensibly cowritten with SEDUE, in fact the Mexicans did not even see the report until they were handed a completed draft of it in Mexico City. As many as five drafts of the report were produced before any draft was released to the public (Varady, 1992).

No input or review was sought from border residents until very late in the plan's development. Nogales was not even included in the plan until Santa Cruz County officials learned of the omission and complained to the EPA a month before the plan's release in August 1991. This exclusion was particularly surprising to Zurick and other local officials given the efforts they had made to involve the EPA in the Nogales Wash sewage problems and the repeated difficulties the city has had with the EPA over its failure to meet air quality standards.[36]

When the draft plan was finally released in August 1991, a highly structured process of public hearings was announced. A hearing was scheduled for Nogales, Ariz., on September 26, 1991, and similar hearings were scheduled for five other pairs of sister cities along the border, from Brownsville/Matamoros to San Diego/Tijuana. The EPA made no concerted effort to publicize the hearings, and many people claimed that they had been given little or no advance notice that a hearing was even to be held.[37] On August 16, local officials learned that the EPA had set stringent restrictions for participation in the hearing, including a requirement that 20 copies of any written testimony must have been sent to Washington, D.C., at least four weeks before the hearing, and another 30 copies must be brought for distribution at the hearing. In response to strong public objections, this four-week requirement was later reduced to three weeks. Remarks at the hearing were limited to five minutes per person, and the seating capacity of the hearing room was woefully inadequate for the 140 local people who attended the hearing on September 26. The time allotted for the hearing was too short for the limited remarks of even the 40 people who qualified to speak.[38]

By the time the round of hearings on the draft IBEP had ended, the EPA was besieged with criticism. Not only were border residents indignant over the exclusion of their views during the drafting of the plan, many also resented the manner in which public hearings and public comment had been handled by the agency. Moreover, the substance of the plan raised even greater concerns. During the hearings and in prior and subsequent communications to the media, border scholars, officials, and activists alike criticized the plan's shortcomings. Of particular concern was its lack of specificity, most notably in procedural and financial recommendations. Despite its length (200 pages), the draft contained no analysis of how needed infrastructure and other proposed solutions would be paid for, or how solutions to growing environmental problems would be shared equitably between the United States and Mexico. Nor did it address the troubling nonurban environmental problems in the border region, ones affecting national parks, wildlife sanctuaries, and other protected and rural areas. In spite of its trade-related impetus, the IBEP contained no explicit discussion of the anticipated impacts of NAFTA, or of what should be done to address those impacts.

An Evaluation of the EPA and SEDESOL as Binational Actors

Given the history of the implementation of the La Paz Agreement, the handling of the IBEP should not have surprised anyone. During the entire period since the agreement was signed, there has been little cooperation between the EPA—the designated coordinator of the agreement—and other federal agencies, let alone state or local agencies. The working groups established by the EPA meet infrequently and are largely unrepresentative of border interests. With no defined role or mandates, the working groups have not produced implementable plans or programs for dealing with border environmental problems.

When the EPA and SEDESOL were charged in November 1990 to develop a plan for dealing with border environmental problems, they had but a few months to accomplish what they had been unable to do in the previous seven years.[39] As a substantive exercise, the IBEP was vague and nonthreatening, lending little insight into the problems it was supposed to address. But even as a procedural, symbolic exercise the plan failed to accomplish its mandated goal of coordination and cooperation. Input from Mexican officials was solicited after the fact rather than allowing them to share in the plan's development. By essentially excluding border residents, environmental groups, and local officials from the process, the EPA lost any opportunity to gain supporters for its plan and to defuse opposition to NAFTA.

In its defense, one could argue that the EPA's record as coordinator of the U.S. response to border environmental problems reflects its own mission and priorities. The agency was created to deal with the myriad environmental issues facing the United States. As a regulatory agency, it has an enforcement mentality that does not easily translate into cooperative decision making and shared responsibility. In pursuit of its mission, the EPA has developed expertise in "top-down" standards setting and rule promulgation but has little experience in "bottom-up" planning and implementation strategies. The problems and needs of the border region do not fit neatly or easily into the kinds of activities the EPA routinely handles. Beset by other pressing issues, and with responsibility for the entire country, the EPA has been, perhaps, understandably remiss in addressing the special needs of the U.S.-Mexico border region.

Local border officials trying to cope with the many water resource and environmental problems facing their communities encounter a number of jurisdictional dividing lines: they must sort through the various local, state, and federal agencies with partial and often overlapping authority to deal with particular issues; they must seek needed funding from state and federal legislators; and they must work with the IBWC and the EPA when transboundary issues are involved. For local officials, these overlapping jurisdictional lines are barriers that retard action and impede accountability. Our review of the experiences of Nogales, Ariz., officials trying to address transboundary sewage contamination clearly points to the existence and evident impermeability of these barriers. And while many local officials of nonborder communities face similar frustrations, the special circumstances created by the international boundary amplify problems on both sides.

A binational institution that is appropriately aimed, well designed, and responsive would do much to overcome the barriers now faced by border officials trying to carry out their responsibilities. Such an institution could provide border residents with at least three elements critical for addressing border environmental problems: (1) information about the nature of the problems they face; (2) monetary resources and authority to act, or clear avenues to gain such authority and resources; and (3) political support from state and federal officials, and from the affected public, for proposed actions.

This chapter has demonstrated that the sole existing "binational" institutions—the IBWC and the La Paz Agreement—do not give border officials these critical elements. The two institutions have done little to build a border environmental database, nor have they enhanced local capacity to respond to problems. They have been slow to act and have done so only in response to crises rather than proactively. In excluding participation by local officials, NGOs, and the public in their decision-making processes, the IBWC, EPA, and SEDESOL have failed to develop broad political support for their programs, even among the residents such programs are meant to serve.

With the passage of the North American Free Trade Agreement, trade between Mexico and the United States will greatly expand. The increased trade and border activity will exacerbate water and other environmental problems in the border region. There is no certainty that the growth will be arithmetic rather than geometric. In the absence of an effective binational institution, border officials must continue to rely on informal contacts across the line and on ad hoc, piecemeal responses to comprehensive, interrelated problems.

Yet this is also a time of great opportunity. The debate over NAFTA has brought these issues onto the national political stage. Many local border officials are pressing for a greater voice in making decisions that affect the region. National environmental NGOs are pushing for a new institution that will be better able to address border environmental problems. The trends toward decentralization and privatization in Mexico provide local border officials with new opportunities to more efficiently and effectively operate and fund their local utilities. But this newfound independence will have little practical meaning if local Mexican officials do not get critically needed assistance in building infrastructure and management capability. When communities share transboundary resources, improvements on one side of the border invariably result in improvements on the other side as well.

The jurisdictional lines that divide border communities have left local officials largely powerless to comprehensively address the problems that threaten their communities' water resources. Binational institutions provide the promise of shared information, cooperative decision making, and joint action. While that promise has not yet been realized, the need for binational cooperation continues to grow. We explore this theme further in Chapter 6.

Chapter 6

Reinventing the Border
A Framework for Transboundary Water Management

Borders have powers of magnification. Problems, including pollution and poverty, become more difficult to solve at borders. Conflict or cooperation among neighbors along borders becomes conflict or cooperation among nations. At borders, trends appear in bold relief, making them easier to recognize and interpret. Chapters 1 through 5 explored the premise that the U.S.-Mexico border in general, and the border community of Ambos Nogales in particular, provides an optimum vantage point from which to observe the interplay of global forces. This chapter summarizes what has been learned and makes some suggestions for modifying decision making with regard to important transnational natural resource questions, particularly water.

Global Forces Revisited

Two major currents of change are sweeping the globe. The deterioration of the global environment is increasingly evident in the general depletion of natural resources, the widespread pollution of air and water, the fragmentation of ecosystems, and the toxification of soils. An international environmental movement is forming to oppose that trend. Not yet sufficiently powerful to stay environmental degradation, and at least partly in reaction to it, global environmental consciousness is on the increase. Evidence of environmental concern is emerging even in poor countries, where economic development is the primary concern. Further, the transnational impact of environmentally damaging action has prompted environmentalists in developed countries to take an interest in activities outside their own nations.

Nationalism, the second of the two global forces, is on the

increase. Previously subjugated peoples in various parts of the world are clamoring for political self-determination. The number of new nations is growing. At the same time that parts of the world are moving toward increased political differentiation, however, the dividing lines between some nations are becoming irrelevant as mutual dependencies and partnerships are developed through international trade. The trend toward global economic integration expressed in the North American Free Trade Agreement (NAFTA) and the General Agreement on Tariffs and Trade (GATT) limits the ability of the signatories to vent their nationalistic feelings through unilateral actions damaging to trade. The economic advances promised by increasingly open trade may make environmental protection affordable to lesser-developed nations. Even before the anticipated economic benefits take place, however, poor and disadvantaged populations in less-developed countries with lax environmental laws and/or implementation are being subjected to greater health risks as polluting businesses move in.

Binational and multinational agreements under which nations pledge to employ wise environmental practices have emerged as common strategies to deal with environmental degradation. In the case of NAFTA, an attempt was made to include protections against the adverse environmental effects of increases in polluting industries spawned by more open trade. Yet, just as governments seem to be increasing their ability to reach decisions at the international level, their capacity and will to implement laws in specific local contexts is diminishing. In many countries, including the United States, a wide gap exists between ambitious environmental legislation and its actual enforcement.

Among the major impediments to the implementation of national and international laws is growing resistance at the local level to directives from the top. Communities everywhere are demanding a voice in decisions that affect them. As central governments carry increasing levels of debt and are increasingly encumbered by slow and unresponsive bureaucracies, local people are turning to their own private and public institutions to solve problems. Such solutions are frequently at odds with federal goals and mandates.

Borders: Maelstroms or Bridges?

Nowhere on earth are contending forces so sharply in focus as at international borders. By their very nature, borders create stresses and contradictions. The growing scarcity of resources, especially fresh water, is highlighted when border conflicts erupt over water rights. A cry of alarm dependably comes from the nations on the receiving end of pollution of shared transboundary resources. Border economies are especially vulnerable to economic markets, and booms and busts are easily triggered by changes in international and national policies and politics. The legal substructure on which international environmental law is now being built is made up of long-standing customs and practices developed among neighboring nations to deal with shared interests.

The way contending trends sort themselves out on borders foreshadows future global directions. If environmental quality and economic development are made to occur in concert on borders, the achievement will be widely reproduced. If border residents can gain control of natural resources through making their own decisions and effecting their own destinies, grassroots democracy will spread elsewhere. Chapters 1 through 5 treat the U.S.-Mexico border and the border community of Ambos Nogales as a test case. We have seen that borders (1) separate problems from solutions, (2) create perverse economic opportunities, (3) aggravate perceived inequalities, (4) marginalize the interests of border residents during the policy-making process, and (5) erect barriers to grassroots problem solving. Each of these characteristics is clearly illustrated by the Nogales case, and each holds implications for border communities elsewhere.

But borders also can be effective bridges. Boundary zones are crucibles for binational and multinational cooperation on day-to-day issues. This chapter uses the Ambos Nogales case to illustrate the cultural, familial, and commercial linkages that exist on the border as they facilitate the resolution of conflict. Although in many ways these links have strengthened over time, the current demographic and environmental changes driven by global trends such as those just described provide new challenges. Whether the contending global trends will play out in such a way that the welfare of border populations is well served will depend in large measure on how border relationships and institutions evolve.

Never has there been a more favorable climate for institutional innovation on the U.S.-Mexico border. The usual wariness resulting from old injustices has diminished as a result of the new trade agreement. As much as any border community, Nogales is poised for change. The penultimate section of this chapter seeks to "reinvent the border" through a set of principles for transboundary water management that rely on the Nogales experience. We suggest that institutional innovation at the regional level is necessary, and we describe in general terms how changes, including those embodied in NAFTA, should be evaluated. Finally, the chapter returns to the issue of whether the bridging effect of borders can be sufficiently strengthened to overcome the many centrifugal and divisive forces that might otherwise overwhelm the best intentions.

Borders Separate Problems from Solutions

Political boundaries, whether domestic or international, often separate the location where problems are experienced from the location where the most effective and efficient solutions need to be put into place. When they are international, the lines frequently appear as gulfs that are enormously hard to bridge. The Ambos Nogales setting typifies this phenomenon.

Both the Santa Cruz and Nogales Valleys are bisected by the international boundary, and portions of each lie within the United States and Mexico. The many water problems experienced in the two valleys include flooding, drought, inadequate water supply, surface and groundwater contamination, and the disappearance of riparian habitat; we discuss these issues in Chapter 3.

Too often, the most frustrating aspect of dealing with an issue is that the most rational solution is not situated in the same nation that faces the brunt of the problems. For instance, from the perspective of securing a long-term water supply, wells that serve the region should optimally be located in the northern parts of the basin, where the water-bearing sediments are deepest. Yet, Mexicans have no alternative but to depend on shallow and vulnerable wells and expensive interbasin transfers. Flooding downstream would best be prevented by many small upstream structures that retain runoff water and by careful upstream land use planning that avoids erosion of hillsides. Unfortunately, Mexico, which has jurisdiction over upstream management, has failed to implement such a strategy, and the downstream areas are left with less effective and more expensive options such as the deeply carved, covered channels that have been constructed through the central parts of Ambos Nogales. Maintaining the water supply for riparian areas means that the upstream areas that produce the water must allow it to continue to flow. Surface flow and riparian vegetation in the Santa Cruz River is now almost entirely downstream of the Nogales International Waste Water Treatment Facility (NIWWTF), which treats effluent coming from, and by treaty belonging to, Mexico.

Because water flows downhill, the consequences of pollution tend to be felt in locations some distance from the area of origin. As is the case with flooding, the best location to address problems of water pollution is in Mexico, while residents of the United States have the greatest incentive to get the problems solved.

Comparable problems of floods and drought, groundwater overdraft, habitat reduction, and declining quality are manifest elsewhere along the U.S.-Mexico border as well. And as in Nogales, solutions are too often impeded by the misplaced locus of power and decision making. For instance, the habitat of endangered aquatic species in Organ Pipe Cactus National Monument in Arizona may be adversely affected by new wells developed to serve adjacent Mexican agriculture. In turn, Mexican agriculture in another location may be adversely affected by the lining of the All American Canal in California. The interconnectedness of hydrologic systems, which transcend political borders, is also characteristic of ecosystems, wildlife migration patterns, and the spread of noxious weeds and diseases affecting plants and animals, including humans. Thus, the anthropogenic internationalization of issues relating to physiographic resources and processes is accompanied by another political feature: the separation of problems and solutions. Both characteristics are artificial, and both usually aggravate already difficult situations.

Borders Create Perverse Economic Opportunities

The economic opportunities that exist at borders create a number of perverse incentives from a water management perspective. Border enterprises spring up and prosper because they can offer easy access to an item that costs more or is of lower quality on the other side. Because water is a small part of costs of production on borders, business locations will poorly reflect the scarcity of water. Competition among water users in arid lands to gain at others' expense is exaggerated at borders because restraint may simply mean surrendering the opportunity to use the dwindling resource. Restraint is especially unlikely when the forces of global economic competition reinforce the focus on immediate economic opportunities for profit.

If a border region of a developing nation has a potential for strong economic growth, the long-term consequences of overexploitation of shared transnational water resources are not likely to be viewed as much of an impediment. Today, every nation is forced to compete against every other nation within complex, linked blocs and networks. In our historical overview in Chapter 2, we noted that economic forces and central Mexican government policy have worked together to dictate an industrial boom along the border that has had serious consequences for the environment and water resources. Offers of tax advantages and the use of public infrastructure for a very low cost have specifically encouraged industry to locate along the border. The maquiladora program's major benefits to Mexico are the jobs the maquilas provide and the inflow of foreign currency. But while maquila operations employ large numbers of workers, they contribute a relatively small amount to tax revenues used for water distribution, sewers, schools, hospitals, and other public projects. The wages paid to the workers are so low that the taxes on them are relatively insignificant. In addition, maquila industries are structured so that the location of their taxable assets is often very far from the border cities in need of public infrastructure investment.

Global economic forces and border industrialization have greatly increased water resources management problems in Nogales. Maquilas now dominate the economy in Nogales, Son., where they employ 43 percent of the city's workforce. The many immigrants attracted by the newly created jobs have caused a marked population boom, particularly on the Mexican side. The only affordable housing close to workplaces for maquila workers in Nogales is in *colonias*, squatter settlements often perched precariously on hillsides. These settlements have poor drainage, abet erosion, aggravate monsoon flooding, and are a source of surface water pollution.

The colonias in Nogales, Son., have strained the water and sewer systems beyond their capacity. Chapter 3 describes how the difficult topography combined with too little investment in expansion and maintenance have resulted in an inadequate water supply and wastewater removal for many residents there. The original system was never designed to deal with so many people and such a large area. Finding enough water to pump into the system has also been a problem. The low pressure in the system, poor maintenance, and frequent outages have led to contamination of the water supply through sewage infiltration into leaky pipes. Efforts to extend sewer lines have not been matched by expenditures on upkeep, and poorly maintained sewer lines are subject to frequent breakages.

The Mexican government's desire to attract industry to the border by offering low wage rates, low utility costs, and low taxes is clearly an impediment to any rational user-pays water supply and sewerage system. Supplying services to rapidly built, unplanned housing in difficult terrain requires expensive engineering and is a strain on any self-financed water supply system, at least in part because the demand for new connections outstrips revenue from users. The lack of control over hookups makes matters even worse. An unknown but potentially large number of industries, businesses, and housing developments have managed to build their own water supply systems. The drilling of new wells is supposed to be regulated by the federal government, but there is a widespread perception that many wells are not registered. Further, maquila owners contribute little to the public coffers to fund water supply and sewerage systems to serve the factories and the workers attracted to them. Maquiladora factories pay payroll taxes, but because wages are low, the taxes are not substantial. Further, the taxes are collected by the national government and often are not returned to the states, which in any case may not invest them in water system maintenance.

The same perverse incentives that have caused water problems in Ambos Nogales also operate elsewhere. The border industrialization policy has encouraged population explosions in places such as Juarez, where irreplaceable groundwater is being mined, and Tijuana, where there are no adequate collection and treatment facilities to handle the additional waste loads. Perverse economic incentives also affect other natural resources in the border region. The demand for mesquite charcoal in the United States has led to widespread cutting of mesquite forests and ironwood trees in Mexico. The loss of these species does irreparable harm to birds and other wildlife as well as to the Seri, Native Americans whose exquisite ironwood carvings are one of their few accesses to the cash economy. Even though the cutting of live ironwood is prohibited in Mexico, the profits to be made from selling it appear to be overwhelming law enforcement capabilities (Nabhan and Carr, 1994).

These perverse incentives, though intrinsic and often unintentional, nevertheless constitute a palpable barrier to self-sufficiency. Water systems, expensive to develop and maintain, are particularly vulnerable to pressures from counterproductive financial incentives. As a consequence, problems with water systems continually outpace solutions. Border residents depend on infusions of money and expertise from distant decision makers to resolve local problems. Further, false signals are being sent to industry and residents relocating to the border that natural resources are limitless. Low costs and lack of effective regulations carry the wrong message about resource scarcity.

Borders Aggravate Perceived Inequalities

Fairness and equity, even more than efficiency, are key values associated with water management. Perceptions of inequity in the allocation of water from the Colorado River and Rio Grande have long plagued U.S. relations with Mexico. Inequitable access to and use of shared groundwater aquifers promises to be a matter of increasing controversy among border residents. In Ambos Nogales, residents on the two sides of the border, who share an aquifer and river basin, encounter inequalities in access to, quality of, and cost of water supply, as well as quite different levels of health risks. If such differences come to be perceived as unfair, they are bound to contribute to transboundary disputes.

As Chapter 3 describes, the water supply system in Nogales, Ariz., is generally well managed and has been upgraded to match the city's population expansion. Water is continually available at constant pressure. In contrast, residents of Nogales, Son., have limited access to the public water supply system, which is often unreliable, and are often obliged to find alternative means of supply. Some do what their counterparts in many developing countries do: they buy from water vendors and use bottled water. As a consequence, residents of Nogales, Son., actually pay more for less reliable, lower-quality water than their counterparts in Arizona. Further, as we document in Chapter 4, there are additional costs associated with waiting for, carrying, and boiling the water. The fundamental issue is whether such marked differences are acceptable among close neighbors whose lives and welfare are intertwined. Perceptions of injustice and unfairness would seem natural. Unfortunately, the disparity in service between the two Nogaleses is likely to widen rather than narrow. However responsive and flexible the water vendors are, money spent on private water vendors and bottled water is not invested in public water supplies and does not pay for upgrading the public water distribution system.

What is true for water undoubtedly applies as well to other aspects of environmental quality where access to shared resources is very unevenly distributed. Free trade, although it may be expected to diminish wage and price differentials between the two countries, will not eliminate such disparities unless a greater public investment is made. Of course, some of the resources necessary for increased public investment accrue to the United States through sales tax receipts from maquila workers, who spend a high proportion of their wages there, as well as from corporate profits taxable in the United States. The inequalities noted above will persist unless deliberate corrective measures are taken to bring greater equity in services and exposure to health risks resulting from pollution.

Borders Marginalize the Interests of Border Residents During the Policymaking Process

Borders delineate the areas furthest from the political center, marginalizing the concerns of border residents with respect to those who live closer to the center of power. The problems of border residents are regarded as not central and therefore of lesser concern in policymaking, and it is therefore hardly surprising that policies framed in national and state contexts are often at odds with border needs and priorities. Water managers on both sides of the border must deal with laws, institutions, and decision-making processes that are unresponsive, complicate their problems, and impede cooperation.

In Arizona, state water laws are written with the two largest metropolitan areas, Tucson and Phoenix, paramount; Nogales is an afterthought. The Arizona Groundwater Management Act establishes Active Management Areas (AMAs) in areas of critical groundwater overdraft. Users within the areas are subject to a number of restrictions. Nogales, Ariz., is included in the Tucson AMA; its Mexican counterpart, of course, is not.

Rather than place absolute pumping limits on Arizona cities, AMAs regulate per capita water use. The per capita water use in Nogales, Ariz., exceeds the established limits, and the city is thus under pressure to lower its per capita water use. One reason for the very high usage, however, is that the per capita figures do not include the estimated 40,000 or so people who cross the border each day from Mexico.

AMA mandates may obligate Nogales, Ariz., to take measures that will interfere with the informal means through which the city has tried to ease water problems in Nogales, Son. For instance, some Sonoran businesses located near the border have connections of historic origins to the Nogales, Ariz., municipal water supply system. Two of the three active accounts are large enough to appear on a list of the Nogales Water Department's 50 largest water customers. Public spigots in city parks and open access to private supplies provided by Nogales, Ariz., residents to neighbors, friends, and family from Sonora all increase the city's water consumption.

Nogales, Ariz., is often overlooked when federally funded projects come to Arizona. The relatively minor importance of the city to any member of the Senate or House of Representatives and the reduced seniority of the Arizona congressional delegation have further limited the city's access to public funds. Although the Central Arizona Project, a large-scale water transfer project bringing water from the Colorado River as far as Tucson, was initially planned to include Nogales, the high costs of construction and the poor benefit-to-cost ratio do not justify further extension. As Chapter 5 explains, in recent years Ambos Nogales has been unable to attract congressional support for additions to the NIWWTF.

The federal laws administered by the EPA were not fashioned with border circumstances in mind. For instance, the EPA requires a moratorium on the construction of new sewer lines to waste treatment plants that have exceeded their capacity. In 1991, such a moratorium was placed on new hookups to the NIWWTF, even though it was actions taken by the International Boundary and Water Commission (IBWC) that caused the overload. Similarly, the EPA has applied laws that hold large plants to stringent standards for pretreating effluent to remove heavy metals. Nogales, Ariz., officials have no control over the pretreatment practices of industries in Mexico, and, furthermore, a smaller plant that served only their own needs would not have to meet such strict standards. Reducing the degree of cooperation with Mexico in waste treatment is a tempting alternative to contending with the problems generated by federal regulations.

The needs of Nogales, Son., also seem to have been marginalized by the state of Sonora and the highly centralized federal system in Mexico, outlined in Chapter 5. Federal and state agencies are responsible for construction and operations, respectively, leaving minimal responsibilities for the local government. The investment of national funds in border water and sewer projects has increased, but it remains out of step with the government's pro-growth industrialization policies and lags far behind the growth of demand. The border is remote from Mexico City, which is the beneficiary of most of the public's concern about the deteriorating environment. With considerable fanfare (and often around election time) the president of Mexico visits the hinterlands to dedicate a new water project designed to resolve water issues, such as Nogales's water basin transfer project, completed in 1991. The expected improvement in service frequently fails to materialize.

Residents of Ambos Nogales complain that they had practically no input into the environmental plan that was supposed to be a joint product of the United States and Mexico during the NAFTA negotiations. Border residents are almost never informed of or involved in decisions made to control drug traffic along the border, even though those decisions greatly affect their lives. They were ignored by the General Services Administration during the long and costly upgrading of the downtown border crossing.[1] Similarly, both opponents and proponents of the erection of a steel fence to prevent neighborhood border crossings, and presumably to reduce crime, charged that they were not included in the decision-making process.[2] The marginalization characteristic of frontier zones also inhibits the ability of local grassroots organizations to pursue their constituents' interests.

Borders Erect Barriers to Grassroots Problem Solving

If official policies often ignore the interests of border residents, they can also directly inhibit bottom-up, grassroots problem-solving efforts. The Nogales experience shows that the two influences are not unrelated. In fact, it is the very maze of regulations, awkward institutional frameworks, and lack of official interest that inhibits and frustrates community-based action.

While border residents have strong reasons to search for understanding and cross-boundary agreements, they lack sufficient power to make good on any cooperative agreements they might negotiate. It is clearly in the interests of both sides in Ambos Nogales to narrow the existing gap in the quality of water service and sewage disposal. Reliable water service would greatly enhance the quality of life for residents of Sonora, and better water delivery and sewage collection systems in Sonora would make it easier to control contaminants flowing into the United States, an issue of great concern to Arizona residents.

Better management of the water supply and exchanges of information about planned projects would also benefit residents on both sides of the border. Both communities are sinking wells and developing new water supplies without coordinating their activities. The border creates a dividing line where issues of national sovereignty are paramount over the common interests and shared resources of border communities.

International treaties and agreements that represent the sovereign national interest as dictated by central governments may poorly reflect the needs and preferences of border people. Further, international agreements that depend on the political processes internal to national governments may fall short of achieving their goals precisely because they fail to consider local actors whose behavior will determine the extent to which the laws are implemented.

Incentives for national and international institutions generally do not reflect the realities encountered at the border. High-level policymakers are rewarded for setting ambitious goals, but too often they do nothing to provide the appropriate understanding, tools, and capacity at the local level to transform the goals into actualities. Overambitious goals and objectives therefore become burdens and impediments to local actors.

The existing formal agreements between the United States and Mexico that authorize joint action on water resources (see Chapter 5) are seriously flawed. They do not permit sufficient public participation to ensure that decisions reflect border values or that local residents will participate in implementation. The treaty and related law that created the IBWC) and its Mexican counterpart, the Comisión Internacional de Limites y Aguas (CILA), as well as the La Paz Agreement of 1983, are both inadequate in this regard.

The boundary commission is an institution designed to facilitate joint action while protecting national sovereignty. The two sections and their commissioners represent and operate solely under national jurisdictions and are responsible only to their respective governments. In recent years the commission has been criticized for its lack of foresight, its conservatism in responding to environmental issues, and its exclusion of outsiders from its planning, operations, and information gathering. The reluctance of both sections to allow outside participation has occasioned the strongest criticism from scholars and activists.

The IBWC and CILA have a long history of responding to flooding, drainage, and sewage problems in Ambos Nogales, but almost always after the fact. Their responses have been limited to engineering fixes such as channelization of washes and construction of waste treatment plants, the latter frequently outdated by the time they were completed because of the protracted period required for a proposed project to run the political gauntlet. The crises usually persist because the engineering solutions address neither fundamental planning problems nor the lack of capacity of local water utilities.

The commission has not taken a comprehensive view linking quantity to quality in water management and has purposely avoided pursuing any kind of water allocation agreement for the Santa Cruz River. Local officials have little access to the IBWC's data on transboundary water resources.

The EPA's actions as U.S. coordinator for the 1983 La Paz Agreement have been only marginally better than those of the IBWC when it comes to facilitating grassroots participation. The agreement calls for cooperation in finding solutions to mutual problems, but there is no institutional structure for implementation other than to designate the EPA and its counterpart in Mexico as coordinators. Border residents and environmentalists have been particularly critical of the general lack of public representation and participation in decision-making activities under the agreement (Kelly, 1991; Mumme, 1992).

Border Links

The divisive characteristics of borders listed and discussed above would make effective problem solving next to impossible in the absence of counteracting forces. Fortunately, along many borders, the U.S.-Mexico border especially, long-standing cross-national ties exist to facilitate cooperation. What formal governmental machinery treats as distinct and separate national interests, informal arrangements unite into a less fragmented border-community interest. These cross-national ties interact to create a binational border region that is neither American nor Mexican in character, but combines much of the best of both nations. This transitional region softens the hard lines of political boundaries and facilitates binational cooperation. The integrating forces described in Chapters 2 and 4 include a common history, shared border culture, kinship ties, a common language, integrated economies, and informal networks among officials and groups. One of the most important lessons to be learned from the 500 years of border experiences since the Spaniards invaded the New World is that political dividing lines are temporary social constructs. What is often portrayed as a fixed and inviolable line may in fact be of fairly recent origin. The Gadsden Purchase culminated a series of U.S. expansions during which U.S. residents, like many Mexicans today, fiercely resisted staying within established boundaries. Native Americans and their ancestors migrated, often seasonally, from one place to another in the border region. Thus, the defining characteristic of the U.S.-Mexico border is actually the fluidity of its population. The shared history of border residents has imparted an expectation and tolerance for new and different neighbors; residents view the influx both as inevitable and as an opportunity. After all, as Chapter 2 describes, Ambos Nogales was founded by peddlers and tradesmen taking advantage of the location.

Thus the border region, more than other parts of either the United States or Mexico, is poised to accept diversity and to profit from increased commerce. When relationships sour between Washington and Mexico City, it is the border residents who suffer most because it is they who are inconvenienced by the artificial delays imposed at border crossings. Consequently, border residents have a larger stake in good binational relations. Since border residents suffer when the politics or the economy of either nation falters, they have a heightened desire to see decisions that are mutually beneficial to both nations.

The border culture, which is a mix of Anglo and Latin cultures but quite different from both, provides a further unifying influence for its residents. The special character of the border is recognized by others in both nations. El Norte is believed to be practically a different nation by many Mexicans, and U.S. citizens visiting U.S. border towns often describe them as more Mexican than American. Bolstering and transmitting this separate culture are a number of border institutions, including cultural centers, historical societies, research organizations, newspapers and electronic media, and social organizations. The optimism, flexibility, and creativity found at the border create a society that works to accommodate the interests of all. The many binational families are an inducement toward binational integration. The population of Ambos Nogales is more than 90 percent Hispanic, and many families have members on both sides of the line. Kinship ties stimulate the flow of resources and family members to the areas of need and opportunity. The border thus is characterized by an empathy that favors common understanding between people in different nations. Many of the people who reside there share attitudes that we termed "binationalist" in Chapter 4. They are capable of speaking English but are often more comfortable in Spanish, and they visit friends, family, and business associates on the other side of the line with some frequency. In Chapter 4, we noted that people with a binationalist outlook in Nogales, Ariz., tend to more closely mirror the attitudes about water resources prevailing among Sonoran residents.

The integrated border economy is a powerful stimulus for agreement. The economies of Nogales, Ariz., and Santa Cruz County depend heavily on purchases made by Mexican visitors. Schools, hospitals, and other infrastructure are supported by sales taxes paid by Mexicans, and many residents are employed in enterprises that in one way or another relate to Mexico. The shopping patterns of most residents of Ambos Nogales are binational; people search for the best values and find them on both sides of the line. The movement of goods and services across the border extends beyond the city to include transportation routes that span both nations. A large share of the winter fruits and vegetables consumed in the United States comes through the Port of Nogales. Trade routes are ties that bind nations together.

The links between border residents are matched by networks that have grown up between professionals and public officials trying to deal with shared problems. Medical personnel exchange information, equipment, and patients. Local police have informal arrangements to cooperate in the pursuit of offenders and the prevention of crime. Firefighters and disaster rescue teams go where they are needed, even if that means ignoring the border from time to time.

Chapter 3 documents a number of informal arrangements that have evolved at the border. The Nogales, Ariz., Water Department serves customers in downtown Nogales, Son., and during periods of extreme drought transfers water to the Mexican side. Local public health officials maintain informal contact, and as we illustrate in Chapter 5, are often able to share information informally that is unavailable through official channels.

Border ties such as these have remained strong over time, and new links have been forged as new needs have arisen. For example, a growing number of local nongovernmental organizations, such as the Border Ecology Project (BEP), operate on both sides of the border. Binational groups such as the Arizona-Mexico Commission, appointed by the governors of Arizona and Sonora, have intensified their activities. The Border Trade Association, initiated by U.S. and Mexican businesspeople involved with maquilas, exemplifies the channels of cooperation that are expanding as trade relationships intensify.

Although the binational ties are strong, the stresses to which they are being subjected are increasing. The population boom and accompanying environmental degradation have introduced problems that are difficult to handle through informal, face-to-face contacts. As Chapter 5 shows, however, official action usually means the preemption of informal networks; when the federal government becomes involved, local people, and their spirit of cooperation, are often set aside.

The mechanisms through which newcomers have long been socialized into the border culture have been swamped by the large influx of immigrants to the border from other parts of the United States and Mexico. As the survey data reported in Chapter 4 reveal, there are a number of higher-income, monolingual (English only), relatively new residents who lack ties to, and empathy with, Mexico and Mexicans. They depend on different sources of information, have very different concerns about water resources, and hold attitudes at odds with the attitudes found among Mexican residents. Such newcomers exert influence beyond what would be expected from their relatively small numbers because they are politically active. In their voting and their contacts with public officials, they are more likely to express attitudes that run counter to the spirit of cooperation exhibited by other border residents. Further, they are more likely to believe that border water problems are the concern of the federal government, which has not been sympathetic to autonomous community action.

Bridging Borders through Improved Institutional Design

Far-reaching reforms of international conventions that fully recognize that environment is global, not just local, are long overdue. Comprehensive global and multinational treaties that include targets and standardization of environmental regulations are among the ideas that have been suggested to stop environmental deterioration. To achieve such reforms, national governments will have to relinquish some of their sovereignty to collective bodies that can take a transnational perspective; for example, NAFTA's supplemental annex on the environment adopts this model. However, some critics believe that this focus on high-level negotiations of new, more comprehensive environmental regulations is misguided. They argue instead for the creation of grassroots institutions that take into account the motivations, interests, and resources of local actors, the nature of the problems, and local traditions of problem solving (McGinnis and Ostrom, 1992).

The need for a bottom-up approach is especially critical in border areas. Border regions need to be thought of as coherent entities in their own right. When borders are viewed as centers of concern rather than as peripheries, possibilities for transnational bargaining and accommodation emerge. The Nogales case study illustrates what can be accomplished when border watersheds are treated in a holistic manner. Each side has something to gain from applying a hydrologic systems perspective to the placement of water supply wells, waste treatment facilities, and flood control structures.

Rather than pursuing either comprehensive or locally based solutions exclusively, a better approach would be to nest existing and new institutions at all levels—the border region, the nation, and internationally—and to place authority appropriately at each level depending on knowledge, political will, and resources. New regional institutions with transboundary jurisdiction need to be established and given the authority to collect and disseminate data, make planning decisions, and apply for and dispense funding for needed and deserving environmental projects (Ingram, 1993).

The climate of the mid-1990s is highly favorable for launching regional approaches. Changes in the Mexican government, described in Chapter 5, position it positively toward delegation of responsibility and resources. Citizen activists on the border have made it clear that the secretive practices of remote national bureaucracies are no longer acceptable. Such developments and attitudes are largely responsible for the inclusion of the Border Environmental Cooperation Commission (BECC) in the side agreements to the North American Free Trade Agreement. President Clinton's executive order establishing the BECC and the North American Development Bank is in Appendix A. Appendix B is our description of an ideal border institutional model, which can be used as a point of comparison.

Regional commissions represent an old, well-tested idea. They date back to the recognition, in the 1960s, of the problems associated with the fragmentation of ecosystems. Some regional commissions, particularly river basin commissions, have been harshly criticized for their inability to command and control the other players in their region. Measured by different criteria, however, these institutions have performed well. Regional commissions provide a forum for communication, information exchange, network building, joint planning, and raising public and agency awareness of issues and opportunities. Multiple public and private institutions with overlapping jurisdictions and diverse interests are a fact of modern governance. Hierarchical arrangements that appear to grant clear authority to a single agency encounter opposition not only from other agencies but also from grassroots constituencies who feel unrepresented. The multiple perspectives that exist in binational settings certainly require a more collaborative, consultative, and consensus-building structure.

While far from ideal, BECC has a number of the characteristics and attributes necessary to improve water resource and environmental decision making. What follows is a discussion of the attributes and actions that will enable BECC or some future border institution to contribute to improved environmental management. Appendix B discusses these ideas in greater detail.

Criteria for Successful Border Institutions

1. Regional institutions must be truly binational and broadly inclusive of state, local, and nongovernmental interests. The number of delegates from each nation must be equal, and they must represent diverse geographical and other interests.

BECC, as it was structured in the NAFTA side agreement, is governed by a binational board that includes the commissioners of the IBWC and EPA/SEDESOL as ex officio members, and six other directors with expertise in environmental planning, economics, engineering, finance, and related matters.[3] Both nations are to have one state, one local, and one public member. Which interests to represent will surely be an issue. In particular, it may prove difficult to determine which of the border states is to be represented. However, BECC represents a substantial gain in terms of inclusiveness.

A common problem faced by regional commissions is the need to maintain the interest and commitment of their members. Inclusiveness is meaningless without full participation, and participation will depend largely on members' perception that their tasks are important, which leads to the following principle.

2. Regional institutions must have jurisdiction over a broad range of border environmental issues, not just water resources. Although the focus of our analysis has been on Ambos Nogales and its water resources, it is our judgment that border water issues need to be placed in the larger context of sustainable development. That is, water resources must be considered in conjunction with solid and hazardous wastes, air quality, toxic pollutants, pesticides, and environmental health issues, all of which are necessarily interconnected.[4] BECC's jurisdiction includes environmental infrastructure in the border area, especially water pollution, wastewater treatment, municipal solid wastes, and related matters. This mandate appears more narrow than is desirable. Of course, it is not clear whether infrastructure includes, as it should, assembling of the general environmental and

land use data necessary for good environmental planning. The regional environmental commission's effectiveness will depend on whether it is able to take a more comprehensive binational approach to environmental protection so that border development becomes sustainable and the downward trend in border environmental quality is reversed.

3. Regional institutions should be able to deal proactively with needs and problems before they reach the crisis stage and without the necessity of seeking separate authorization and funding for each project from the national governments. It is more likely that a regional institution will gain the necessary support if it offers positive inducements for action rather than negative sanctions.

BECC does not itself develop or manage projects. Instead it certifies projects in concert with the affected states and localities. This does not necessarily preclude the commission from encouraging localities to plan ahead and perhaps help to arrange financing for planning. In line with this recommendation, BECC has no regulatory authority and provides benefits rather than sanctions. It certifies or may refuse to certify environmental infrastructure projects for funding by the North American Development Bank or other entities. If sufficient funding is made available, it is possible that regional commissions will contribute to a more rational and timely process of responding to environmental problems.

BECC's certification decisions are made on the basis of an environmental assessment that the project meets ecological, environmental, economic, and other criteria. This certification process is clearly superior to the ad hoc, crisis-driven responses to border environmental problems of the past that have failed to produce lasting positive results. The cyclical water "crises" in Ambos Nogales over the past 50 years amply demonstrate the failure of the congressional appropriations process, under which projects receive funds based on the interest and clout of the congressional delegations from the states affected. A different but no more disciplined kind of presidential politics drives the location and funding of projects in Mexico.

4. Regional institutions must contribute to building the capacity of local environmental agencies, particularly municipal water agencies. Agency capacity includes not just assurance of professional and

technical skills but, more importantly, substantial self-financing and application of user-pays rate assessments.[5] At the local water utility level, the lack of agency capacity in Mexico is among the most important reasons for the vast inequities in water service on the two sides of the border. The failure of water utilities to apply pay-as-you-go and user-pays principles in designing tax and rate structures is common in the border region.

It is a serious error for national governments or donor agencies to continue to fund water infrastructure development projects without assurances that the operating agency has the ability to operate them. Radically reducing the federal subsidy and increasing the local cost share offers some clear advantages to border areas like Ambos Nogales. Politically driven expenditures from national and state governments are not very reliable; cost-of-service fees collected from local water users would provide a more consistent source of funds for operations, maintenance, and infrastructure expansion. Local self-financing, rather than financing through national taxes, involves fewer economic distortions and greater efficiency. Further, decentralization of control over water resources and reduction of federal subsidies is fully consistent with present Mexican national water resources policy, as discussed in Chapter 5.

Pricing the water services is a critical part of local capacity building. Setting the appropriate rates not only allows the utility to pay its bills and expand in a timely manner, it also sends appropriate signals to users about the scarcity of water. Commercial and industrial users, even if they have private wells, inflict a cost on others who share a common aquifer, as in the case of Ambos Nogales, and they should pay for the water they use.

The preamble to the BECC proposal affirms that, to the extent practicable, environmental infrastructure projects in the border region should be operated and maintained through user fees paid by polluters and those who benefit from the projects. It will be important for the commission to insist on financial plans that provide resources for expansion, as well as operations and maintenance, if future crises are to be avoided in the fast-growing border region.

5. Regional water institutions should be responsive and accountable to the public, particularly to local residents. Local opinions, atti-

tudes, and experiences must be reflected in the identification of issues, priorities, and programs. Regional forums are needed in which local public officials and representatives of nongovernment organizations can come together to explore areas of common interest.

Local support is critical to the long-term success of any regional institution. All too often in the past, as exemplified by the NIWWTF, subsidies have been incorporated into local border problems. The difficulty has been that local residents are reluctant to oppose projects that are paid for by outside interests, even if a project is seriously flawed. An effective binational institution needs to garner public support on the basis of its long-term ability to identify and fund environmentally beneficial actions.

The input and cooperation of local officials in decision-making processes are essential. Open meetings and public participation requirements can avoid the secrecy and elitism that have discouraged many NGOs and others from becoming involved in the activities of the IBWC and the La Paz working groups. When important local actors have the opportunity to participate, they are much more likely to cooperate in implementing the projects decided upon. As Chapter 5 illustrates, the residents of Ambos Nogales lack public arenas in which to express their opinions with a realistic hope that these may make a difference. Among the unfortunate consequences of the absence of forums is the inability to compare and contrast perceptions. It is altogether possible that the different attitudes about water on the two sides of the border reported in Chapter 4 could be moved toward greater consensus through discussion and meaningful dialogue.

To a significant degree, grassroots participation is built into the structure of BECC. The board of directors includes two members of local government and two members from the public. In addition, an advisory council that meets regularly is to consist of at least one member of each border state with six such members appointed from each nation, and six members from the public with at least two from nongovernmental organizations. Further, BECC is directed, to the extent possible, to publicize documentary information on all the projects it considers. BECC is also required to provide opportunities for public comment on applications for certification of projects. Clearly, BECC provides unprecedented opportunities for public involvement.

6. Credible, balanced information about the environmental problems associated with proposed projects, as well as their environmental, economic, and social impacts, need to be made equally available on both sides of the border.

Ignorance and secrecy have been principle impediments to good environmental management in the border region. Chapter 5 documents the very different kinds and levels of information officially provided to the public by the U.S. and Mexican governments. Because no credible binational source exists, the media in each nation tend to interview different officials and put forward very different interpretations of the available facts and perspectives. Fragmented and inconsistent sources of information neither adequately inform nor help to forge public consensus for action.

While its purview is limited to proposed infrastructure projects, BECC promises to improve the supply of credible information provided from a binational perspective. An environmental assessment that considers potential environmental benefits and risks, costs as well as available alternatives, and the environmental standards and objectives of the affected area is required of applicants for certification. If the board of directors takes their mandate seriously and interprets it broadly, the commission will require that projects justify their construction on the basis of real benefits to local populations and without saddling residents with impoverishing debt.

7. Regional border institutions must fit into the already crowded space of existing institutions by (a) helping existing institutions reach their goals, and (b) working cooperatively together. Direct threats to existing institutions might well endanger the survival of any new institution. To be politically feasible, the new border commission must create a niche for itself in which it does not supplant or duplicate institutions already performing important functions. A regional commission should serve roles not now being adequately performed. In the densely packed bureaucratic environment of the border, there are a welter of agencies with narrow missions, none of which are really responding to environmental problems. What is needed is an institutional network that connects actors at various levels. Up until now, most binational linkages have been informal—and routinely ignored by formal institutions.

A clear advantage of the design of the BECC Board of Directors is the inclusion of the IBWC and EPA/SEDESOL as nonvoting members. It will be far easier for existing agencies working on the border to accept a new institution in which they can play a part. Through the inclusiveness of its membership on the board of directors and the advisory council, BECC provides for formal linkages between state and local officials in both countries that have not previously been available. Further, by insisting on truly binational infrastructure projects that are likely to be both more efficient and more environmentally beneficial, BECC can encourage state and local officials and NGOs to cooperate. Rather than working against grassroots binational linkages and informal networks, as federal-level institutions have so often done in the past, BECC can include grassroots organizations through project plans and decision processes that fortify them.

There are other roles that BECC is not designed to serve directly, but which are badly needed. The numbers and status of environmental professionals need to be increased, especially in Mexico and particularly in the area of water resources. Professionalism and binational linkages can be increased through short courses and workshops offered by U.S. universities or agency counterparts. BECC's focus on infrastructure projects is unfortunate because much of the investment on the border should be put into upgrading the capacity of local officials. Among the skills especially needed is the ability to communicate effectively with the public in the unique border cultural context. It is unfortunate that different segments of the border public are receiving very different messages about water quality, as our data in Chapter 4 indicate. The emergence of attitudinal cleavages along ethnic and racial lines such as those we describe undermines the conditions necessary for cooperative decision making. Environmental professionals need a strong binational understanding of the issues and must be able to communicate with a broad public, including those who are bilingual and depend on the radio to learn about issues as well as those who rely on newspaper articles.

Borders, more than any other geographical locations, are experiencing the contending forces of environmentalism, nationalism, the global economy, and popular democratic participation. Consequently, it is in border regions that the great issues of our time will be decided: whether the desire to prevent environmental deterioration will result in the improvement of the quality of life in developing countries or environmental quality will continue to be the privilege of wealthy nations; whether the creativity and flexibility of ethnic diversity will be embraced as an advantage or people will separate themselves into warring ethnic enclaves; whether more open global trade will lead to improved living standards and quality of life in poor nations or polluting industries will gravitate to areas of lax labor and environmental standards; whether governments will become more responsive and democratic so that ordinary people gain greater control over issues affecting their lives or decision making will continue to be dominated by an elite.

Borders are not only bellwethers of the ways global trends will play out, they also introduce special problems with particular impediments to resolution and opportunities for gain. Borders are multiplying everywhere, as are border problems—many of them relating to transboundary water resources. While not often cited for the good example it provides, the U.S.-Mexico border has much to teach the world; despite great economic and cultural disparities, the two nations have been able since 1848 to resolve most of their differences peacefully. Further, a unique border culture has evolved, one that displays many of the best characteristics of both nations. However, resolution of transborder water problems has been neither as effective nor as sensitive to actual hydrologic and social conditions as is desirable. Both the United States and Mexico are prepared, more than they have ever been, to work together to solve problems. The Mexican government in particular is initiating rapid and innovative changes in water resources institutions. The time is appropriate to remodel border relationships to reflect the closer ties developing between the United States and Mexico and the growing importance of the border region.

The water resources experience of Ambos Nogales portrays common border difficulties. Borders separate the locus of problems from the source of their solutions. The economic opportunities that exist on borders encourage irrational development. Differences in water service at borders aggravate perceptions of inequity. The preferences of border residents are often ignored even though their cooperation is essential to successful implementation of policy. The informal ties that allow border residents to resolve day-to-day problems are often ignored by central governments and international agencies.

Open, binational forums created within the border region are needed to develop empathy and shared understandings of problems. The limitations of hierarchical institutions that centralize power and authority in bureaucratic structures at national or international levels, but are unable to implement solutions, are increasingly obvious. At a time when officials and the public are receptive to ideas of reinventing government, structures need to be designed to engage border residents in binational approaches to resolving their water problems. Whether successful innovation can take place at the regional level to enable local residents to both have greater control and to strengthen their binational links will largely determine whether the many divisions and differences discussed here can be successfully bridged.

Appendix A

Implementation of the Border Environment Cooperation Commission and the North American Development Bank

By the authority vested in me as President by the Constitution and laws of the United States, including the North American Free Trade Agreement Implementation Act ("the NAFTA Implementation Act"), it is hereby ordered as follows:

Section 1. It is the policy of the United States that the U.S.-Mexico Agreement Establishing the Border Environment Cooperation Commission and the North American Development Bank will be implemented consistent with United States policy for the protection of human, animal, or plant life or health and the environment, so as to advance sustainable development, pollution prevention, and biodiversity preservation, environmental justice, ecosystem protection, and biodiversity preservation, and will be implemented so as to promote transparency and public participation.

Section 2. (a) The Administrator of the Environmental Protection Agency and the United States Commissioner, International Boundary and Water Commission, United States and Mexico ("Commissioner"), shall represent the United States as members of the Board of Directors of the Border Environment Cooperation Commission, in accordance with the Agreement Between the Government of the United States of America and the Government of the United Mexican States Concerning the Establishment of a Border Environment Cooperation Commission and a North American Development Bank, signed on November 16 and 18, 1993.

(b) The policies and positions of the United States in the Border Environment Cooperation Commission shall be coordinated through applicable inter-agency procedures, which shall include participation by the Department of State, the Department of the Treasury, the [Department of Housing and Urban Development and the] Environmental Protection Agency, and other Federal Agencies, as appropriate.

(c) The Commissioner shall promote cooperation, as appropriate, between the International Boundary and Water Commission and the Border Environment Cooperation Commission and the developing, and carrying out border sanitation and other environmental activities.

Section 3. (a) The United States government representatives to the Board of the North American Development Bank shall be the Secretary of the Treasury, the Secretary of State, and the Administrator of the Environmental Protection Agency.

(b) For purposes of loans or guarantees certified by the Border Environment Cooperation Commission, these representatives shall be instructed in accordance with the procedures of the National Advisory Committee on International Monetary and Financial Policies ("Council"), as established by Executive Order No. 11269 of February 14, 1966. For purposes of this section only, the membership of the Council shall expand to include the [Secretary of the Department of Housing and Urban Development and the] Administrator of the Environmental Protection Agency.

[(c) For purposes of loans or guarantees certified by the Border Environment Cooperation Commission, these representatives shall consult with the Community Adjustment and Investment Program Advisory Committee, established pursuant to section 543(b) of the NAFTA Implementation Act, concerning any community adjustment and investment aspects of such loans or guarantees.]

[(d) For purposes of loans, guarantees, or grants endorsed by the United States for community adjustment and investment, these representatives shall be instructed in accordance with procedures established by the Community Adjustment and Investment Program Finance Committee established pursuant to section 7 of this executive order.]

Section 4. The functions vested in the President by section 543(a)(1) of the NAFTA Implementation Act are delegated to the Secretary of the Treasury.

Section 5. The functions vested in the President by section 543(a)(2) and (3) of the NAFTA Implementation Act are delegated to the Secretary of the Treasury, who shall exercise such functions in accordance with the recommendations of the Community Adjustment and Investment Program Finance Committee established pursuant to section 7 of this executive order.

Section 6. The functions vested in the President by section 543(a)(5) and section 543(d) are delegated to the Community Adjustment and Investment Program Finance Committee established pursuant to section 7 of this executive order, which shall exercise such functions in consultation with the Community Adjustment and Investment Program Advisory Committee, established pursuant to section 543(b) of the NAFTA Implementation Act.

Section 7. (a) There is hereby established a Community Adjustment and Investment Program Finance Committee (the "Finance Committee").

(b) The Finance Committee shall be composed of the Department of the Treasury, the Department of Agriculture, the [Department of Housing and

Urban Development and the] Small Business Administration, and any other Federal agencies selected to assist in carrying out the community adjustment and investment program pursuant to section 543(a)(3) of the NAFTA Implementation Act.

(c) The Department of the Treasury shall serve as Chair of the Finance Committee. The chair shall be responsible for presiding over meetings of the Finance Committee, ensuring that the views of all other members are taken into account, coordinating with other appropriate United States government agencies in carrying out the community adjustment and investment program, and requesting meetings of the Advisory Committee pursuant to section 543(b)(4)(c) of the NAFTA Implementation Act.

Section 8. Any advice or conclusions of review provided to the President by the Community Adjustment and Investment Program Advisory Committee pursuant to section 543(b)(3) of the NAFTA Implementation Act shall be provided through the Finance Committee.

Section 9. Any summaries of public comments or conclusions of investigations and audits provided to the President by the ombudsman pursuant to section 543(c)(1) of the NAFTA Implementation Act shall be provided through the Finance Committee.

Section 10. The authority of the President under section 6 of P. L. 102-532 of October 27, 1992, 7 U.S.C. section 5404, to establish an advisory board to be known as the Good Neighbor Environmental Board is delegated to the Administrator of the Environmental Protection Agency.

Section 11. This Executive Order is intended only to improve the internal management of the Executive Branch and is not intended to, and does not, create any right to administrative or judicial review, or any other right or benefit or trust responsibility, substantive or procedural, enforceable by a party against the United States, its agencies or instrumentalities, its officers or employees, or any other person.

William J. Clinton

The White House

Appendix B

Proposal for a U.S.-Mexico International Boundary Environmental Commission: A Binational U.S.-Mexico Border Environmental Management Institution

Introduction

The U.S.-Mexico border is truly a region under stress. With increasing economic development and explosive population growth, it is essential to strengthen the institutional capability for protecting labor and the quality of the environment in the border region. With rapidly changing conditions, existing institutions are finding it increasingly difficult to cope with the tasks of providing environmental protection in a transboundary context.

The International Boundary and Water Commission has a long and respected record of achievement, but its treaty mandate focuses primarily on water quantity. The La Paz Agreement of 1983 provides an important vehicle for coordinating the border activities of the environmental agencies of the two countries—EPA and SEDESOL—but the energy and attention that these hardworking agencies can give the border region has to be shared with compelling concerns throughout their respective countries. The many demands placed on these two agencies makes it difficult for them to provide the focus and continuity essential to addressing the full range of the difficult transboundary issues.

The border area now requires a binational institution whose exclusive mandated responsibility is the protection of the environmental quality of the border region itself: a commission that would build on the advances of the La Paz Agreement and the achievements of the IBWC. It would supplement, not supplant, existing binational institutions.

The NAFTA negotiations now provide an opportunity for environmental institution building—at the trilateral level in the form of a North American Commission on the Environment (NACE), and at the bilateral level with an International Border Environmental Commission (IBEC), a regional entity whose focused responsibility would be the protection of the U.S.-Mexico border region. The NACE and the IBEC would coordinate their activities and thus work in tandem to provide environmental oversight at both the continental and regional levels.

An International Boundary Environmental Commission

We strongly recommend the creation of a new border environmental institution with oversight jurisdiction over water quality (surface and groundwater), air quality, hazardous material, and toxic waste management, and other environmental quality and health matters in the U.S.-Mexico border region. This should be done through codification of the annexes under the La Paz Agreement in treaty form with designation of the IBEC as the lead agency with responsibility for border environmental protection.

Criteria for an Effective Binational Institution

A. It must have adequate jurisdiction over transboundary natural resources contamination and health issues to permit it to collect data, prepare comprehensive plans, and improve environmental and health management along the border.

B. It should be capable of anticipating problems, setting priorities, and acting before the emergence of crises that erode institutional trust. Priorities should be set on the basis of the seriousness of problems, efficient allocation of scarce resources, and sustainability of solution.

C. It must have sufficient financial resources to enable it to deal proactively with needs and problems before they reach the crisis stage and without the necessity of seeking separate authorization and funding for each project from the national governments.

D. It should be interdisciplinary, with capacity and incentives to generate broad support for its programs, building from a base of local grassroots support as well as state and federal backing.

E. It must be responsive to local communities with local attitudes and experiences built into the development of plans and priorities and with the goal of building the capacity of local institutions to solve problems in a sustainable way that does not initiate or perpetuate a cycle of dependence.

F. It must fit into the already crowded space of existing institutions by helping them meet their goals and work together more cooperatively. Other agencies, officials, NGOs, and individuals should be able to look to the institution for information and expertise.

G. It should be flexible, so that it can grow and change with differing conditions and mandates.

I. Structure
Binational commission with strong local involvement in the border region.

A. A binational commission supported by advisory boards.

1. Commission co-chaired by appointees of the Presidents of Mexico and the United States (in the United States confirmed by the Senate) who serve at the pleasure of the respective Presidents. Each co-chair would be a full-time paid employee of the IBEC. The co-chairs shall have demonstrated expertise in environmental affairs, and shall not have vested economic interest in trade and investment arising under the North American Free Trade Agreement.

2. Eighteen commission members including the two co-chairs, the Mexican and United States Commissioners of the IBWC, twelve members appointed by the governors of the border states (one member for each of the six Mexican border states, two each for Texas and California, one each for Arizona and New Mexico), and one each appointed by SEDESOL and EPA. The terms for the governor-appointed members would be six years.

3. Technical advisers and local advisory boards are to be appointed by the Commission to provide special expertise and local input on specific issues under consideration by the Commission.

4. Agency resource people from such agencies as Public Health Service, SALUD, and HHS should be designated to work with the IBEC and be funded by their respective agencies.

B. Regular, open IBEC meetings in border communities.

1. The headquarters of the IBEC should be binational and in a border community, perhaps alternating between the two countries on a periodic basis. Meetings of the Commission should be held in various communities along the border, giving local residents convenient opportunities to attend.

2. The IBEC should meet on a regular basis, no less than four times a year.

3. Commission meetings should be open to the public with opportunity for public comment and presentation of proposals. Notice of all meetings shall be publicly made at least 15 days in advance. Executive sessions shall be held to a minimum.

4. The IBEC also would be empowered to hold public hearings, technical meetings, workshops, and briefings relating to border environmental matters under its own auspices or in cooperation with other authorities and organizations. Persons and organizations may petition the IBEC to schedule a meeting or invite written statements concerning environmental issues in the border region, or urge the IBEC to take action under its jurisdiction.

C. The secretariat for the IBEC should be binational, interdisciplinary support staff with broad expertise in environmental affairs.

1. The technical staff should emphasize social, legal, planning, and economic as well as engineering and scientific expertise to permit it to collect, analyze, and synthesize data and to make recommendations in accord with the IBEC mandates.
2. The secretariat will be responsible to the entire Commission but will report on an ongoing basis to the co-chairs.
3. Staff will be responsible for chairing and organizing the working groups created by the Commission.

D. Critical Environmental Management Areas (CEMAS) may be designated in border areas identified as having significant environmental problems.
1. Designation of the CEMA would be the responsibility of the IBEC, but nominations could come from the IBEC staff or from local areas who wish to be designated as a CEMA.
2. Each CEMA must be provided with adequate resources to establish a planning office to receive technical assistance from the IBEC professional staff and work with local agencies, officials, and NGOs.

II. Functions and Powers
  A. Information collection, analysis, and dissemination.
    1. The first task of the IBEC will be to collect, maintain, and update an inventory of border environmental resources and threats to air quality and water quality, hazardous materials and toxic waste problems, environmental health issues, and bioresource problems and to prepare the outlines of a plan for border environmental management and sustainable economic development which identifies initial CEMAS.
    2. Preparation of an annual "State of the Border Environment" report that incorporates information and experiences from the CEMAS as well as the rest of the border region. These reports should include the following kinds of information and should be provided to local, state, and federal agencies and NGOs for coordinated implementation of solutions.
      a. Actions necessary to protect and manage the quality of shared water resources to ensure adequate supplies of water for the border region's population, economic development and wildlife.
      b. Procedures necessary to ensure adequate tracking of hazardous toxic and radioactive wastes from "cradle to grave."
      c. Actions necessary to encourage the reduction of municipal, industrial, agricultural, and radioactive wastes generated within the border region.
      d. Measures necessary to ensure environmentally sound treatment,

storage, and/or disposal capacity for toxic and radioactive wastes located within the border region.

3. The environmental agencies of each country shall report annually to the IBEC on environmental conditions and the implementation of environmental programs and legislation in their respective border areas in order to assist the IBEC in its information-gathering tasks and in preparing its State of the Border Environment report.

4. IBEC will act as a clearinghouse for information about environmental problems and related information along the border providing information and technical assistance services to agencies, officials, NGOs, and private individuals.

5. CEMA planning office and/or IBEC technical staff will work with local communities, governmental agencies, utilities, and locally based NGOs to develop more detailed environmental management plans for local areas. The goal will be to empower local officials, not to supplant them.

B. Public participation and local border community involvement.

1. The IBEC and its staff will be mandated to provide opportunities for direct participation by interested individuals and organizations in the planning process leading up to the annual State of the Border Environment report and supplementary reports. Some suggested means for encouraging such participation include

    a. "Scoping workshops" in which interested parties are provided background information, problem identification, and proposed solutions and are given an opportunity for oral and written comments.

    b. Public hearings and participation of the public in working groups to provide information and foster support for recommended actions.

    c. Public bulletins and newsletters describing the work and proposed actions of the IBEC.

    d. Use of computer electronic mail and bulletin board systems to disseminate information, questions, and comments to interested individuals and groups.

C. "Ombudsman" environmental oversight and enforcement function.

1. The IBEC will be authorized to receive and investigate citizen complaints of nonenforcement of environmental laws or other potential problems within the Commission's jurisdiction.

    a. The IBEC's technical staff may be directed to investigate the matter and issue a report to the IBEC.

    b. If further action is deemed advisable by the Commissioners, an official IBEC report may be issued on the matter with findings and actions to be taken.

2. The IBEC will also be mandated to regularly review the existing environmental programs in the border region to identify gaps and weaknesses and recommend needed changes. This information would be presented through the annual State of the Border Environment reports and in supplementary reports as needed.

D. Border Environmental Trust Fund (BETF) to provide secure financing for operation of the IBEC and ongoing border environmental planning and project implementation.

1. The BETF should receive appropriations from the two national governments. However, it must also have a stable source of funding outside the federal authorization and appropriation process that is logically connected to the increased burden on the border environment resulting from the removal of trade restrictions. This could be provided by a "customs processing fee" dedicated to environment, health, and other purposes, which would be a percentage of the value of transboundary trade at a rate low enough to avoid distortion of trade or investment activities.

2. In addition to financing the administrative costs of the IBEC and CEMAS, monies from the Trust Fund should be made available to border communities through grants and low-interest loans for needed infrastructure projects identified during the planning process. Such grants and loans should be directed toward building better management capacity and opportunity for environmentally sustainable and financially self-sufficient development in the local border areas.

3. Particular emphasis should be placed upon improvements in planning, management, and infrastructure to enhance the match between user fees and cost-of-service requirements for local utilities.

4. Funding decisions should be based on flexible cost-sharing that acknowledges the difference in resources that exist in different communities and on different sides of the border.

E. Strengthen the binational linkages of border communities to facilitate joint problem solving.

1. Acknowledge and understand the different priorities and perceptions of different cultural and economic groups, looking for commonalities that reach across the border.

2. Develop public information and education campaigns that strengthen the capacity of local bilingual media to cover natural resource and water stories while also emphasizing the binational aspects of water problems to nonbilingual residents.

3. Host binational meetings and facilitate collection of binational data.

III. Nested Institutions Design

The IBEC will not duplicate or supplant existing institutions, but instead will serve a needed coordinating and service role in environmental matters along the U.S.-Mexico border.

A. The treaty and related jurisdiction of the International Boundary and Water Commission (IBWC) over boundary waters will continue. This would permit the IBWC to continue its important historic role in regard to border waters while allowing for coordinated management of border environmental problems by the IBEC.

B. The IBEC would relieve existing institutional problems faced by EPA and SEDESOL in meeting the needs of the border area at the same time these agencies are faced with pressing national environmental issues and programs to administer. The IBEC would provide an institutional structure for addressing the unique border environment with information and needed expertise supplied by EPA and SEDESOL. Mechanisms initiated in the La Paz process, such as working groups, will be transferred, and where appropriate, carried forward by the IBEC.

C. If the proposed trilateral North American Commission on the Environment (NACE) is established, the IBEC will work in cooperation with it in matters affecting the U.S.-Mexico border area. NACE's primary focus can be expected to be national legislative issues, upward harmonization of standards, and trade sanction–type authority among Canada, the United States, and Mexico. NACE will be responsible for those transboundary environmental impacts that have geographic implications that extend beyond the U.S.-Mexico border region. The IBEC, in contrast, will focus its efforts on the specific environmental issues, construction of facilities, and implementation of environmental programs in the areas contiguous to the U.S.-Mexico border.

IV. Mandate and Goals

Assuring that water quality, air quality, hazardous material, and toxic waste management and environmentally related health concerns in the U.S.-Mexico border area will be addressed in ways that will permit sustained economic development along the border. Attention should also be paid to preservation of important ecosystems and endangered habitats and species.

A. Defining sustainable economic development to take into account a healthy environment for quality of life, tourism, and protection of the environment for today's border residents and for future generations.

B. Oversight jurisdiction covering the entire U.S.-Mexico border with the ability to designate local areas as having critical environmental management needs.

C. Avoiding supranational law enforcement authority, but rather relying on the "intrusive sunshine" of regular reports to the public and governments evaluating the state of border environment and enforcement programs of the various governmental agencies.

D. Empowering local governments and agencies to become self-supporting through improved information, planning, and management, and enhanced infrastructure, metering, fee collection, and bonding capability. Emphasis should be placed on supplementing existing state and local cost-sharing arrangements.

E. Obtaining adequate and ongoing sources of revenue to permit the IBEC to fund proactive planning and management activities and to provide low-interest loans, grants, and other incentives to local areas to build infrastructure and management capability.

F. Striving to incrementally improve the quality of the environment and access of water users on each side of the border to good-quality water supply and wastewater services with ongoing emphasis on what users themselves want and are most concerned about.

G. Developing and maintaining the capability for production and open access to environmental data in the border region through development of a border database and generally promote binational cooperation in the development of right-to-know programs and public participation.

H. Working toward the goal of self-sufficient, self-supporting utilities with cost-of-service fee structures as users develop more confidence in the system and rely less on individual solutions.

I. Strengthening positive binational linkages along the border, recognizing that the border culture provides an important unity to the binational region.

> The Udall Center for Studies in Public Policy
> The University of Arizona
> July 1993

Contributors to This Proposal

This proposal is a collective effort that builds on the thought and work of many different scholars from both academia and NGOs.

On March 6, 1993, a group of border policy scholars met in Tucson,

Arizona, under the auspices of the Udall Center for Studies in Public Policy and the Centro Internacional de Recursos Transfronterizos (International Transboundary Resources Center, or CIRT) to review a range of proposals and arrive at a common set of recommendations incorporating the principal points of agreement and emphasis. Those attending the meeting were Helen Ingram and Nancy Laney from the Udall Center, Professor Albert E. Utton from CIRT, and Professor Stephen D. Mumme from Colorado State University.

As a result of this meeting, a draft proposal was prepared and circulated for comments; the draft was then revised to reflect the input and suggestions offered. Especially helpful suggestions were made by Paul Ganster, San Diego State University; Roberto Sánchez, El Colegio de la Frontera Norte; Dick Kamp, Border Ecology Project; Ty Fain, Texas General Land Office; Mary Kelly, Texas Center for Policy Studies; and Alberto Székely, CIRT–Mexico City.

Certainly, no single contributor is in total agreement with every aspect of this proposal. The present proposal is just that, a proposal. It is neither the last word nor perfect in every detail, but it is offered in the spirit of furthering the development of binational institutions to improve the quality of life of the inhabitants of the border region.

Notes

Chapter 1   Global Trends and Border Consequences

1. Adding the new African nation of Eritrea increases the number of new borders from 46 to 49.
2. "World of Change," *Arizona Daily Star*, June 10, 1992.
3. *World Resources 1992–93*. As of 1990, 81 percent of urban areas and 58 percent of rural areas worldwide had access to safe water supplies; 78 percent of urban areas and 48 percent of rural areas had access to sanitation. Polluted water affects the health of some 1.2 billion people and contributes to the death of some 15 million children under five years of age every year (Rodda and Young, 1992). Roughly 153 billion cubic meters (40 trillion gallons) are discharged in urban wastewater streams annually, with as little as one-third receiving any kind of treatment (Rogers, 1992). The World Health Organization (WHO) has set 150 liters (40 gallons) per day as the water needed per household in the cities of the developing world; 75 liters (20 gallons) per day per household is considered adequate to protect against waterborne diseases (Falkenmark and Suprapto, 1992).
4. "U.S., Mexico Take on Border Pollution," *Wall Street Journal*, February 25, 1992.
5. "Border Waste Not Tracked," *Arizona Daily Star*, November 25, 1991.
6. *Wall Street Journal*, February 25, 1992.
7. Population control is not a significant part of the Mexican environmental agenda, for example, and nature has taken a backseat to protecting public health (Graham, 1991).
8. "Environmentalists Fight Each Other over Trade Accord," *New York Times*, September 16, 1993.
9. "Subsidized Homes Are Not Readily Available to Mexican Citizens," *Arizona Republic*, November 8, 1992.
10. Ostrom's arguments in favor of "nested" regimes are in McGinnis and Ostrom, 1992.
11. "Nogales Air Pollution Exceeds EPA Limits," *Nogales International*, July 10, 1991.
12. "Nogales Wash Fire Being Probed: Pollution Concern Is Raised Again," *Arizona Daily Star*, May 31, 1991.

Chapter 2 Shared Encounters: Ambos Nogales

1. "Tourism Spoiler, Rules for Visits to Mexico Still Frustrating," *Arizona Daily Star*, April 8, 1992.

2. U.S. drug policy has sanctioned—without any requirement to file an environmental impact statement—road building along the border, which has denuded and scarred the desert. Further, the presence along the border of the Mexican military, supported by the United States, has encroached on the habitat of the pronghorn antelope, and armed personnel sometimes shoot at anything that moves. Finally, U.S. Air Force supersonic overflights of the Tohono O'odham reservation are adversely affecting wildlife, and, in the opinion of the Tohono O'odham themselves, are responsible for splitting many saguaro cacti.

3. "Nogales Arizona 1880–1980 Centennial Anniversary," Nogales Centennial Commission, 1980. Much of the history of Nogales, Ariz., that we present is derived from this report.

4. Much of what we document about the history of the borderlands is derived from this book.

5. *WPA Guide to 1930s Arizona*, 1989. Information about Ambos Nogales in the 1930s comes from this book.

6. Due to its small population and the small geographic area encompassed by Santa Cruz County, U.S. census data have been broken down by county rather than by city. Because most (two-thirds) residents of the county live within the city limits, and because our references to the people and issues of Nogales, Ariz., are, unless stated otherwise, intended to apply beyond the actual city limits to encompass the entire Nogales area, we feel that it is appropriate to use census data for Santa Cruz County to represent "Nogales, Arizona." All U.S. census data are from the 1990 count.

7. All Nogales, Son., census data are from this source unless otherwise noted.

8. As of September 1993 there were 77 maquiladoras in Nogales, Son. (Maquila Association, Nogales, Son.); the mayor has requested a halt to further maquila construction (see Chapter 2, n. 18).

9. Santa Cruz County has a 0.5 percent sales tax, which brought in $1,673,000 in 1992 (County of Santa Cruz, Treasurer's Office, pers. comm., 1993). The state of Arizona reimbursed the county an additional $2,184,000 from the state sales tax of 5 percent. The total represents 35 percent of the county's 1992 revenue. The 1 percent city sales tax raised $3.6 million for Nogales, 42 percent of the 1992 revenue; in addition, the state returned $1,259,000 from the state sales tax (City of Nogales finance director, pers. comm., 1993). Thus, sales taxes constituted 57 percent of the city's revenues in 1992.

10. Robert Hathaway, executive vice president, West Mexico Vegetable Distributors Association, Nogales, Ariz., pers. comm., 1993.

11. "Maquiladoras: Are Plants along the Border a Boon or Bane to Workers?" *Tucson Weekly*, March 23–29, 1988.

12. Martin Guerrero, statistician, COLEF-Nogales, pers. comm., 1993.

13. INEGI, 1990a; and Martin Guerrero, pers. comm., 1993. Some of the maquila workforce are not residents of Nogales, Son.

14. When the maquilas first began operations, the workforce was largely female; in recent years, the male:female ratio has been changing, as figure 2.3 indicates.

15. "The Border Boom: Hope and Heartbreak," *New York Times Magazine*, July 1, 1990.

16. "Fighting for a Piece of the Rock," *New Times* (Phoenix), November 4–10, 1987.

17. "The Future of Nogales," *Tucson Citizen*, April 5, 1993.

18. In Mexico as in the United States there is a certain stigma associated with identification with the border culture. "That reality has caused Mexicans in the interior to view fronterizos as a different breed within the nation's society, a group whose lifestyle has been conditioned by their 'addiction' to foreign tastes and products" (Martinez, 1988 p. 113).

19. "The Future of Nogales," *Tucson Citizen*, April 5, 1993.

Chapter 3   The Troubled Waters of Ambos Nogales

1. G. W. Marx, "Sanitary Sewage Disposal Problem, Nogales, Sonora, Mexico—Nogales, Arizona, U.S.A." Report of the Director, Sanitary Engineering Department of the Arizona State Department of Health, 1946, Arizona State University Libraries, Tempe, Department of Archives and Manuscripts, The Carl T. Hayden Papers MSS-1 [hereinafter cited as Hayden Papers].

2. IBWC, "History and Development of the International Boundary and Water Commission, United States and Mexico," 1952, Hayden Papers MSS-1.

3. Marx, "Sanitary Sewage Disposal Problem."

4. IBWC, "International Border Sanitation Problem, Nogales, Arizona—Nogales, Sonora: Recommended Measures for Solution." Report to J. F. Friedkin, Commissioner, by the Board of Consultants to the U.S. Section, February 1963, Hayden Papers MSS-1.

5. L. M. Lawson, Letter to Senator Carl Hayden from the Commissioner, U.S. Section of the IBWC, 1949, Hayden Papers MSS-1.

6. "$290,000 Disposal Plant to Be Constructed Soon; Robins Signs Resolution," *Daily Herald*, May 9, 1950, Hayden Papers MSS-1.

7. IBWC, Status Memorandum: "International Sewage Disposal Facilities, Nogales, Arizona—Nogales, Sonora." Memo attached to a letter from J. F. Friedkin, Commissioner, to Arizona Senator Carl Hayden, November 26, 1963, Hayden Papers MSS-1.

8. U.S. Senate, S.960, 82nd Congress, 1st session, 1951, Hayden Papers MSS-1.

9. "An Increasing Health Hazard," *Austin American Statesman*, March 27, 1988.

10. Mariana Celaya, administrative assistant of operations, Nogales Water Department, pers. comm., 1993; prices effective in 1992 and 1993.

11. "City to Get Kino's Water," *Nogales International*, October 12, 1988.

12. The elevation ranges from 1,200 to 1,400 meters in Nogales, Son. (a change of 656 feet).

13. *La Voz del Norte*, June 5, 1991. Boletin Bimensual mayo–junio, Sistema de Información Fronteriza (SIF), COLEF, 1991.

14. The results of this survey are discussed in more detail in Chapter 4.

15. *La Voz del Norte*, May 12, 1991. Boletin Bimensual mayo–junio, SIF, COLEF, 1991.

16. For comparison, approximately 30 percent of the connections to the public water supply in Mexico City are not registered (World Bank, 1992).

17. The cost is $15.96 for the first 15,000 liters and $1.40 for each additional 1,000 liters (1 gallon = 3.785 liters).

18. Letter from Gary Woodard, Division of Economic and Business Research, University of Arizona, to the Udall Center, August 27, 1991.

19. Letter from Gary Woodard, August 27, 1992.

20. According to the World Health Organization, 75 liters (20 gallons) per day per household is considered adequate to protect against waterborne diseases (Falkenmark and Suprapto, 1992).

21. "Chemicals Catastrophe Lurking Behind Border," *Austin American Statesman*, March 27, 1988.

22. Original prices as reported by COLEF in October 1993, when one (new) peso was exchanged at U.S. $0.293.

23. Water delivery prices are discussed in World Bank, 1992.

24. G. W. Marx, Letter to the Commissioner of the IBWC from the Director and Chief Engineer, Arizona State Department of Health, October 14, 1957, Hayden Papers MSS-1.

25. IBWC, "International Border Sanitation Problem, Nogales, Arizona—Nogales, Sonora: Recommended Measures for Solution."

26. R. C. Weaver, Summary of the situation in Nogales, addressed to Senator Carl Hayden of Arizona from the Administrator, Housing and Home Finance Agency, December 1961, Hayden Papers MSS-1.

27. IBWC, Status Memorandum: "International Sewage Disposal Facilities, Nogales, Arizona—Nogales, Sonora."

28. IBWC, "International Border Sanitation Problem, Nogales, Arizona—Nogales, Sonora: Recommended Measures for Solution."

29. IBWC, "Nogales Border Sanitation Problem: Memorandum of Current and Proposed Course of Action," 1965, Hayden Papers MSS-1.

30. IBWC, Position Paper: "Nogales International Wastewater Treatment Plant, October 1987," Hayden Papers MSS-1.

31. IBWC, Position Paper: "Nogales International Wastewater Treatment Plant, October 1987."

32. "Nogales Wants Mexico to Pay Bigger Share," *Arizona Daily Star*, November 25, 1991.

33. The activities surrounding this event are discussed in greater detail in Chapter 5.

34. "Nogales Wants Mexico to Pay Bigger Share," *Arizona Daily Star*, November 25, 1991.

35. IBWC, Position Paper, "Nogales International Wastewater Treatment Plant, October 1987."

36. "High Bacteria Count Found in 7 Wells along Wash," *Nogales International*, November 7, 1990.

37. "A History of Pollution in Mexico Casts Clouds over Trade Accord," *New York Times*, August 16, 1993.

38. "Chemicals Catastrophe Lurking Behind Border," *Austin American Statesman*, March 27, 1988.

39. "The Border Boom: Hope and Heartbreak," *New York Times Magazine*, July 1, 1990.

Chapter 4 Divided Neighbors

1. Unless otherwise noted, the following analyses are based on comments and data taken from two surveys conducted in 1991. One survey, conducted by El Colegio de la Frontera Norte (COLEF, 1992), interviewed residents of neighborhoods in Nogales, Son. The other survey, conducted by the Udall Center for Studies in Public Policy at the University of Arizona (Udall Center, 1993c), interviewed water department customers in Nogales, Ariz.

2. Unless otherwise noted, all Nogales, Son., census data are from these sources.

3. "Fighting for a Piece of the Rock," *New Times* (Phoenix), November 4–10, 1987.

4. *La Voz del Norte*, July 1, 1991. Boletin Bimensual julio–agosto, SIF, COLEF, 1991.

5. Teresa Leal, community activist and organizer, Nogales, Son., pers. comm., 1992. The survey was performed in April 1992.

6. Teresa Leal, pers. comm., 1992.

7. The COLEF survey, performed several months after Los Alisos was com-

pleted, found that very few residents have access to water 24 hours per day, and many do not have any access at all to the piped water system.

8. "Nogales Sonora Water Shortage Tests Friendship, Family Ties," *Arizona Daily Star*, August 7, 1987.

9. "State Water Company Is Object of Scorn of Residents in Flood-Damaged Sonora," *Arizona Daily Star*, January 30, 1993.

10. *La Voz del Norte*, June 13, 1991. Boletin Bimensual mayo–junio, SIF, COLEF, 1991.

11. *La Voz del Norte*, June 14, 1991. Boletin Bimensual mayo–junio, SIF, COLEF, 1991.

12. Survey numbers 202, 505, and 354, from Udall Center for Studies in Public Policy, University of Arizona, Tucson, 1991 Nogales, Ariz., Water Survey.

13. Survey numbers 361 and 63, from Udall Center for Studies in Public Policy, University of Arizona, Tucson, 1991 Nogales, Ariz., Water Survey.

14. We have watched illegal crossings of the border by way of a hole in the railroad gate. Returnees to Mexico often carry plastic grocery bags that contain a variety of mundane items such as toilet paper and paper towels.

15. U.S. Immigration and Naturalization Service, Mariposa Office, Nogales, Ariz.

16. We observed a line of people casually crossing through one such hole that was plainly visible from the official downtown crossing point, and only about 20 meters distant. That such crossings are common is evident from the well-worn trails leading up to and through the fence. People cross illegally for a number of reasons, convenience and excitement among them. Many others cross illegally because it is difficult to obtain the documentation necessary to cross legally. To obtain a 72-hour crossing card, a Mexican citizen may need to produce a letter verifying employment, a birth certificate, income tax receipts, or bank account statements.

Chapter 5 Stranded Communities and Failed Crossings

1. Earth Technology Corporation, "Water Quality Assurance Revolving Fund," Phase I Report, Nogales Wash Study Area, final draft, March 1990.

2. CFU/100 ml is the number of colony-forming units per 100 milliliters of water.

3. Following Zurick's 1990 emergency declaration, Cerro Pelon Wash was fenced off, preventing public access.

4. The stop has since been relocated to prevent the childrens' contact with the wash.

5. As of October 1993, Zurick was still receiving calls from Nogales residents asking if they could picnic along Nogales Wash. These calls are particularly

prevalent in springtime. The concrete-lined channels of Nogales Wash are also used by teenagers for skateboarding.

6. In the Nogales sector, the U.S. Border Patrol apprehended 70,937 undocumented persons in fiscal year 1992, and 92,639 in fiscal year 1993 (Steve McDonald, pers. comm., October 1993). While exact breakdowns are unavailable, the Border Patrol confirms that the two tunnels are used largely by three groups of people: (1) *plasmáticos* (those crossing the border to donate blood plasma), (2) those wanting a relatively clandestine route to the train station (one of the tunnels surfaces next to the station), and (3) criminals, who use the tunnels as conduits for stolen property and drugs. See "Violence, Kids Run Together in Nogales Canals" (p. A1), and "Nogales 'Tunnel Kids' Survive in Dark Underworld," pp. B1, B4, B5, both in *Arizona Daily Star*, April 24, 1994.

7. "IBWC Cites Lack of Funds for Delay in Aiding Wash Cleanup," *Nogales International*, October 31, 1990.

8. SEDESOL is the successor agency to SEDUE and the counterpart to the EPA in Mexico.

9. San Francisco is the EPA's regional headquarters, with jurisdiction over Arizona.

10. At last count (1990), 89 Nogales households were still connected to private wells. The number once was much higher.

11. "Cross-border crime is rampant, [Santa Cruz County] officials said. The county has 10 to 12 times more criminal cases than other comparably-sized counties in Arizona, [Santa Cruz County Superior Court Judge Roberto] Montiel said.... Sheriff Tony Estrada told [Attorney General Janet] Reno that 38 percent of the county's $11.5 million budget is eaten up by criminal justice costs" ("Reno Tour in Arizona Emotional," *Arizona Daily Star*, January 16, 1994).

12. "Invisible Enemy," *Tucson Citizen*, October 21–23, 1993; "'Cancer Street' Viewed," *Tucson Citizen*, December 1, 1993; "Cancer Answers Being Sought," *Tucson Citizen*, December 3, 1993.

13. In addition, BEP (and other NGOs) strongly objected to the plan prepared by the EPA, not only on the basis of its inadequacies, discussed later in this chapter, but also because local groups were excluded from participation in its development.

14. The primary cause of death is classified as "respiratory"; however, at this level of analysis it is impossible to determine how many fatal respiratory infections may have been caused by windborne pathogens that were directly related to human wastes improperly disposed of in the environment.

15. El Ley General Equilibrio Ecológico y la Protección al Ambiente, enacted in March 1988, contains 25 chapters and 194 separate articles.

16. *Carro completo*, "a full cart." This idiomatic expression means that the PRI is opening new political space; while there will be room in the cart for

different political parties, the PRI will still be the driver (i.e., will still be in charge).

17. Charles Dumars, co-chair of the Committee on the Use of the Mexico City Aquifer as a Water Supply Resource, National Research Council, pers. comm., 1993.

18. When it was signed, the agreement designated the Ministry for Urban Development and Ecology (SEDUE) as the responsible Mexican organization; SEDUE was succeeded in 1992 by SEDESOL.

19. Letter from H. Karns to L. Douglas, January 21, 1931, Pimería Alta Historical Society Files, Nogales, Ariz.

20. Letter to Senator Hayden from Secretary of State Stimson, January 30, 1931, Pimería Alta Historical Society Files, Nogales, Ariz.

21. G. W. Marx, "Sanitary Sewage Disposal Problem."

22. Letter from L. M. Lawson to C. Hayden, July 30, 1949, Hayden Papers MSS-1.

23. Letter from J. Robins to C. Hayden, May 23, 1951; letter from L. M. Lawson to C. Hayden, May 23, 1951; letter from C. Hayden to Conolly, July 13, 1951; all in Hayden Papers MSS-1.

24. Letter from W. Moore to J. Quigly, March 29, 1966, Hayden Papers MSS-1.

25. Letter from L. M. Lawson to C. Hayden, October 30, 1953, Hayden Papers MSS-1.

26. IBWC, Office of the Commissioner, "Santa Cruz River Development—United States and Mexico," September 2, 1954, Hayden Papers MSS-1.

27. Minutes of the meeting held May 9, 1956, 11:00 A.M., in the offices of the Interstate Stream Commission, Mayer-Heard Building, Phoenix, Ariz., Hayden Papers MSS-1 [hereinafter cited as May 9, 1956, Minutes].

28. Letter from E. Felix, delegate in charge, to C. Ronstadt, chairman, Santa Cruz River Committee, May 9, 1956, Minutes.

29. May 9, 1956, Minutes.

30. Further, under Mexican water law, secondary treated sewage belongs to the person operating the sewage treatment plant, so long as it is not reintroduced into the "Nation's waters" (Dumars et al., 1993). This is a clear incentive for some private operator to construct and operate a sewage treatment facility in Sonora.

31. IBWC, Position Paper, "Nogales International Wastewater Treatment Plant, October 1987."

32. IBWC, "Nogales Border Sanitation Problem."

33. This is a small fraction of the maquilas that produce hazardous wastes in their operations (Mumme, 1992).

34. Letter from Daniel McGovern, EPA Region IX administrator, to Senator Dennis DeConcini, dated November 13, 1990.

35. "Botched Rescue," *Tucson Weekly*, November 12, 1991.

36. Ibid.

37. "EPA Slights Area Officials," *Nogales International*, August 28, 1991.

38. "Border Plan Won't Work, EPA Told," *Nogales International*, October 2, 1991.

39. As this book went to press, the responsibility for water issues passed from SEDESOL to a newly created ministry (under a December 1994 decree by newly elected President Ernesto Zedillo), the Ministry of Environment, Natural Resources, and Fishery (Secretaria de Medio Ambiente, Recursos Naturales, y Pesca).

Chapter 6   Reinventing the Border:
A Framework for Transboundary Water Management

1. "Border Project Beset by Overruns, Wage Dispute," *Arizona Daily Star*, December 26, 1993.

2. "Public Excluded from Debate over Nogales Border Wall," *Arizona Daily Star*, December 13, 1993.

3. See note 39, Chapter 5, above.

4. Water resource problems have traditionally been handled with end-of-the pipe physical solutions. Water managers who want to take a broader, human approach have only recently begun to affect domestic water policy. As we indicate in Chapter 5, the IBWC exemplifies the kind of agencies that dominated the supply and project approach to water management that had its heyday in the 1950s.

5. Daniel Okun has identified capacity building of water agencies in developing countries as an acute need (Okun, 1991).

Bibliography

Alger, C. F. 1984–1985. Bridging the micro and the macro in international relations research. *Alternatives* 10(3):319–44.

American Chamber of Commerce in Mexico [AMCHAM]. 1988. *Maquiladora Handbook*. Mexico City, D.F.

Anderson, J., and M. de la Rosa. 1991. Economic survival of poor families on the Mexican border. *Journal of Borderland Studies* 6(1):51–68.

Arizona Department of Health, Sanitary Engineering Division. Feb. 7, 1946. "Report: Sanitary Sewage Disposal Problem, Nogales, Sonora, Mexico—Nogales, Arizona, U.S.A."

Arizona Department of Water Resources [ADWR]. 1990. *Santa Cruz County Water Issues Report*. Tucson: Arizona Department of Water Resources.

Arizona–Sonora Desert Museum. 1991. Riparian habitats. *Sonorensis*. Tucson: Arizona–Sonora Desert Museum.

Ayer, H. W., and R. M. Layton. 1974. The border industry program and the impacts of expenditures by Mexican border industry employees on a U.S. community: An empirical study of Nogales. *Annals of Regional Science* 8(2):105–17.

Bahl, R. W., and J. F. Linn. 1992. *Urban Public Finance in Developing Countries*. Washington, D.C.: International Bank for Reconstruction and Development [World Bank].

Bennett, V. 1995. *The Politics of Water: Urban Protest, Gender, and Power in Monterrey, Mexico*. Forthcoming from the University of Pittsburgh Press.

Caldwell, L. K. 1993. Implications of the 1992 Rio conference for environmental policymaking. *Policy Currents* 3(3):5–6.

Colegio de la Frontera Norte [COLEF]. 1992. *Manejo Transfronterizo del Agua en los Dos Nogales: Estrategias para Nogales, Sonora*. Technical report. Tijuana, B.C.: El Colegio de la Frontera Norte.

Comisión Nacional del Agua. 1990. *Water Policies and Strategies*. Mexico City, D.F.

——— . 1992. *Situación Actual del Subsector Agua Potable, Alcantarillado y Saneamiento*. Mexico City, D.F.

Cornelius, W. A., J. Gentleman, and P. H. Smith, eds. 1988. *Mexico's Alternative*

Political Futures. San Diego: Center for U.S.-Mexican Studies, University of California.

Dickinson, R. E. 1992. Changes in land use. In *Climate System Modeling*, ed. K. E. Trenberth, pp. 689–700. Cambridge: Cambridge University Press.

Duda, A. M., D. R. Lenat, and D. L. Penrose. 1982. Water quality in urban streams—what we can expect. *Journal of the Water Pollution Control Federation* 54:1139–47.

Dumars, C. T., R. Martinez, and G. Ortiz. 1993. Institutions controlling water quantity and quality allocation in Mexico. Second draft. Comments in the report to the National Academy of Sciences Committee on the Use of the Mexico City Aquifer as a Water Supply Resource, October 2, 1993. University of New Mexico School of Law, Albuquerque.

Environmental Protection Agency [EPA]. 1991. Mexican environmental laws, regulations and standards. Preliminary report of EPA findings (revised June 27). Office of the General Counsel, Washington, D.C.

EPA and Secretaría de Desarrollo Urbano y Ecología [SEDUE]. 1991. *Integrated Environmental Plan for the Mexico-U.S. Border Area. First Stage, 1992–94*. Washington, D.C.: Government Printing Office.

Falkenmark, M., and R. A. Suprapto. 1992. Population-landscape interactions in development: A water perspective to environmental sustainability. *Ambio* 21(1):31–36.

Frederick, K. D., and D.C. Gibbons. 1986. *Scarce Water and Institutional Change*. Washington, D.C.: Resources for the Future.

Graham, W. 1991. MexEco? Mexican attitudes toward the environment. *Environmental History Review* 15(4):1–17.

Herzog, L. A. 1990a. *Where North Meets South: Cities, Space and Politics on the U.S.-Mexico Border*. Austin: Center for Mexican-American Studies, University of Texas.

———. 1990b. Border commuter workers and transfrontier metropolitan structure along the United States–Mexico border. *Journal of Borderlands Studies* 5(2):1–20.

Hey, E., and A. Nolkaemper. 1992. The Second International Water Tribunal. *Environmental Policy and Law* 22(2):82–88.

Heyman, J. M. 1991. *Life and Labor on the Border*. Tucson: University of Arizona Press.

Hjern, B. 1992. Illegitimate democracy: A case for multiorganizational policy analysis. *Policy Currents* 2(1):1–5.

Hogwood, B. W., and B. G. Peters. 1985. *The Pathology of Public Policy*. Oxford: Oxford University Press.

Hopkins, R. G. 1992. The economic impact of Mexican visitors to Arizona. *Arizona's Economy* (November):1–5.

Ingram, H. 1993. Transnational water resources management: Learning from the U.S.-Mexico example. Abel Wolman Distinguished Lecture, National Research Council, Washington, D.C.

Ingram, H., and A. Schneider. 1990. Improving implementation through framing smarter statutes. *Journal of Public Policy* 10(1):67–88.

Ingram, H., and D. R. White. 1991. The U.S. section of the International Boundary and Water Commission: Expanding state and local involvement; Ambos Nogales and the need for change. Presented at the Tri-National Conference on the North American Experience in Managing International Transboundary Water Resources: The Boundary Commissions of Canada, the United States, and Mexico, held at Gasparilla Island, Florida, April 19–23, 1991.

Instituto Nacional de Estadística, Geografía e Informática [INEGI]. 1990a. *XI Censo General de Población y Vivienda, 1990 (Sonora)*. Mexico City, D.F.

———. 1990b. *Nogales: Indicadores Sociodemográficos*. Mexico City, D.F.

Katko, T. S. 1991. Reselling and vending water. *Journal of the American Water Works Association* 83(6):63–69.

Kelly, M. 1991. *Facing Reality: The Need for Fundamental Changes in Protecting the Environment along the U.S.-Mexico Border*. Austin: Texas Center for Policy Studies.

Korten, D.C. 1991. Sustainable development: A review essay. *World Policy Journal* 9(1):157–90.

Leonard, H. J. 1988. *Pollution and the Struggle for World Product: Multinational Corporations, Environment, and International Comparative Advantage*. Cambridge: Cambridge University Press.

Levy, D., and G. Székely. 1987. *Mexico: Paradoxes of Stability and Change*. 2d ed. Boulder, Colo.: Westview Press.

Martinez, O. J. 1988. *Troublesome Border*. Tucson: University of Arizona Press.

———. 1990. Transnational fronterizos: Cross-border linkages in Mexican border society. *Journal of Borderland Studies* 5(1):63–78.

McGinnis, M., and E. Ostrom. 1992. Institutional analysis and global climate change: Design principles for robust international regimes. In *Global Climate Change: Social and Economic Research Issues*, ed. M. Rice, J. Snow, and H. Jacobson, pp. 45–85. Proceedings of a conference held at Argonne National Laboratory, Chicago, Ill., February 11–13, 1992.

Mumme, S. P. 1984. Regional power in national diplomacy: The case of the U.S. Section of the International Boundary and Water Commission. *Publius* 14(4):115–35.

———. 1991. Clearing the air: Environmental reform in Mexico. *Environment* 33(10):7–11, 26–30.

———. 1992. New directions in United States–Mexico transboundary environmental management: A critique of current proposals. *Natural Resources Journal* 32(3):539–62.

Nabhan, G. P., and J. L. Carr, eds. 1994. *Ironwood: An Ecological and Cultural Keystone of the Sonoran Desert.* Occasional Paper in Conservation Biology. Washington, D.C.: Conservation International.

O'Connor, R. E., R. J. Bord, and A. Fisher. 1994. Quality, quantity, and availability of fresh water: Public perceptions in the United States. *Research and Exploration* 10(3):318–41.

Okun, D. A. 1991. Meeting the need for water and sanitation for urban populations. Abel Wolman Distinguished Lecture, May 1991, Natural Research Council, Washington, D.C.

Orianne, P. 1973. *Difficulties in Cooperation Between Local Authorities and Ways of Solving Them.* Study no. 6, Local and Regional Authorities in Europe. Strasbourg: Council of Europe. Cited in C. F. Alger. 1984–85. Bridging the micro and the macro in international relations research. *Alternatives* 10:319–44.

Ostrom, E., J. Walker, and R. Gardner. 1992. Covenants with and without a sword: Self-governance is possible. *American Political Science Review* 86(2):404–17.

Pavlakovic, V., and H. Kim. 1991. Outshopping by maquila employees: Implications for Arizona's border communities. *Arizona Review* (Spring):9–16.

Pavlakovic, V., and A. Silvers. 1988. Survey of the maquila plants in Sonora, Mexico. Project report prepared for the Arizona Department of Commerce, Arizona-Mexico Commission, Phoenix.

Repetto, R. 1993. What can policymakers learn from natural resources accounting? Paper delivered at the Organization of American States Seminar on Natural Resource and Environmental Accounts for Development Policy, Washington, D.C., April 13–14, 1993.

Rodda, J. C., and G. J. Young. 1992. Foreword to *Keynote Papers.* International Conference on Water and the Environment: Development Issues for the 21st Century, January 26–31, 1992, Dublin, Ireland. Geneva: World Meteorological Organization.

Rogers, P. 1983. The future of water. *Atlantic Monthly* 252(1):80–93.

———. 1992. Integrated urban resources water management. In *Keynote Papers.* International Conference on Water and the Environment: Development Issues for the 21st Century, January 26–31, 1992, Dublin, Ireland. Geneva: World Meteorological Organization.

Sánchez, R. A. 1993. Public participation and the IBWC: Challenges and options. *Natural Resources Journal* 33(2):283–98.

Sand, P. 1990. *Lessons Learned in Global Environmental Governance.* Washington, D.C.: World Resources Institute.

Schneider, A., and H. Ingram. 1993. The social construction of target populations: Implications for politics and policy. *American Political Science Review* 87(2):334–47.

Sellers, W. D., and R. H. Hill, eds. 1974. *Arizona Climate 1931–1972*. Tucson: University of Arizona Press.
Sellers, W. D., R. H. Hill, and M. Sanderson-Rae, eds. 1985. *Arizona Climate*. Centennial ed. Tucson: University of Arizona Press.
Sjöstedt, G., ed. 1993. *International Environmental Negotiation*. International Institute for Applied Systems Analysis. Newbury Park, Calif.: Sage Publications.
Sloan, A., J. W. West, and J. P. West. 1977. The role of informal policy making in the U.S.-Mexico border cities. *Social Science Quarterly* 58(2):270–82.
Solley, W. B., E. B. Chase, and W. B. Mann. 1983. *Estimated Use of Water in the United States in 1980*. Circular 1001. Alexandria, Va.: U.S. Geological Survey.
Spicer, E. H. 1992. *Cycles of Conquest: The Impact of Spain, Mexico, and the United States on the Indians of the Southwest, 1533–1960*. 10th ed. 1962. Tucson: University of Arizona Press.
Stoddard, E. R., and J. Hedderson. 1987. *Trends and Patterns of Poverty along the U.S.-Mexico Border*. Borderlands Research Monograph Series, no. 3. New Mexico State University, Las Cruces.
Striegl, R. G. 1987. Suspended sediment and metals removal from urban runoff by a small lake. *Water Resources Bulletin* 23(6):985–96.
U.S. Department of the Army. 1987. Nogales Wash and tributaries draft feasibility report and environmental assessment. Los Angeles District, U.S. Army Corps of Engineers.
U.S. Fish and Wildlife Service. 1992. Fish and wildlife needs related to the North American Free Trade Agreement (Region 2). Executive summary. Albuquerque, N.M.
U.S. General Accounting Office. 1991. *U.S.-Mexico Trade: Some U.S. Wood Furniture Firms Relocated from the Los Angeles Area to Mexico*. Document NSIAD-91-191. Washington, D.C.: Government Printing Office.
Udall, S. L., and R. G. Varady. 1993–94. Environmental conflict and the world's new international borders. *Transboundary Resources Report* 7(3):5–6.
Udall Center. 1993a. State of the U.S.-Mexico border environment. Report of the Public Advisory Committee, EPA U.S.-Mexico Border Environmental Plan. Prepared by the Udall Center for Studies in Public Policy, University of Arizona, Tucson.
———. 1993b. *Ambos Nogales Water Resources Study: Santa Cruz Watershed and Nogales, Arizona*. Prepared under the auspices of the Udall Center Ambos Nogales Water Resources Project by the Technical Task Group.
———. 1993c. Water in Nogales: Survey of use, issues, and concerns. Report prepared by the Udall Center for Studies in Public Policy, University of Arizona, Tucson.
van Tongerin, J.A.N., S. Schweinfest, E. Lutz, M. Gomez Luna, and F. Guillen Martin. 1991. Integrated environmental and economic accounting: A case

study for Mexico. World Bank Environmental Working Paper no. 50, Washington, D.C.
Varady, R. G. 1992. Are EPA and residents speaking the same language? In *The U.S.-Mexico Border Region under Stress: A Binational Symposium on Ideas for Future Research*, pp. 33–35. Proceedings of the October 1991 symposium sponsored by the Ford Foundation at Guaymas, Sonora.
Velez-Ibañez, C. 1988. Networks of exchange among Mexicans in the U.S. and Mexico: Local level mediating responses to national and international transformations. *Urban Anthropology and Studies of Cultural Systems and World Economic Development* 17(1):27–51.
———. 1994. Plural strategies of survival and cultural formation in U.S. Mexican households in a region of dynamic transformation: The U.S.-Mexico borderlands. In *Diagnosing America: Anthropology and Public Engagement*, ed. S. Foreman. Forthcoming from the University of Michigan Press.
Vlacos, E., A. Webb, and I. Murphy, eds. 1986. *The Management of International River Basin Conflicts*. Proceedings of a Workshop held at the headquarters of the International Institute for Applied Systems Analysis, Laxenburg, Austria, September 22–25.
Water Environment Federation. n.d. *Clean Water for Today: What Is Wastewater Treatment?* Alexandria, Va.: Water Environment Federation.
Weiss, E. B. 1993. International environmental law: Contemporary issues and the emergence of the new world order. *Georgetown Law Journal* 81(3):675–710.
Weiss, H., M. A. Courty, W. Wetterstrom, F. Guichard, L. Senior, R. Meadow, and A. Curnow. 1993. The genesis and collapse of third millennium North Mesopotamian civilization. *Science* 261:995–1004.
Whipple, W., and J. V. Hunter. 1979. Petroleum hydrocarbons in urban runoff. *Water Resources Bulletin* 17(1):36–45.
World Bank. 1992. *World Development Report 1992: Development and the Environment*. Washington, D.C.: International Bank for Reconstruction and Development.
World Resources 1990–91. Washington, D.C.: World Resources Institute.
World Resources 1992–93. Washington, D.C.: World Resources Institute.
WPA Guide to 1930s Arizona. 1989. Tucson: University of Arizona Press.
Zurick, Patrick. Personal interview conducted by Nancy Laney and Helen Ingram, Jan. 22, 1992.

Index

Acid rain, 10
Active Management Area (AMA), 66–67, 212
Arizona Department of Water Resources (ADWR), 67, 68
Arizona Groundwater Management Act (AGMA), 66–68, 212

Bilingualism, 46, 129, 134
Binational orientation, 136, 141. *See also* Transnational fronterizos
Border crossings, 131
Border Ecology Project (BEP): against air pollution, 164; and binational nongovernmental organizations, 219; dissemination of information, 154
Border Environmental Cooperation Commission (BECC), 221–227
Border Health Task Force, 160
Border Industrialization Program, 37
Border Patrol, 35
Bottled water: assumed purity of Arizona-manufactured, 105, 106, 108, 128; contamination in, 99; for drinking and cooking, 110; impact on public water supply system, 84; individual initiative for, 123; industrial solvents in, 120; in planned neighborhoods, 125; price of, 79; purchased by Nogales, Ariz., residents, 139; in summary, 211
Bracero program, 37

Central Arizona Project (CAP), 54, 66, 213
Clean Water Act, 21
Colonias, 19, 112; cooperation among residents, 115; public health, 114, 118–119; sewerage, 110; water supply, 116
Comisión Internacional de Limites y Aguas (CILA), 179. *See also* International Boundary and Water Commission
Comisión de Agua Potable y Alcantarillado del Estado de Sonora (COAPAES): and bacterial contamination, 120; chlorination systems, 121; community groups, 123–124; disconnection of nonpayers, 177; illegal connections, 74; pipas, 77; policy toward a Mexican wastewater treatment plant, 94; price disparities, 81; relationship with CNA, 175; relationship with SEDESOL, 178; responsibility, 71; revenues, 72; water demand, 122, 176; water quality, 73
Comisión Nacional del Agua (CNA): focus of, 173; jurisdiction, 171; proposed restructuring of water resources management, 174; role vis-à-vis COAPAES, 175
Community spigots, 80
Connection fees, 64
Cost-of-service charges, 64, 71, 81, 173
Cross-border networks, 47

Deforestation, 10
Drought, 53, 68, 70, 78

Environmental Protection Agency (EPA): and BECC, 222, 227; as binational actor, 200–202; contribution to NIWWTF, 188; development of IBEP, 198–199; grassroots representation, 216; and La Paz Agreement, 179, 195–197; and Santa Cruz County Health Department, 150, 153–158; sewer line moratorium, 91–93, 213
Environmental regulations (general discussion), 23–24

Floods, 62, 96, 122

Gadsden Purchase, 30, 33, 34, 217
General Agreement on Tariffs and Trade (GATT), 204
General Ecology Law, 172
General Services Administration (GSA), 214
Great Depression, 32, 36, 42
Greenhouse gases, 10
Groundwater mining, 8, 66, 212

Immigration formalities, 35–36
Integrated Environmental Plan for the Mexico-U.S. Border Area (IBEP), 198–200
Interbasin water transfers, 70
International Boundary Commission (IBC), 180
International Boundary and Water Commission (IBWC): Army Corps of Engineers, 97; and BECC, 225, 227; chlorination facilities, 99, 113; engineering solutions, 213, 215–216; jurisdiction, 101, and La Paz Agreement, 195; local officials and, 201–202; NIWWTF of, 61–62, 87–92; overview of, 179–182; policy toward a Mexican wastewater treatment plant, 94; and Santa Cruz County Health Department, 150–157; wastewater treatment issues, 184–192

La Crisis, 41
La Frontera, 28, 49
La Paz Agreement, 194–197; and EPA, 198; flaws in, 215–216

Maquiladoras: benefits to Mexico, 208; Border Trade Association and, 219; definition of, 37; economic impact on Nogales, Ariz., 131, 159; and EPA, 155; hazardous chemical wastes, 91–92, 101–102, 127, 177, 196; in Nogales, Son., 38, 42–43, 48, 63–65, 113; private wells, 74–75; taxes paid by, 209; use of chemical drums for water storage, 110; workers' salaries, 43–44; workforce turnover, 44–45
Mesquite charcoal, 210
Mexican legal system, 169
Mexican Revolution, 32, 36
Minimum water requirements, 58

National fronterizos, 47, 143
National Groundwater Law, 174
National orientation, 136, 141. *See also* National fronterizos
National Pollution Discharge Elimination System (NPDES), 89–90
Nested institutions, 24, 220
Nogales International Wastewater Treatment Facility (NIWWTF): bacteriological contamination from, 92–93; as first completed, 62; funding for, 194; and industrial wastes, 91–92; NPDES and, 89–90; overcapacity, 87, 91; riparian areas, 102,

191–192, 207; treatment processes, 90–91
Nogales Wash: as covered channel, 62–63; description of, 50; and public health, 97, 99–101, 177; Santa Cruz County Health Department and, 148–152; wellfields underlying, 70
Nogales Water Department (NWD): emergency response, 78; general description, 65–66; Sonoran accounts of, 75–76
North American Development Bank, 223
North American Free Trade Agreement (NAFTA): border environment, 14–16, 198, 204; and Border Trade Association, 219; IBEP and, 200, 214; nongovernmental organizations and, 194, 197; supplemental annex on the environment (environmental side agreement), 220–222

Operation Blockade, 131
Organ Pipe Cactus National Monument, 207

Partido Revolucionario Institucional (PRI), 21
Pipas: associated costs of, 84; community groups solicitation for, 124; description of, 76–79; increasing water prices, 81; and water contamination, 120
Poverty level, 116
Private wells, 66, 74, 99, 150
Public health: and the international border as artificial line, 183; affected by canalization of Nogales Wash, 97; and chlorination, 99; COAPAES water and, 73, 120; in colonias, 114; perceptions of, in Nogales, Ariz., 127; perceptions of, in Nogales, Son., 165; and Santa Cruz County Health Department, 149, 151, 154; affected by sewer line breaks, 87–88, 98, 119; and wastewater pathogens, 90

Railroad depot, 36
Reagan–de la Madrid Accord, 195. *See also* La Paz Agreement
Riparian areas, 55–58, 94–95, 102, 142, 191–192

Santa Cruz River, 50–52, 60, 69, 108, 127, 142, 157
Secretaría de Agricultura y recursos Hidráulicos (SARH), 171
Secretaría de Desarrollo Social (SEDESOL): BECC and, 222, 227; relationship with COAPAES, 178; IBEP as exercise of, 200; La Paz Agreement and, 179, 195, 197, 202; mission, 172
Secretaría de Desarrollo Urbano y Ecología (SEDUE): La Paz Agreement and, 195, 197, 198; mission, 172
Six Weeks' Revolution, 32
Solidaridad, 172
Sonoran wastewater treatment facility, 191
Summer monsoons, 53
Sustainability, 5, 10
Sustainable development, 6, 10, 17, 24, 68, 103, 125, 222–223

Tariff Act, 32
Tetrachloroethylene, 100, 102, 158
Tijuana, 100, 130
Transnational fronterizos, 143
Treaty of Guadalupe Hidalgo, 29, 33

Work Projects Administration, 33

About the Authors

Helen Ingram is the director of the Udall Center for Studies in Public Policy at the University of Arizona. She is also a professor in the Department of Political Science and the School of Public Administration and Policy, with a joint appointment in the Department of Hydrology and Water Resources. Dr. Ingram's research specialties are the policymaking process and policy implementation as well as, more recently, policy design. In the field of water resources she is best known for her contribution to the understanding of the politics of policymaking. Dr. Ingram has served on a number of National Research Council committees. She is also one of four U.S. members taking part in the NRC's binational study, "The Use of the Mexico City Aquifer as a Water Supply Resource." Since 1989 Dr. Ingram has been the principal investigator of the research project on which this book is based.

Her recent publications include *Public Policy for Democracy* (with S. R. Smith, 1993), *Water Politics: Continuity and Change* (1990), *Does Anybody Win? The Community Consequences of Rural-to-Urban Water Transfers* (with C. R. Oggins, 1990), and *Water and Poverty in the Southwest* (with L. Brown, 1987).

Nancy Laney is the deputy director of the Arizona–Sonora Desert Museum, an internationally recognized zoological park and botanical garden located in Tucson, Arizona. Between 1988 and 1993 she was an attorney for the University of Arizona specializing in environmental, water, real estate, and intellectual property law. She also worked for four years in the U.S. District Court as a staff attorney assigned to multidistrict securities litigation arising out of the default on $2.25 billion in municipal bonds issued by the Washington Public Power Supply System. Ms. Laney has served as a consultant on several research projects, including the present Ambos Nogales study, and she is the author of a number of articles and book chapters on natural resources policy and water law, including "Natural Areas: Issues and Opportunities" (in *Preserving Arizona's Environmental Heritage*, 1991), and "Does Arizona's 1980 Groundwater Management Act Violate the Commerce Clause?" (*Arizona Water Review*, 1983). She is the coauthor of two books: *Saving Water in a Desert City* (with H. Ingram, 1984) and *Policy Approach to Political Representation* (with H. Ingram and J. R. McCain, 1980).

About the Authors

David Gillilan completed his B.A. degree in economics and public policy at Swarthmore College in 1983, and earned a master's degree in water resources administration from the University of Arizona in 1992. During 1991 and 1992, Mr. Gillilan focused on border water issues. He is currently a research associate in the Department of Earth Resources at Colorado State University in Fort Collins, where he is writing a book about instream flow protection in the Western states. His particular interests lay in the field of natural resources and environmental policy.